Book Recommendations

Christmanship: A Theology of Competition and Sport is crystal clear, **biblically informed, and full of wisdom**. This is what we have come to expect from Dr. Greg Linville. Greg is a man who has given his body, his mind, and more importantly his heart to the field of sports ministry for more than 30 years. Read this book. Its more than a book about sports ministry; it's insight into Greg Linville, a man worth getting to know.

Rob Burns
Former Professional Soccer Player—Dallas Stars
Missional Leadership Consultant—Evangelical Alliance
Cardiff, Wales, U.K.

Many years ago we met Dr. Greg Linville through our church's sports ministry and were truly blessed by that experience! He taught our family what it means to be passionate and genuine about whatever you do—even sport! *Greg lives out what he writes in his book*. He believes in nurturing relationships with others and God should be a priority.

Mark Murphy
12-year NFL Veteran and Green Bay Packer Hall of Famer
Assistant Dean of Students and Coach—Akron St. Vincent St. Mary
Pam Murphy
Former college athlete;
Parents of 4 college athletes
Grandparents to 2½ beautiful babies!

Dr. Linville has been *a lone voice for more than 25 years, crying in the wilderness of sport*. His cries have been trying to point the Christian view of sport to a theological basis that will build a philosophy of ministry that establishes sound methodological models. *Christmanship: A Theology of Competition* will put the cries into multiple forms of delivery for all to understand.

Tim Conrad
Former Collegiate Athlete and Coach
President, UW Sports Ministry
Hilton Head, South Carolina, USA

Having known and called Dr. Greg Linville a friend for over 20 years has been a blessing for me and my family. His wisdom and guidance with regard to sport, competition, and life has been invaluable to so many. Dr. Linville's ability to communicate the value of perspective, passion, and the significance of being excellent at the important things in ones' life is truly a gift.

Mike Birkbeck
Former Major League Baseball Pitcher
Current Division I Baseball Coach—Kent State University
Husband to Sue & Father to John

Greg Linville is rare among authors. He deftly manages on the Sports Ministry stage to combine a profound understanding of theology with his years of practical experience in local Church Sports Outreach. He is *a "dreamer of the day," one who fills the gap between vision and reality*. All Sports Ministers should have this book in their "kit" bag.

Bryan Mason
Former Physical Education Teacher, Christian in Sport
Church Director and CSRM European Director,
Currently Executive Director, Higher Sports
Crakehall, Yorkshire Dales, England, U.K.

Greg's book on **Christmanship: A Theology of Competition and Sport** *will stimulate much thinking in Australia as we set about developing sports ministry leaders* in churches, schools, and community sports clubs. In a nation as passionate about sport as we are, there is much work to be done in envisioning and equipping those who will be raised up to serve God and others in and through sport. In particular, worldview thinking and habits adopted from sport need to be critiqued from a biblical perspective. Greg's work achieves all of this and I commend him and this book as worthy of your attention.

Jim Dayhew
Founder of Sports Serve
Director of Christian Education, Thomas Hassall Anglican College
Sydney, Australia

Dr. Greg Linville has presented local Church Sports Ministries with a unique understanding and method of engaging with the current world of competition and sport. His insights bring about both an internal (personal) and external (community) dialogue challenging Christians today to examine the ever increasing cultural influence of sport on our lives. Whether you are a weekend warrior, spectator, or active participant, Dr. Linville's look at *"Christmanship" should be at the top of your reading list.*

Barb Wagenfuhr
Retired Sport and Recreation Minister
1st Presbyterian Church
Colorado Springs, Colorado, USA

Greg Linville is passionate about applying God's word to sport. He is ***one of the foremost thinkers on the subject***. His concept of "Christmanship"—not merely Sportsmanship—as the standard required of the Christian athlete is not only a unique and original contribution to an understanding of competition from God's perspective . . . it is also immensely challenging!

Stuart Weir
Former Christian In Sport Director; Author and Editor
Verite' Sports Director
Oxfordshire, England, U.K.

It is my pleasure to recommend to you Greg Linville's book on CHRIST-MANSHIP. In this day of "win at all costs," it is imperative Christian athletes understand they are not athletes who happen to be Christians, but rather they are Christians who happen to be athletes. The difference is found in one's identity in Christ and not sports or the scoreboard and, therefore, requires the athlete to manifest Christ in their athletic endeavors. ***This book will help the athlete understand how to honor Christ in his/her competition*** and be the ultimate witness of an empowered, submitted, and enriched life. I highly recommend this book.

Rodger Oswald
Former Athlete and Coach
Retired founder of Church Sports International
CSRM Staff—Emeritus
San Jose, California, USA

In my sports ministry courses at Azusa Pacific University, *I have relied on Greg Linville's writings and resources on athletic competition and exhibiting Christmanship*. All of my students know various Linville-isms—like, our opponent in a competitive endeavor is "not our enemy but a co-competitor." Every year I highlight in our Integration of Faith and Sport course Greg's materials on the value of each component of competition—coach, referee, co-competitor, winning/losing, teammate, etc. I'm so excited that Greg has decided to put all these concepts together in one book.

Steve Quatro
Professor of Sports Ministry Azusa Pacific University
Executive Director Sports Outreach Los Angeles (SOLA)
Pasadena, California, USA

———————

For many years, I have challenged teams to pursue character above the "almighty win." Coaches and athletes aren't defined by the scoreboard but rather by what occurs deep in their souls. Greg's powerful teachings over many years, now contained in this excellent book, provides *an excellent combination of biblical truth and practical insights* on how athletes can maximize their performance on and off the field, and more importantly, develop a deep character that will benefit them "all the days of their life."

Rod Handley
Former COO of FCA
Founder and President, Character that Counts
Kansas City, Missouri, USA

———————

Dr. Greg Linville has been *one of the leading thinkers in the world on the engagement of Christianity with Sport* for the last couple of decades and we in the U.K. love him because of his authenticity, attention to detail, and his appreciation of a historical context to the cases he presents.

David Oakley
CEO Ambassadors Football
Bolton, England, U.K.

Dr. Greg Linville is one of those rare people who naturally inspire people both in ministry and in sports. I have always enjoyed reading Greg's material because he combines both his understanding of biblical exegesis with his vast understanding of sport. *His knowledge of first-century sport and how the early church interacted with sport is unparalleled.* "Christmanship" is a concept Greg brilliantly addresses for Christians all over the world. This is a must read for all who struggle with applying their faith in the sporting realm.

Rev. Alec Wallis
Pastor—Grace Chinese Christian Church
Sydney, Australia

Dr. Linville is a true Man of God with the special gift of inspiring, empowering, equipping, and transforming the people of sport. *I consider him to be the Apostle Paul of this generation—a Christian sports missionary taking the Gospel of Christ to the sports world.* Our sports world is in desperate need of the theological truths, philosophical principles, and methodological models Dr. Linville so eloquently espouses in his book—*Christmanship.* I highly recommend this book.

Susan Stewart
Former Collegiate/Olympian Basketball Player and
Sports Ministry Student
Mississaugua, Ontario, Canada

I have known Greg Linville for a number of years and always found him to be *a person of integrity, scholarship, and vision.* I have used his material on the mission field and found it not only helpful, but also relevant to those that I come into contact with through sport. His book, *Christmanship: A Theology of Competition and Sport,* is welcomed by all who are involved in "reaching the world of sport and/or reaching the world through sport" for Christ.

Todd James
Former Coach and Missionary with Evangelical Friends Mission
Castleknock, Dublin, Ireland

Dr. Greg Linville has served as *a pioneer and mentor for sports ministers across the globe*. From Young Life, the YMCA, and FCA to numerous universities and seminaries where he has coached and instructed, he has raised up an army of sports ministers who are empowered, educated, and equipped to teach and model Christmanship within their sphere of influence. And having coached with, competed with, and competed against Greg, I can tell you this is not just a book he's written, but a principle he models.

Michael T. Brown
Former Collegiate Athlete and High School Coach
Executive Director/CEO—Danville Family YMCA
Danville, Illinois, USA

The mix of sport, faith, and competition—and how these three sit together—is a challenge each Christian sportsman or athlete has to face. In this book Dr. Linville has used his wealth of knowledge, experience, and insight to help us dig deep and find the answers we need on this key issue. *I highly recommend this book*, which is a gift and a resource to anyone who is serious about honoring God on the track, field, or pitch.

Rob McAvoy
Sport and Youth Pastor
Long Lane Church, Liverpool, England, U. K.

I highly recommend *Christmanship* to anyone who wants to know what the Bible has to say about living out their faith in the arena of athletics. Dr. Linville's book is a compilation of many years of research, observation, prayer, and praxis. At FCA, we are in need of Christian athletes who can reflect Jesus to a lost world on and off the field. **Christmanship *will help athletes know how to compete in ways consistent with verbal claims of Christ's Lordship*.**

Al Schierbaum
Former Athlete, College Coach and Author
State Director—Ohio FCA
Twinsburg, Ohio, USA

For years Dr. Greg Linville has been an exemplar of what sports ministry should look like. I am excited his theological, philosophical, and methodological concepts and thoughts are finally on paper. Linville's book—**Christmanship** *will serve as a model for all in sports ministry* and help move us forward to do the job God has called us to do.

Bob Johnston
Former Professional Baseball Player
Athletes in Action Staff
Toronto, Canada

Sports practice and theology are two aspects that are never easy to put together. Greg with unique expertise tackles both elements, then weaves them together with great simplicity to come up with a practical theology of sports athletes and coaches can apply in their own context with relative ease. *This is a must read for any sports minister and all athletes* who dare to dream about developing a Christian Sports culture in their own setting.

Benjamin Kawadza
Former Athlete and Coach
Zimbabwe Director CSRM
Harare, Zimbabwe

I am honored to recommend *Christmanship: A Theology of Competition and Sport*. It is a clear and biblically based examination of an issue that gets too little attention by the church. May God use this book to kickstart the church toward greater, deeper, and wider ministry using sport to reach a lost and dying world. **Greg is one of the few who understand the deeper things of sport as intended by God.** Whether you use sport as a ministry tool or not, this book will enrich your life and ministry. Read it, use it, teach it.

John Garner
Former Director of Rec Lab
Professor—Oklahoma Baptist University and
Sports Ministry Consultant
Nashville, Tennessee, USA

Dr. Greg Linville has had a profound influence upon my understanding of the dynamic relationship between sport, theology, and our service to Christ. He is *the most lucid thinker on this subject* I know. I am certain this book will challenge and inspire all who read it. It is my hope and prayer this work will receive a global audience so the example of Christmanship will help reshape and transform the attitude and approach of Christians involved in sports.

Tim Tucker
Former Ambassador in Sport Staff
National Director—The Message South Africa
Capetown, South Africa

There has never been a more important time for "Christmanship." Dr. Linville's book serves as a beacon of light in a very dark world. *This seminal work establishes the theological foundation for competition, sport, athletics, and sport ministry and provides a blueprint for how sport and its participants can be "redeemed"* by outreach ministries founded upon a solid theological foundation. Christmanship is a concept that goes well beyond the arena of sport, applicable to all who "compete" with daily obstacles.

Rev. Brian Nutt
Former Collegiate Athlete and Pastor—Oak Hill Church
Akron, Ohio, USA

CHRISTMANSHIP

A Theology of Competition, Sport, and Sport Ministry

Dr. Greg Linville

Oliver House
Publishing Inc.
Canton, Ohio

Oliver House Publishing Inc.
2521 Landscape N.W.
Canton, Ohio 44709

Copyright © 2014, Greg Linville

ISBN: 978-0-9869250-9-9

Library of Congress Control Number: 2014934954

For any reproduction rights, including federal copying, computer reproduction, etc. contact:

Dr. Greg Linville, CSRM International
C/O The World Outreach Center
5350 Broadmoor Circle N. W.
Canton, Ohio–USA 44709
glinville@csrm.org

Printed in the United States of America.

To my newly born grandson, Raef Benjamin Linville: May this book prove to be catalytic in creating a world of "redeemed sport" in and through which you can "feel His pleasure" when you compete.

TABLE OF CONTENTS

FOREWORD

I have been involved with or around the world of athletics my entire life. My father was a football coach for more than 40 years, beginning as a high school coach, moving on to the collegiate level, and spending the final 16 years of his career as an offensive line coach in the NFL. I began participating in various sporting activities at a very young age and played football, basketball, and baseball through my 4 years of high school. After high school, I attended Penn State University on a football scholarship and was the team's starting quarterback for 3 years. During that time I was awarded the MVP of the Sugar Bowl when the Nittany Lions defeated Georgia to win the National Championship.

In 1983 I was drafted by the NFL's Kansas City Chiefs and played professional football for seven seasons, retiring in 1989. The very next year I began a career in sports broadcasting and have continued in that profession to this day. I give you this background information simply to confirm the statement that I have been involved in sports, in some form or fashion, for my entire life. In 1980, as a sophomore at Penn State, I made the most important decision of my life by accepting Jesus Christ as the Savior of my life and declaring Him as the Lord over my life, dreams, goals, and future. This marked the beginning of a challenging new adventure as my worlds of sports and faith intersected.

From the early years of my faith journey until now, I have been interested in understanding how these two powerful passions of my life can appropriately blend and work together. I know that some people believe sports and competition can have no connection with genuine faith in Christ. I've heard others suggest that the "sacred" and "secular" parts of our lives are both valuable but need to remain separated. I am of the belief that it is possible to live a life of worship, expressing gratitude and praise to our Creator God, through anything we do, including participation in sports.

No one that I have met in the 33 years that I have walked with Christ has taught me more about the dynamic relationship of sports and faith than Greg Linville. My relationship with Greg started when I competed both against and with him on recreational basketball courts and softball fields, including winning a state softball tournament. Eventually, we spent time together in home Bible studies and men's groups. During our time together, I learned about and witnessed firsthand Greg's theology of sport and competition and his concept of "Christmanship."

More than anything he confirmed my belief that Christian athletes should be the hardest working, toughest, and most dedicated members of any team or in any athletic competition. As true "ambassadors of Christ," Christian athletes should set the standards of integrity, humility, fair play, and respect for the game being played.

Greg has always supported his teachings and theology with a deep understanding of Scripture and practical applications of how to live out our faith through athletic competition. As his university and seminary students can well attest, Greg's knowledge of the Bible and how it relates to sports and competition is unprecedented and is bolstered by his understanding of the practices and training methods of ancient Greek athletes. I found it fascinating to learn from Dr. Linville about the Academies, where Olympic athletes were trained. The concept of training the total athlete—body, mind, and spirit—was widely recognized and utilized in the ancient world. It leads one to consider the possibility that the best way to maximize the full potential of a modern athlete is to take a similar three-pronged approach to training.

I highly recommend this book to anyone who aspires or feels led to be involved with sports and recreation ministries. The interest in sports and competition has never been higher in our society than it is today. Likewise, the ugly issues of cheating, poor sportsmanship, greed, and scandal have never been more prevalent in the world of athletics than they are now. Athletes and coaches at all levels in all sports need to be taught and encouraged that there is a better way, a higher way, to enjoy sports and competition. Sports ministry is growing worldwide and with it the opportunity to transform and redeem the way society views competition. The potential harvest is enormous, and we desperately need more workers to invade the playing fields, courts, stadiums, and gymnasiums all around us. Hopefully, as you read and study this book by Dr. Greg Linville, you will be more equipped to share a new vision to athletes and coaches of competing for Christ and expressing our deep gratitude to God by the way we play and instruct.

"I urge you therefore, brethren, by the mercies of God, to present your bodies a living and holy sacrifice, acceptable to God, which is your spiritual service of worship. And do not be conformed to this world, but be transformed by the renewing of your mind, that you may prove what the will of God is, that which is good and acceptable and perfect." (Romans 12:1–2)

Todd Blackledge
Canton, Ohio, USA
September 2013

ACKNOWLEDGMENTS

B ryan Mason came to my rescue during the oral defense of my doctoral dissertation. One of the committee members believed I lacked sufficient citations. Bryan simply stated the reason for a more limited number of citations was because much of the dissertation was seminal information, reflection, and application. The committee member was initially stunned into silence, but as she heard more of my explanations and the affirmations of the members on the dissertation committee, she became significantly excited to be part of such a unique and groundbreaking project. I was truly thankful for Bryan and my other two evaluators, Steve Quatro and John Garner, for their help in reading through my drafts but even more appreciative for the years we have shared working through the concepts put forth in my dissertation and in this book. Bryan, Steve, and I made up the CSRM staff "triumvirate," and John and I have partnered on many speaking and writing projects. I thank them and many others for their input into my thinking and my life.

The honest truth is this book is what I really wanted to write for my dissertation. I felt called to articulate and assemble these thoughts and was extremely frustrated to put this project on hold until the dissertation was done. Yet, as this book finally comes to fruition, it becomes increasingly clear each additional year adds more clarity and allows for more expansive contemplation of a lifetime of experiences, conversations, and reflection. I have come to realize the final product will never be completed because God continues to mold me and my thinking via continued revelation through the study, instruction, and reflection upon the divine Word of God and through the interaction with, and participation in, the natural revelation of creation and the human experience.

All of this to say, there have been so many people, institutions, and experiences that have shaped my thinking and I wish to thank all who are mentioned here. I also seek to indicate I recognize that what follows flows through my "pen" but is truly the property of a much larger community. The Scottish Enlightenment of the mid-eighteenth century (which eventually found its fulfillment in the American Declaration of Independence, Constitution, Bill of Rights, and capitalism) emerged from a group of moral philosophers, clergy, and thinkers who all interacted on the streets of their neighborhood in Edinburgh, Scotland. In a similar fashion, the concepts of this book have emerged via the modern "technological communication village" of the late twentieth and early twenty-first centuries. I have been fortunate enough to personally take part in symposia, discussions, and dialogues in the United States, Canada, England, Greece, New Zealand, Australia, and Egypt where these concepts have been discussed. The core of what is contained in the chapters of this book has been continually bantered back and forth via Skype, webcams, emails, and websites. This has enabled an ever increasing ease for the necessary international "check and balance," which ensures clarity and theological orthodoxy.

I gratefully recognize the input of many colleagues who have pioneered these areas with me. Each has directly or indirectly influenced my thinking and much of what follows stands on the shoulders of many others. I am indebted to all who are cited or mentioned in this treatise. Though I attempt to give proper credit where it is due, I do not always use traditional citations because (a) much of what follows has never been written, only discussed and (b) it is hard to determine the genesis of a specific thought or concept when it is born in the midst of a CSRM roundtable discussion, academic symposia forum, or while relaxing in an English pub. The scarcity of specific citations does not indicate a lack of appreciation for the influence of others, nor should it be thought I assume all credit for what follows. Rather, it should suffice to state what a privilege it is to live during this time period and to have the opportunity to interact with such gifted and inspired people who stimulate seminal thoughts and concepts. There truly has been a unique convergence and confluence of people and ideas.

A few specific activities bear special mention . . .

Beginning in 1997 the Association of Church Sports and Recreation Ministers (CSRM) held an almost yearly academic symposium on topics related to the theological and ethical aspects of competition and sport. This symposium has featured a "who's who" of sports theologians and practitioners, including Dr. Vickie Byler, Dr. Steve Conner, Graham Daniels, John Garner, Dr. George Hunter, Caz McCaslin, Lowrie McCown, Dr. Steve Moroney, Dave Oakley, Professor Rodger Oswald, Dr. Andrew Parker, Professor Steve Quatro, Frank Reich, Barb Wagenfuhr, Stuart Weir, and I. To anyone interested in these topics, I would greatly recommend the resources found at www.csrm.org, including many hours of unpublished recordings of academic symposia on these topics by many of the following authors and speakers.

In addition, I was asked to participate in two symposia in the United Kingdom. The first was sponsored by Christians in Sport (CIS), where I was asked to dialogue with then-CIS directors Stuart Weir and Graham Daniels on the topic of Lord's Day considerations for sport. The other was to make a presentation on the same topic at the York St. John University Sport and Spirituality Symposium. These and other symposia, including numerous CSRM and CSKLS conferences, have been foundational in establishing and clarifying much of my thinking about competition and sport.

I am the grateful recipient of the information attained by listening to hundreds of seminar presenters via conferences and recordings. I have been shaped by listening to every CSRM seminar ever recorded and greatly influenced by these faithful men and women of God.

A number of special people also bear special mention . . .

My Students: I have been extremely blessed by the thousands of students who have graciously allowed me to "test" my theories on them. They will never know how valuable their debating of these concepts with me was in the development of what is written here. Their feedback and push-backs have helped shape much of what I believe and teach today. In addition, the rubrics contained in these chapters were at least partially formed over my years of teaching the Theology of Competition and Christmanship Sports Ethics courses to Sports Outreach Ministry students. I specifically recall Matt Snyder and Dave Williams, who greatly shaped my ideas about templates for determining biblically defensible sports and actions within sport. I could specifically name literally hundreds of students who all have made impressions upon me, but Dave garners additional, special mention for his holding me accountable and supporting me, CSRM, and all things "sports ministry." Of course, all errors of thinking, logic, or theology are my own and not the responsibility of my students.

First Friends Church: Every theoretician needs a laboratory to test theories and learn experientially. To that end . . . I am grateful for the people and colleagues at First Friends Church. For 15 of the most fulfilling years of my life, the leaders, congregational members, and participants of the Sports Outreach Ministry of First Friends Church afforded me the opportunity to minister and be ministered to. We worked, ministered, and experimented together. I am truly thankful for each of the three senior pastors I served under and a fourth I served with. I wish to offer special thanks to Dr. John Williams and his wife Carol for hiring me and for their belief in me and my visions for reaching the world through sport. The late George Robinson was a unique inspiration and truly attempted to enable my dreams to come true, including embracing the vision for the building of a 40-acre ministry site in which "a field of dreams" could be realized. The third was Mark Engle who was a great collegiate athlete and shared the passion of using sport to reach others for Christ and actively participated in the church's Sports Outreach Ministry. And last is my good friend and current Lead Pastor Stan Hinshaw, who supports and empowers what may well be the most effective local church Sports Outreach Ministry in the country. Stan allows me to continue as a volunteer in that outreach ministry, and he ensures the church's ongoing support of my efforts in and through CSRM.

In addition and perhaps more importantly, I was privileged to work with an incredible Sports Outreach Ministry staff. Tanya Hockman came as an intern, was eventually hired to direct all of our women's ministries, and without a doubt developed it into the model for all other churches. Tanya and I continued our sojourn together for another 15 years as we co-taught courses at a local university where we constantly dialogued about the theology, theory, and pragmatics of sport and faith integration. Tanya is truly one of the most gifted and committed people I have ever had the privilege of knowing. She has been a true partner, colleague, and a major influence in my thinking and life. Her modeling of Christmanship as a daughter, sister, wife, mother, and coach is unparalleled. Todd Larson was one of the best outreach-oriented Sports Ministers I ever encountered and was a phenomenal partner for many years. Paul Johnson, Tom Schooley, and Angela Arrington have paid me the highest compliment. They continued to oversee one of the finest local church sports outreaches in the world on the foundation we collectively created. Upon my departure as their director, they continued in their endeavors to redeem both the sports person and the sports culture.

Two other Sites—The Canton Stearn Center Boys Club & Heritage Christian School: Two other important places and a few significant people significantly impacted the development of Christmanship concepts. Tim Haverstock, Dave Miday and Smoke Monnot—staff and board of the Boys Club—and all who played in the leagues there, were greatly influenced by and constantly challenged by the Christmanship ethic. Their insights were profound and their friendship is irreplaceable.

The coaching staff—Larry Hackenberg and Mike Brown—and players at Heritage provided a unique opportunity to live out Christmanship at the scholastic level. Over a period of 8 years, Coach "Hack" and our staff was eclipsed by only Canton McKinley, who won only one more game than did Heritage. Coach Brown brought a rare combination of passion, love and strategy to the team, and Coach Hackenberg possesses one of the greatest basketball minds I've ever encountered. He has shaped my views of Christmanship more than any other single person. I have a very unique bond with these two men and count them among my greatest friends.

Mentors: Mentors include Jim Leedy and Bob Starcher, both of whom the Lord saw fit to take home in the past few years. They taught me, encouraged me, and modeled for me the essence of Christmanship. I miss them and their guidance. Many others have served as mentors through their writings and life, including Eric Liddell, D. L. Moody, John R. Mott, James Naismith, Robert McBurney, Kynaston Studd, and his better known brother, C. T.

Oliver House Publishing: A big thank you to John Oliver, John Geib, Peter Guiler, Marge Oliver, and Stan Terhune for their constant encouragement to write this book and especially for the extraordinary efforts Stan Terhune made in his diligent and vigilant editing of the text.

Colleagues: I am greatly indebted to fellow travelers along this journey with whom I've had regular times of dialogue: Tim Adcox, Dr. Vickie Byler, Dr. Steve Conner, Tim Conrad, Graham Daniels, Jim Dayhew, John Garner, Jay Martin, Bryan Mason, Lowrie McCown, Rodger Oswald, Steve Quatro, Wade Salem, Bob Schindler, Barb Wagenfuhr, Stuart Weir and Ken Youngson. Many of these ministry partners have also authored works that greatly influenced this book.

Other authors who have graciously granted me a day or more to dialogue or have taken time at a conference to think together include Dr. John Byl, Dr. Robert Higgs, Dr. Shirl Hoffman, Dr. George Hunter, Frank Reich, and Dr. John White.

To all of these and the countless hundreds of others I pause to say thank you and to recognize each person's role in shaping who I am and what I write here. This book is truly a result of a collective genius of which I am just the mouthpiece.

CSRM Staff and Board of Trustees: I have shared more than 25 years of common ministry with my Administrative Assistant Martha Wertz. Martha, more than any other staff person, deserves special credit for overlooking my foibles and for covering my administrative deficiencies. I can never thank Martha enough. She is the epitome of a willing servant, team player, and loyalty.

Maranda Curl is perhaps the most genuinely nice person I've ever met. Maranda is also incredibly gifted and capable. She and her husband Brent deserve special commendation for also enduring their tenure with me. They have clearly been the driving force behind the CSRM Sports Outreach Summits from which I have attained so many of the insights that make up this book. Their incredible abilities to plan, organize, and implement the world's largest and most significant conference for local church sports outreach has produced a forum from which the concepts in this books emerged.

Don Renninger has been a longtime colleague and friend. This book would be greatly lacking without Don's artistic and technical gifts. I provide a scanty idea for a graph or picture and he takes it from there. All the graphic and artistic work in this book are directly the result of this most gifted man.

Rob Wagler has become a more recent colleague and a great sounding board. He is insightful, supportive, and one of the most encouraging men of God I've had the privilege to know.

Three other previous CSRM staff members have already been mentioned but deserve additional, special mention here: Bryan Mason, Steve Quatro, and Dr. Vickie Byler. I owe each a special recognition for countless hours of doing sports ministry together and thinking about its theological foundations.

A Special Bible Study: For nearly 3 years, I had the special privilege of meeting with a group of Christian athletes and coaches, many who played and coached professionally and who remain in high profile positions within sports to this day. I owe much of the rudiments of Christmanship to those men as we engaged in weekly dialogues around what the Bible had to say about competition, sport, family and life. I am truly honored they wrote the Foreward and some of the endorsements that appear in this book. I count a decades-long friendship with each of them as one of my life's true blessings.

Four special groups: Four special groups (the Young Life Family, the "Camping Buddies," my prayer partners, and our "TLC" group) have been incredibly influential in my life and each person within each of the groups has played a part in making this book a reality. From the most important support—prayer—to personally encouraging me and for many even financially supporting the ministry of CSRM and/or the publication of this book, I say thank you. To each of you—you know who you are—thank you.

Family: How can I not give credit to my family?

My first coach was my father, and it is he and my mother who bear the major responsibility for shaping my faith–sport integration and for establishing the spiritual, ethical, and theological foundations of my life. Their guidance, love, encouragement, and lifetime of prayers are appreciated more than I can communicate.

Crediting my son and daughter goes beyond a common obligatory thank you. They truly have influenced my thinking more than anyone else. We have shared so much in our common competitions and sporting experiences. They evidence Liddell's "pleasure" in their playing and coaching, perhaps better than anyone I've ever observed. They are the first people I want to discuss the latest Cleveland Indians, The Ohio State Buckeyes, or local high school game with. I cherish all the years we attended the state high school basketball tournament games. Is it any wonder the greatest sports movies ever made always end with a kid and a dad in the back yard "having a catch"? I imagine at least part of eternity playing catch with my dad and my kids.

My wife is truly the joy and love of my life, and although she is the least athletic person in our family, she certainly is the one from whom I have learned the most about the world of "competitive" ideas. She has been my biggest fan, my best critic, and the consummate life's partner. Jane inspires me to excel and to "walk humbly" with Christ. She has watched far more games than she ever imagined possible.

Sacred Place: Much of this was originally written and all of it was repeatedly edited on the shores of Lake Erie at the Lakeside Chautauqua. There is indeed something sacred and inspiring about the Chautauqua community. Jesus Christ has redeemed and inspired hundreds of thousands of people through the religion pillar of Lakeside, and generations of people have benefited intellectually, spiritually, culturally, and physically through the various expressions of all four pillars of Lakeside. As Lake Erie's blue, green, and sometimes turbulent gray waters broke upon the rocky shore of Lakeside Chautauqua's Island View Park, God repeatedly spoke to me. Computer in hand, I typed, trying to record as best I could what I heard from Him. I would encourage anyone needing a "thin place" for rest, recreation, great entertainment and spiritual renewal to consider visiting Lakeside Chautauqua. (www.lakesideohio.com)

A Final Word: It is hard to know exactly where one idea inspired another and it is just as hard to know who inspired whom. It is easier to recognize I owe much to all who are cited here and many others. It must be stated, however, that although much credit should go to others for all that is true and positive in this work, I am completely responsible for any flaws or shortcomings presented and in no way wish to suggest any of my errors in reasoning, remembering, or hermeneutics to be the fault of any of my colleagues. To put it bluntly, although I take full responsibility for this work, I very much realize it is a product of the years I entertained these ideas and discussed these issues with those mentioned and many others who are not mentioned—far too many to mention. To all who have had an impact or an influence, I say thanks. To any who believe I have not given adequate or appropriate credits for their influence, please bring it to my attention so I can apologize and give proper acknowledgment in future editions. I recognize this to be much more God's work than mine, a true Kingdom effort, and I have felt a weight of responsibility to undertake the exhausting effort to bring it all together in an attempt to further His Kingdom, rather than my personal portfolio. It is to His glory and for the purpose of redeeming the people of sport as well as redeeming the world of sport that I write.

PREFACE

I am a practicing theologian and have been about my practice since 1972, when I graduated from high school and served a center-city church as the director of a "drop in" teen center. Within the next year, I expanded my practice to include center-city ministries with two other para-ministries: Young Life and the YMCA. My practice continued for the next 13 years as I used athletics, motorcycles, camping, and other activity-based tools to reach out to urban kids, gangs, and their families. During this time I began to practice my theology in a new area—coaching. Coaching doors continued to open for me, first at local high schools and then at a Christian college. Building upon my experiences as a multi-year letter-winner in three high school sports and a brief stint as a collegiate coach, I was called to a sports and recreation ministry at a local church, where I continued to practice my theology until 1999. During this time, in the early 1990s, I started teaching as an adjunct professor of sports ministry. This role expanded a class at a time, ending with a tenure-track position as an assistant professor of ministry, which began in 1999. I also assumed the position of executive director for the association of Church Sports and Recreation Ministers (CSRM) in 1999. Thus, I have been a practicing theologian for more than four decades.

In addition to having been a practicing theologian, I experienced many years' worth of informal theological training and extensive formal theological training from a Christian college and three different theological seminaries. The completion of an M.A., an M. Div. Equivalency, and a D. Min. could only be eclipsed by the unbelievable privilege of having been granted an Honorary Doctorate of Divinity in Sports Ministry from Brier Crest Seminary. I believe theology—the study of God—is a lifelong process, and yet it is worthless unless practiced in daily life. That belief is the driving force for this book.

So I have been at this notion of learning about, and practicing, theology for some time now. Not nearly as long as many, but certainly long enough to have learned a few things and because of the varied experiences in different cultural, ministerial, and academic settings, both in North America and other countries, I have been able to integrate both the theological and methodological sides of theology. These experiences have cumulatively brought me to this place and time. They enable me to put together what follows in this book. Because of my experiences and training, I am able to provide some insights that only a practicing, trained theologian can realize and comprehend. God has graciously allowed me to receive and comprehend not only His natural revelation, which comes from meditating on the natural order and experiences of life, but He has also placed in my path a plethora of theological mentors, some of whom I've met as teachers, coaches, and professors, others whom I've only encountered through books or stories. These mentors have helped me to comprehend the divine revelation of God's word. Therefore, the strength of what follows is twofold. First, this work is intended to make the ministry of future sports and recreation outreach ministers pragmatically easier to comprehend and practice. Second, it will offer to the formal theologian insights into Scripture and theology that can only come from a life of applied and practiced theology.

I do not claim to be the final authority on the theological and pragmatic aspects of what follows, as God alone reserves that right. I only hope to aid those of us in the process of being seekers of God and of truth. I recognize the dilemma faced by anyone who has ever set about to put words into print. That dilemma is what looks good or right today may not look as bright a few years from now. Therefore, my hope is this treatise will be used of God to spur more right thinking, which will cause more right living, which will ultimately aid those who are practicing their theology in sports and recreation outreach ministries, and as a result, these ministers will be used to invite more people to enter into a personal relationship with Christ. If there is ultimate wisdom and truth in this work, it will be so proven, and if not, it will still aid the movement by preventing others from falling into the same trap.

As I write this, sports and recreation ministry in the local church stand at a crossroad. Sports outreach is a relatively new but maturing movement within the church. Though most churches are still not involved in sports ministry, this methodology has been utilized by a growing number of local congregations since the early- to mid-twentieth century. At the very least, sports ministry is no longer novel and, unfortunately, has begun to show signs of fatigue. It is evidencing an increasing need to be re-envisioned through solid theological truths and biblically based philosophical principles. In fact, *and I cannot state this strongly enough*, if the people, ministries, and institutions of the current Sports Outreach Movement do not take seriously the call to reestablish their *methodological models* upon *theological truths* and *biblically based philosophical principles*, the movement will fade into irrelevance as did its predecessor—Muscular Christianity. Nonetheless, I believe the Sports Outreach Movement is beginning to awaken, and I look forward to its regaining its momentum at the start of the twenty-first century. It is hoped this book will prove to be catalytic in equipping and empowering the Sports Outreach Movement to be an ever increasing force for evangelism, mission work, church planting, and church growth. It is further hoped this humble work will inspire the Sports Outreach Movement to accelerate its Kingdom efforts and help it remain true to its roots of calling people to Christ.

Logically, and it should not be a surprise to anyone, since the Sports Outreach Movement in local churches is relatively new and underdeveloped, the accompanying body of literature can be no further along in its development. Although a few authors have written upon the topic of sport and religion or athletics and faith, very little has been written about either the theology or Christian ethics of sport, nor has much been penned about sports ministry. I believe this is due to the fact that competition is not an area of concern to most theologians, and most athletes and coaches don't have the theological training needed to interact with the more substantive issues. Moreover, much of what has been written on these topics has been very critical of competition and the Sports Outreach Movement. These critical views need to be challenged with the truths found in this book—the author's treatise on the theology of competition. It is hoped new light will be shed by the concepts and truths portrayed in this work, and although I do not claim to be either a great theologian or an athlete of much reputation, I do have a substantial background and interest in both and hope to make a contribution that can encourage and inspire those involved with sport and ministry.

This work is intended to aid in the theological, philosophical, and methodological development of three communities. The first community is the sports and recreation outreach minister. The concepts presented in this book are set forth so as to be a catalyst for thinking and planning new and more vital sports outreach ministries of the future—missional *methodological models* (Level 3) that are founded on strategic *philosophical principles* (Level 2), which emerge from biblically based *theological truths* (Level 1). If the models found in this book help just one sports and recreation outreach minister be more effective in reaching the athletic world for Christ, I will consider my efforts to be a success.

The second community this is intended for is the academy. It is hoped this book will help meet the need for quality texts for those training future sports and recreation ministers at Christian colleges and seminaries. The third community is the world of coaches and athletes, especially those who are sincerely attempting to honor Christ through and in their sporting endeavors. My hope is any coach or athlete who reads this will know competing in sport is biblically defensible and how to participate in sport in Christ-honoring ways and at Christ-honoring times. Perhaps a few will even come to a personal and saving faith in Jesus Christ. Of course the ultimate hope is God will be glorified. It is to these ends this book is being offered.

This book is a labor of love. I am deeply indebted to "the great cloud of witnesses" who have preceded me. This book is an attempt to give back a small portion of what they have given to me. I hope my efforts to introduce these "fathers and mothers" of the sports ministry movement are worthy of my great debt to them.

Last, it is also a labor of love on the behalf of all who currently serve as a sports and recreation minister. Not only do I love sports outreach ministry and hope to enhance it with what follows, but I also have had the opportunity to meet with thousands of sports, recreation, and activity ministers who are currently reaching out for Christ through sports and recreation. Today's sports outreach minister is usually underpaid, overworked, and underappreciated. People often wonder when he or she will get a real job or at the very least don't realize sports outreach ministers do much more than play. So for all who have spent countless hours manicuring baseball fields, mopping gym floors, training coaches, settling disputes between parents and referees, running camps, and wondering if it was all worth it, I write this book to encourage you. "Don't be weary in well doing," my fellow sports ministers. Though not always appreciated, yours is a great calling, and I want you to know you follow in the line of a rich heritage of sports ministers. Hopefully you will find this affirming and thus you will be encouraged to be even more diligent in your "working as unto the Lord."

Dr. Greg Linville
Lakeside, Ohio
2013

CHAPTER 1

PHILOSOPHIC FOUNDATION OF COMPETITION

This chapter articulates the philosophical foundation from which a discussion concerning the integration of competition and Christianity emerges. It also presents seminal thinking on factors that both positively and negatively influence competition. It includes a pioneering work on charting the predictability of an athlete's fulfillment within his or her athletic endeavors and key definitions of competition, sport, and athletics.

1

I. INTRODUCTION—THE QUESTION

Each time the world focuses on the Olympics, people holding a theistic worldview revisit age-old questions concerning the integration of sport and faith. They ask questions such as: Does God approve of athletics? Would Christ participate in sport? Or, is competition biblical? With regard to sport, Arthur F. Holmes discusses three cautions expressed by Thomas Aquinas. "First, do not take pleasure in indecent or injurious play. Second, do not lose your mental or emotional balance and self-control. Third, do not play in ways ill-fitting either the hour or the man . . . play should have positive moral and other consequences . . ."[1] On the surface this sounds like good advice, but how are competitors who are faithful followers of Christ to ultimately know?

To the great encouragement of such Christian athletes, there are scriptural answers to these age-old questions. Competitors desiring to obey, honor, and worship Christ can find biblical principles to guide their sporting endeavors.

What might frustrate these athletes is to discover their questions are not easily answered—nor quickly attained. Solid answers require committed study, dedicated inquiry, persistent research, and contemplative reflection. This treatise is written to aid, guide, and complement such efforts. Its purpose is to empower all who are on the journey to discover how to honor Christ in and through their athletic endeavors.

The ultimate destination of this journey is to outline how to compete in the image of Christ (Christmanship). Stops along the way will include theological, philosophical, methodological, and ethical discussions. These discussions will determine:

- ⚽ Theologically based truths, foundations, and justifications for competition
- ⚽ Biblically based philosophical principles supporting sports in general
- ⚽ Biblically based philosophical principles supporting specific sports
- ⚽ Historically based methodological models for integrating faith and sport
- ⚽ Ethically based guidelines for how to participate in sport, athletics, and games in Christ-honoring ways

---

[1] Shirl Hoffman (ed.), *Sport and Religion* (Champaign, IL: Human Kinetics Books, 1992), p. 251.

The following is written to all who sincerely desire to be (a) **theologically informed** about sport and competition; (b) **experientially formed** in how they play their sport; and (c) **spiritually transformed** as they worship and honor God through their sport.

Every stop serves as a foundation for the next and each builds upon the former. Each is incomplete by itself, but in conjunction with one another make a strong, unified basis for Christian participation in sport and athletics. Together, they form an exciting, albeit daunting, challenge for anyone attempting to integrate faith and sport in biblically based ways—all for the glory of Christ! Preparing and training for a sport take great effort, time, and commitment. Similarly, establishing a biblical basis for competition and sport is not obtained quickly or easily. The journey is about to begin. All aboard!

II. PHILOSOPHICAL PRINCIPLES OF COMPETITION

The words *competition, sport,* and *athletics* are often used interchangeably but in reality have distinctively different meanings. Sport is a subcategory of competition. As Graph 1 shows, sport is one example of, one manifestation of, competition. Sport is one expression of, but not identical to, competition. To fully understand the biblical basis for sport, one must first have an appreciation for this distinction. By comparing business, politics, and other aspects of life with sport, a more complete comprehension of competition and sport emerges.

Two or more political parties debate issues and "compete" for power. Scores of businesses attempt to "win" new customers by improving their products and/or services. Politicians and businesspeople are tempted to "cheat" or even lie in order to "gain an advantage over their rivals." Even a quick perusal of these concepts reveals their similarities, but clear distinctions are also realized.

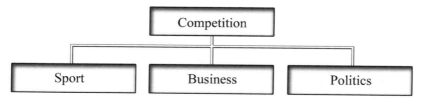

Graph 1

Therefore, to summarize, competition is an overarching concept found in almost every aspect of life, including business, politics, and relationships. As I argue later, competition was created to be a positive force and, when properly understood and utilized, assures many redeeming outcomes. More in-depth definitions enhance a comprehension of what competition, sport, and athletics are (see pages 12–15). These definitions will serve as a foundation to the discussion and help to bring clarity as we progress on our journey to Christmanship. More significantly, I will propose there are two additional concepts crucial to the comprehension of sporting competition. I have termed them (a) the **Progressive Intensity Levels of Competition (PIL)** and (b) the **Motivational Influences on Competition (MI)** and will explain them and their relevance to a proper theology of competition. First, a look at the **PIL**.

A. Progressive Intensity Levels of Competition (PIL)

Vacationing parents are often taken by surprise when a "row" breaks out among children who have been playing peacefully all day while at the beach. They wonder what happened to their blissful reverie. They didn't understand that their kids shifted from children at "play" to opponents engaging in "competition." In more technical terms, what happened was the children unknowingly moved up the **Progressive Intensity Level of Competition (PIL)** scale.

Two children creating sandcastles (**play**) experience no competition until they decide to see who can design the tallest or most intricate castle (**playful games**).[2] The intensity rises until one child's lack of self-esteem (**Internal Motivational Influence on Competition—IMIC;** see section B and Graph 3 on page 6) is threatened by this foray into comparing sandcastles—a form of competition—and manifests itself when the offended child kicks the other child's masterpiece castle to smithereens. The "row" is on. It reignites later as these two youthful competitors take

---

[2] I was first introduced to the descriptive delineation between play and playful games by my friend and colleague Professor John Byl of Redeemer College in Hamilton, Ontario. Byl is the author of many books and has written the best treatise on competition in light of the fruits of the Spirit yet to date.

part in other structured competitions such as **athletic** contests on the lawn or engage in a **game** of Monopoly in the cottage that night. It escalates to yet another level the next day if they form teams with other children they meet at the beach and compete in various **recreational sport** endeavors. "Rows" can, and often do, break out throughout these activities, baffling and frustrating parents.

This common family experience illustrates one reason why it is helpful to have a working knowledge of competition, sport, and athletics and also to understand there are **Progressive Intensity Levels of Competition** that increase as more factors are added to one's activity. This progression is not set in stone, however, as it can either be accelerated or mitigated by both **Internal** and **External Motivational Influences** (see section B). Well-meaning parents who spend the week's vacation breaking up arguments swear they will never take such a "holiday" again. If only someone could have explained the principles of the **Progressive Intensity Levels of Competition** to them, their vacation could have had a much different outcome.

The concept of **Progressive Intensity Levels of Competition** (Graph 2 on page I-1) helps categorize and define competition's escalation along a set of ascendant activities. As sporting commitment and activity increase, they are inherently accompanied and influenced by heightened levels of potentially negative strength and power. Each step taken up the ladder of **Progressive Intensity Levels of Competition** further reduces the likelihood of obtaining competition's goal of fun, enjoyment, fulfillment, or even fitness.

Whereas the stakes are insignificant in unstructured play on a beach (**Play—PIL 1**) or around a Monopoly board (**Games—PIL 3**), they are much more significant for athletes who receive athletic scholarships or those whose livelihoods depend upon how they compete, play, or coach at professional levels of sport (**Pro—PIL 7**). The bottom line is that the higher a sports person progresses up the **Progressive Intensity Level of Competition Scale,** the more they will be challenged to maintain the right attitudes and actions needed to ensure enjoyment and fulfillment. Only when combined with **Motivational Influences** can one's hope of fulfillment be determined or obtained because the two concepts work together in a symbiotic way.

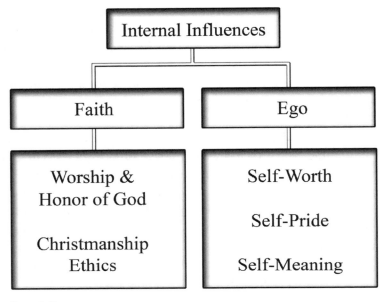

Graph 3

B. Motivational Influences (MI)

The ideal of every athlete devoted to Christ is to experience the words accredited to Eric Liddell: "God made me for the mission field, but He also made me fast and when I run, I feel His pleasure. Not to run would be to hold Him in contempt."[3] However, most sports people will tell you they have rarely, if ever, truly experienced this "pleasure." Most athletes enter into sports, envisioning themselves competing to their fullest, experiencing joy as they run, jump, pitch, catch, kick, and throw. They are often surprised and dismayed when they face the reality of experiencing anger, frustration, failure, and disappointment, which emerge from being cheated by an opponent or from their own inadequate performance and loss of composure. These less-than-satisfying experiences often lead to

---

[3] I've had the privilege of meeting with people who knew Eric Liddell, including his eldest daughter. As best I can tell, Eric never uttered this exact quote, which comes from the script of the movie *Chariots of Fire*. However, each person I've met, from Eric's biographer to fellow POW mates, all agree it is a very fine and accurate representation of what he believed and said.

their own personal disengagement.[4] This book's journey began by clarifying the descriptions of sport and competition. It also describes the **Progressive Intensity Levels of Competition**. Both help define the "playing field" of this discussion. A third step, though, is needed to understand the concept of personal **Motivational Influences** for competing. This is a key element for true competitive joy and fulfillment. These influences stem from either internal needs or external pressures; at times, the more complex and interconnected combinations of the two create incredibly strong forces that threaten to undermine any possibility of achieving the ideals of sport. Graphs 3–6 (see pages I-1 and I-2 for Graphs 5–6) outline many of these influences but are certainly not an exhaustive list.

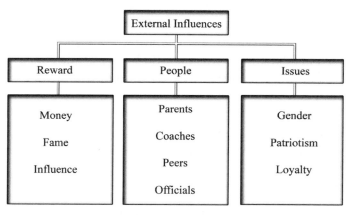

Graph 4

People compete for a variety of reasons. Some are motivated by external forces such as pleasing a parent, friend, child, or spouse; some athletes even compete to prove a social point like gender equality (Billy

---

[4] In their book *Muscular Christianity* (Grand Rapids, MI: Baker Books, 1999), Tony Ladd and Jim Matheson coined the phraseology "engagement, disengagement, and reengagement," which describes the process most athletes and coaches go through. The first step is an excited yet naive involvement in sport by a Christian (engagement). The second step is often followed by a disillusioned walking away from either one's faith or sport when conflicts between one's faith and sport arise (disengagement). Sometimes a more cautious, informed, and mature third step occurs if and when a faith and sport integration can be rationally and theologically comprehended and implemented. I discuss this much more in depth later in a later chapter.

Jean King), religious acceptance (Harold Abrams), or ethnic superiority (Hitler's Nazism). Many compete for personal fame and fortune, while others attempt to secure for themselves a sense of self-worth or significance. These **Motivational Influences** reveal that athletes are not always altruistic in their endeavors and often do not compete to exercise their gifts, fulfill a call in their life, or to experience the joy of Liddell's "pleasure." I believe most athletes have never really contemplated why they compete. Unless they do, they can never truly enjoy their athletic endeavors.

The goal of this treatise—and, to a larger degree, the goal of my life—is to clearly communicate what "feeling His pleasure" in competition really means, and to assist and join with all kindred hearts who desperately desire to experience the deepest of intimacies with their Lord through their sporting and athletic endeavors. My hope is to help people attain joy and fulfillment (**Christmanship**) by clearly defining competition, sport, **Progressive Intensity Levels of Competition, Motivational Influences,** and other concepts, all within a proper theological framework. It is not only necessary to know "right actions" when it comes to sporting activities, but it is also necessary to determine "right attitudes" to truly ensure a biblically defensible participation in sport. To that end, the following discussion explains how and why Liddell's "pleasure" is so rarely attained.

C. Combining Progressive Levels of Intensity with Motivational Influences on Competition

Two forces make experiencing Liddell's "pleasure" a rare phenomenon: competition's **Progressive Intensity Level** and the **Motivational Influences** for competition. Each increase, in either the **Progressive Intensity Level** within competition or in the negative pressures applied to competition from **External** or **Internal Motivational Influences**, results in a higher likelihood of problems developing within competitive activities. Through my experiences I have come to believe both the **Progressive Intensity Levels** and the **Motivational Influences** can be weighted and measured. I also believe they can be assessed through the application of a formula that I call the **Volatility Scale**. This scale predicts a competitor's enjoyment or frustration as illustrated in Graphs 7 and 8 on pages I-2 and I-3.

One's **Volatility Score** will predict whether an athletic activity will be in the **Enjoyment, Encounter, Exasperation,** or even the **Explosion Zone.** **Enjoyment** is obviously the desired zone where competing is truly joyful, but athletes can still experience real competitive pleasure in the **Encounter Zone.** To do so, they must practice **Christmanship** in a supportive environment. **Exasperation** occurs even when the **PIL** of competition is low—if the environment is not conducive for a positive experience. The **Explosion Zone** is not only unpleasant for those involved, but it can also become dangerous, even deadly, when attitudes and tempers flare and are unrestrained. What follows is how to assess, interpret, and apply these concepts to specific athletes and athletic situations.

1. Scoring the Volatility Scale   Each ascending step up the **PIL** scale increases the **Volatility Score**: 1 point for *play,* 2 points for *playful games,* etc., with the top level of *pro* weighing in at 7 points.[5]

Each individual **Motivational Influence** can either increase or decrease the **MI** score anywhere between zero and 3 points: zero points if there is *no MI* one way or the other; 1 point for *little influence*; 2 points for *moderate influence*; and 3 points for *intense influence.* For example, a competitor may experience *intense external influence* from an overzealous and overbearing parent (–3 points); receive *moderate external influence* from a peer who on occasion "bends the rules" (–2 points); and has some minor *self-worth/ego needs (little influence,* –1 point). This totals 6 negative **MI** points to be added into the overall **Volatility Score.**

However, **MI** points can also influence the **Volatility Score** in a positive way. If either an **Internal** or **External Influence** serves either as a guide to enhance one's fulfillment or as a deterrent to one's negative actions, then one's **Volatility Score** moves toward the right side of the scale. For example, an athlete may be motivated by faith to compete with an attitude exemplifying Christmanship (*intense* **Internal Influence**— 3 positive points—see Graph 5 on page I-1); receive *moderate* **External Influence** about sportsmanlike behavior from her coach (2 positive points);

---

[5] The Pro category includes not only all athletes and coaches who are paid to compete but also includes all school coaches who receive a stipend and any college athlete who receives a scholarship.

and receive *little* **External Influence** from an occasional "yellow card" by an official (1 positive point—see Graph 6 on page I-2). This adds up to a positive 6 **Volatility Score** points. The higher the **Motivational Influence Score,** the more likely a positive sporting experience will occur in either the **Enjoyment** or **Encounter Zones,** while lower scores will more likely predict sporting experiences in the **Exasperation** or **Explosion Zones.**

Competitors can chart the likelihood of experiencing Liddell's "pleasure" by establishing their composite score. A composite **Volatility Score** consists of two numbers: (a) the **Progressive Intensity Level** score (ranging from 1–7) and (b) the combined score of the **Internal** and **External influences** (ranging from –25 to +25 or higher). Once this composite number is determined, competitors can then place it on the **Volatility Scale.** If the second number on the composite score is a +1 or above, there is the potential to enjoy positive experiences. The higher the second number is, the more likely this potential becomes. Conversely, any negative score will assure a venture into either the **Exasperation** or **Explosion Zones.** For example, where would a high school varsity boy basketball player competing in a game against his school's rival land on the **Volatility Scale?**

This category of competition is charted at a "6" on the **Progressive Intensity Level (PIL 6).** In determining this player's **Motivational Influences (MI),** he receives **External Motivations** from the following sources: (a) extremely positive support from family (+ 3); (b) encouragement from his coach to strive for **Christmanship** (+3); (c) teammates who are mostly supportive of the **Christmanship** ethic (+2); and (d) playing in a game in which the officials are good and fair (+2). In addition, his **Internal Motivations** include a strong desire to play in a Christ-honoring way (**Christmanship** +3) and a positive self-image keeps his ego needs minimal (+2). Total positive influence points = 15. However, he is playing against a team whose players are only playing to win (gamesmanship) with no regard to **Christmanship** or sportsmanship (–3) and the opposing team is a major rival (–2). The negative **Motivational Influences** totals = –5. Thus, his total combined **MI** is +10 and his composite **Volatility Score** is 6 **PIL**/+10 **MI** (see Graph 8 on page I-3). This **Volatility Score** places the athlete in the **Encounter Zone,** which predicts a reasonable expectation of a fulfilling experience but probably not a totally enjoyable one.

Although it is true that any positive overall **Motivational Influence** score indicates a potentially positive experience, it does not guarantee such an end because each step up the **Progressive Intensity Level** scale produces a more volatile mix of factors that can erupt at any time to overwhelm all the positive influences cultivated in hope of making the endeavors positive experiences. A higher score is required from **Internal** and **External Influences** for there to be even a possibility of such competitive fulfillment. For example, it would take quite a large **MI** to counteract a professional sport activity as even a 7 **PIL**/+1 **MI Volatility Scale** score places the activity perilously close to the **Explosion Zone**. It shows why pure enjoyment is rarely experienced above a level 3 or 4 on the **Progressive Intensity Level** scale because anything above this requires many counteracting positive **Motivational Influences**.[6]

Thus, a combined **Volatility Score** made up of a high **PIL** and a low or negative **MI** predicts potential problems. Conversely, a low **PIL** combined with a high **MI** bodes well for the possibility of enjoyment, but does not guarantee it. The reality is that the higher the **PIL**, the less likely those participating will enjoy their activity, but the competitive activity can still be a positive experience in the **Encounter Zone** if there are enough positive influences to outweigh the negative ones. Often, the determining factor between an **Explosion** or **Encounter Zone,** or an **Encounter** or **Enjoyment Zone,** experience are the choices made by the individual. If they choose negative actions, it will tip to the more negative zone. Choosing positive actions will move it toward the more fulfilling zone. These specific actions are detailed in the chapter on the biblical basis for individual participation in sport and athletics.

It should become apparent from this discussion and these graphs: Real joy and fulfillment are extremely rare commodities but not impossible if there are strong **Motivational Influences**. The ensuing installments

---

[6] This dynamic becomes even more profound with the realization that a normal athletic competition is made up of dozens if not scores of individual people. A college football game could entail some 300 people. If only 5 percent (15 people) become strong negative influences, they can push the entire experience into the **Exasperation** or **Explosion Zones**.

in this book chart a course to stay on the right side of the graph, which is summarized by the overarching concepts found in **Christmanship**.

D. Summary of Philosophical Principles of Competition

Sport, athletics, and play can be subcategorized within the larger concept of competition. Furthermore, understanding **Motivational Influences** for competitions and the **Progression Intensity Level** within competition helps athletes recognize their need in dealing with their competitive desires and endeavors. It is now obvious why a theological foundation for competition is necessary and subsequently why a discussion on the biblical basis for sport and athletics is imperative. Our journey toward **Christmanship** continues.

III. DEFINITIONS RELATING TO SPORT AND FAITH INTEGRATION

The following list, along with Graph 9 found on page I-3, will further define competition, sport, athletics, and play:

⚽ **Competition**—The word *competition* is derived from a Latin root that means "to strive together toward a common goal."

⚽ **External Motivational Influences on Competition (EMIC)** describes the pressures of competing because of, with, or against external forces such as time, obstacles, challenges of weather or other natural causes, courses (golf, race, etc.), and/or other human beings.

⚽ **Internal Motivational Influences on Competition (IMIC)** describes the pressures of competing because of or against internal forces such as one's pride, a personal level of excellence, a personal goal, or unmet ego needs.

⚽ **Sequential**—*Sequential* competition describes the process of one competitor competing in sequence with other competitors as they take turns at a sporting activity such as long jump, pole vault, bowling, golf, shot put, ski jumping, or archery.

⚽ **Simultaneous**—*Simultaneous* competition describes two or more competitors, competing side by side at the same time, in such activities as a marathon, swimming races, sailing regattas, cross-country skiing, or horse racing.

- ⚽ **Synchronized**—*Synchronized* competition combines elements of both *sequential* and *simultaneous* competitions. It describes two or more competitors competing at the same time (*simultaneous*) but playing with and/or vying for the same ball, puck, or other piece of equipment. This type of competition usually has only one team or individual controlling the ball at a time (*sequential*) in such sports as basketball, hockey, football, or baseball. In these examples of sporting competition, teams compete *simultaneously* (both vying for a ball or puck), but upon controlling that ball, they *sequentially* attempt to score with it. In a fairly unique twist, baseball and cricket are the only sports in which the defense has possession of the ball, yet even here the *simultaneous/sequential* process of *synchronized* competition occurs.

- ⚽ **Progressive Intensity Levels of Competition (PIL)**—This phrase is used to describe a concept concerning an ascending progression of seven distinct competitive levels. Each level brings an increasing amount of intensity to the competition, and this increasing intensity carries with it an inherent potential exasperation for all involved.

- ⚽ **MEGA**—Mutually exclusive goal attainment describes the element of competition in which only one person or team can attain a victory or only one person or team can possess a ball, base, or place.

- ⚽ **Sport**—Sport combines many aspects of
  - **Athletics**—Physical activities
  - **Games**—Competitive activities
  - **Play**—Actions that are fun and amusing
  - **Competition**—Competing against others, times, and/or courses or obstacles, and may either be participated in by individuals (golf, bowling, running) or by teams (baseball, rugby, basketball)

- ⚽ **Athletics**—Athletics require activities based upon being physically active and assume one may gain an advantage by being stronger, faster, quicker, or more coordinated. These athletic activities may take place in games, play, recreation, leisure pursuits, or sport.

⚽ **Games**—Games are competitive activities requiring at least one of the following: rules, some level of skill, chance, endurance, strategy, and cooperation in which participants strive to accomplish something or outdo other participants. They may require an athletic ability such as strength, hand–eye coordination, or accuracy needed in games such as horseshoes or may require only thinking, such as a game of 20 Questions, which can be played by a blind quadriplegic and usually rewards those participants who are more strategic or more informed, rather than those who are more athletic.

⚽ **Activities**—Activities are sometimes called sport but are different from sport. They are still competitions (to win a motor race or to hunt/catch/trap an animal) but must be classified in a distinctively different category from sport or even athletics.

⚽ **Play**—Play is defined as an action, exercise, or involvement for one's amusement or recreation. It defines activity that is often more undirected, random, and spontaneous than games or sport. These activities can be building sandcastles, running and jumping, or swinging in one's backyard.

⚽ **Playful Games**—Playful games consist of play with a little direction and organization added in—and possibly with a little playful competition included.

⚽ **Recreation**—Stemming from the concept "to create anew," recreation is used to define the activity that brings refreshment and renewal to an individual usually through the means of a game, pastime, activity, hobby, or sporting endeavor. Within the sports and recreation ministry context, recreation ministry is often used in apposition to sport ministry to refer to activities that are not team or sports oriented. These activities would include such endeavors as hiking, biking, paddling activities, birding, crafts, and camping. There may be competitive elements in leisure pursuits, but normally competition is not a major motivation for the endeavor.

⚽ **Leisure**—Leisure defines the freedom one has from duties or work. It describes the time and activities one participates in during these unrestricted periods. Within the sports and recreation ministry context, it is often combined with the word *pursuits* to describe the activities organized by a local church for people to participate in during their free time.

THEOLOGICAL FOUNDATIONS FOR COMPETITION

This chapter will outline the theological foundation for competition using a traditional rubric of "Creation, Fall, Redemption, and Consummation" as its basic guideline. A lengthy discussion on special and general revelation helps to determine whether or not competition is compatible within a Christian worldview based upon various biblical texts. In addition, arguments against competition will be countered.

I. THE THEOLOGICAL FOUNDATION FOR COMPETITION

A theology of competition is laughable to some, inconsequential to others, and yet an absolute necessity to millions of athletes, coaches, and anyone who has a love for sport and desires to worship God. Two books published in 2009 caught the fancy of many who are critical of sport–faith integration.[1] Tom Krattenmaker's *Onward Christian Athletes* voiced the most extreme attacks upon evangelical sports persons and sports-related ministries, yet both raised appropriate questions about the purpose, role, and methodologies of those actively incorporating faith into their sporting endeavors. These two books are just the most recent examples that demonstrate the need for scholarly theological work on this topic.

For centuries, a theology of competition has either been ignored or easily dismissed by theologians. Often deemed frivolous and not worthy of serious consideration, the subject lacked a truly informed and/or interested constituency. That changed at the end of the twentieth century with a groundswell of people of faith prominently involved in the athletic world pushing for biblical answers to their sports-based ethical dilemmas. As para-ministries and local churches expanded their sport and recreation ministries, more and more theological and ethical dilemmas arose. These ministries were effective in accomplishing their goals of evangelism and discipleship and yet these very outreaches created unique ethical dilemmas and called into question the premise of a faith and sport integration. Biblical clarity and direction are needed.

---

[1] The two books are Tom Krattenmaker's *Onward Christian Athletes* and Shirl Hoffman's *Good Game*. Two critiques of these two books are posted at the CSRM website—www.csrm.org—under the book review page. Krattenmaker is extremely critical in both his purpose and his commentary, and yet some of the questions he raises demand thoughtful, theological responses from the evangelical sports ministry family. Hoffman, an honorable man and a valued colleague, raises questions that challenge his fellow brothers and sisters in the faith. While I heartily agree with much of his thesis, I believe many of his objections will be answered in this treatise. This treatise was not originally meant to directly answer these questions as much of it was written 10 years before the publication of these two books. Had this been published first, I believe it would have made much of what Krattenmaker and Hoffman discuss moot points. Of course it would have verified and strengthened a few of their points as well. I am particularly thankful to Dr. Hoffman, with whom I have had many delightful conversations. Shirl has always warmly welcomed me and my questions. I hope for warm future conversations with Mr. Krattenmaker, who I have yet to meet.

Historically, this biblical clarity has been hampered by the sporting world and the theological world existing in different "silos." Rarely has there been a theologian who has truly experienced or understood competition and sport. Even less frequent was a theologically trained sports person. Furthermore, these communities rarely interact.

Fortunately, a new breed of theologically savvy athletes and coaches developed in the late twentieth century. In addition, the academic world and various sports ministries partnered to strategically answer the raging questions. Personal discussions, conferences, writing collaborations, and academic symposia began to address these issues. Just as the Scottish enlightenment was greatly the result of many keen minds interacting while living in the same geographic neighborhood, a more modern-day "neighborhood" is possible via the wonder of "technological communities," and much of what follows had its roots within this neo-sports-enlightened community. I have been fortunate enough to personally take part in symposia, discussions, and dialogues in the United States, Canada, England, Australia, New Zealand, Greece, and Egypt. Ideas and concepts continue to be bantered back and forth via this "technological enlightenment village," thus enabling an international check and balance that ensures clarity and theological orthodoxy. Graph 10 on page I-4 provides a theological overview and summary I have gleaned from various discussions that have occurred over the last few decades.

A. Theological Template for Understanding Competition

As Stuart Weir, Graham Daniels, Frank Reich, myself, and others have articulated, the biblical basis for competition, sport, and athletics begins with the creation narratives, is supported throughout the Old Testament, and subsequently affirmed in the New Testament.[2] It is defined and

---

[2] I would encourage anyone with a remote interest in this topic to read Frank Reich's article "Competition and Creation," Stuart Weir's *What the Book Says about Sport*, and Weir's collaboration with Graham Daniels' *Born to Play*. In *Born to Play*, Daniels received my blessing to "anglicize" my "Christmanship" concepts, which were unpublished at that time. He did a wonderful job with the material, adding many further insights, but Weir's wise, guiding hand, as editor, should not be overlooked. In addition to these writings, anyone seeking further insight into these concepts should acquire the recordings of CSRM symposia of these three men and others speaking on these topics. The recordings are extremely interesting and can be attained through CSRM's website: www.csrm.org.

guided by a traditional theological fourfold rubric as seen in Graph 10 on page I-4 and articulated in the following list.

- *Creation*—God created all things, including competition.
- *The Fall*—Mankind corrupted the creation, including competition.
- *Redemption*—Of creation, both a specific and personal spiritual redemption (salvation) of individuals involved in competitive endeavors and a general, corporate redemption of the world and culture of competitive sport.
- *Consummation*—There will be a future day in which all will be consummated in glory.

1. Creation—Theological Foundation 1

a. Divine Revelation Support for Competition   God created all things, including competition. Therefore, competition is a "created good" as part of the created order, and although it suffers due to the Fall, it can, and should, be redeemed because it was originally created good. This can be supported from both "divine/special revelation" (the Holy Scriptures) and from "natural revelation." The next stop on our journey will be to look at three components of divine revelation: (i) didactic teachings; (ii) general biblical wisdom; and (iii) biblical narratives.

i. Divine Revelation and Didactic Teachings   Two verses chosen from many others support this thesis from a general perspective. The first is: "Then God saw everything that He had made, and indeed it was very good" (Genesis 1:31). The second verse is: "For by Him all things were created that are in heaven and that are on earth" (Colossians 1:16). Although many other verses could be stated, these two substantiate the point being made, and thus I believe biblical, didactic teaching affirms competition is part of the created order and designed for good.

For clarification, I would also argue these acts of creation included more than the tangible cosmos of planets, rocks, animals, and mankind. They also encompass such intangibles as love, hate, competition, and cooperation. For a deeper discussion of the theology specifically emerging out of the Genesis narrative, I recommend the works of Weir, Daniels, and Reich previously cited. I cannot improve upon their propositions.

ii. Divine Revelation and General Biblical Wisdom   A third verse comes from the Bible's book of common wisdom: the Proverbs. "Iron sharpens iron and one man sharpens another" (Proverbs 27:17). The obvious message is people need others to challenge them in order to grow, mature, or improve. However, some theologians or philosophers would offer the counterargument: "More can be accomplished by encouraging a person than by challenging them." Defining what is meant by the words *challenge* and *encourage* may help, but the real crux of the issue lies in determining what actually occurs in this interaction of "iron sharpening iron."

Take, for example, what has just transpired within the previous paragraph. A competition of ideas has been laid out: argument/counterargument/counter-counterargument. One idea challenges (competes)[3] with the other idea. At the end of the argument, either one idea is seen as being right and the other idea is seen as being wrong or the two have worked together to create a synthesis of ideas far superior than either one by itself. Regardless of whether one idea proves the other wrong or a synthesis is established between the two competing ideas, it results in clear thinking or "sharpened iron." The reality is that both understanding and fulfillment are needed for real growth. It becomes clear by reflecting upon this simple "competition" of ideas about competition: Competition plays a vital role and is a positive force. More importantly, truth cannot be obtained without competition. Thus, the "general wisdom" of the Bible affirms competition.

iii. Divine Revelation and Biblical Narratives   So far, God's divine revelation has served as the foundation for competition from didactic teaching and from the general wisdom of the Proverbs. Competition is also affirmed by examples from narrative stories. Caution is always needed when deducing theological principles from biblical stories, particularly if there is no didactic support from the Scripture. However, I have just demonstrated competition is supported by the clear didactic teaching of Scripture, so the following narratives can be used as further support for competition being biblically supported.

---

[3] Throughout this section, parentheses will appear containing the words *competitor* or *competition*. They are designed to call attention to other words and concepts not always recognized by the uninitiated as being competition. At points, this may become monotonous and even annoying, but I include this technique to emphasize the crucial profundity and prevalence of the overall argument.

Biblical Narrative 1: Paul and Barnabas

Paul and Barnabas had reached an impasse (competition). Barnabas assumed John Mark would join their missionary team. Paul was absolutely convinced otherwise. These two God-fearing and wise men had a "sharp disagreement" (competition) (Acts 15:39). They experienced a competition of ideas or beliefs. This narrative describes two men striving (competing) to be the leader. It outlines their differing (competing) views about John Mark. Luke doesn't sugarcoat this disagreement (competition). It was not pretty. Years later, both men regretted their split and reconciled, including Paul's renewed appreciation of John Mark (2 Timothy 4:11). Nonetheless, at the time, their words were harsh and their relationship was damaged. Perhaps a better understanding of competition would have helped.

Some would offer this narrative as proof for competition being evil or negative. I strongly disagree as I believe it shows how the Fall, which is the root cause of all sin and brokenness, negatively impacts mankind's entire world and endeavors including competition. This narrative does not prove competition to be evil but rather it demonstrates how competition can be misused, perverted, and mishandled, even by two God-fearing men. Rather than realizing competition to be a gift from God, they allowed it to negatively impact them and to some degree allowed it to negatively impact the gospel ministry they were called to.

When properly understood and utilized, competition is a gift. Understanding the gift of competition is a key to interpreting this narrative passage. This narrative reveals competition's overall purpose.

God had given Paul one set of criteria for selecting missionary mates: loyalty, perseverance, and steadfastness. Paul's focus was on the here and now—the success of the current mission work. Barnabas was also concerned about the present, but not exclusively, as he also had an eye for the future. His priorities for selecting missionary partners had more to do with finding young men who had potential—men who could be trained for both current and future ministry. Barnabas realized young, untested disciples would sometimes fall short of expectations and jeopardize a current missionary effort, but he was willing to take such a risk because he knew he was investing in the very foundation upon which future missionary endeavors would be built. Barnabas is a prime New Testament model for how to identify and develop leaders, including, ironically, Paul.

There was, however, more to this altercation (competition) than whether or not John Mark would join them. The discussion (competition) between Paul and Barnabas went deeper. Who was the real leader; who was the one with true spiritual insight; who held the position of authority? Paul probably thought Barnabas was getting old and past his prime. He believed Barnabas was way too soft on holding John Mark accountable for his previous lack of faith and ultimate desertion. Conversely, Barnabas believed Paul to be too young and too inexperienced, lacking in graciousness and long-term vision. He wondered if Paul had forgotten his own past errors and hadn't truly appreciated how much of a risk Barnabas had taken in setting sail with Paul and becoming his mentor. Both men were right in what they were looking for. Both made great points during their argument (competition). Both were ordained to be leaders and both were God-fearing men who had deep spiritual insights. There is no "good guy, bad guy" in this story. I contend their basic problem was they did not understand the principle of competition. They did not recognize they, and their "competing" ideas, were God's gift to one another. This is a great example of the how the Fall negatively impacted the ordained role of competition.

By not recognizing that God had given them a gift in the other person (competitor) and his perspectives (competitive ideas), they failed to reap the benefits of competition. Instead, they only experienced the ugly side of competition. They focused upon winning and losing the debate (competition), rather than focusing on the goal of competition: "iron sharpening iron." Had they enthusiastically engaged in the competitive exchange of ideas with the goal of being sharpened rather than winning or losing, they could have experienced a whole new level of being filled, led, and used by God. They may still have parted ways but with a clearer understanding of their roles, purposes, and mission. In addition they could have parted with each other's blessings.

They could have handled the conflict (competition) in a more gracious and humble manner, and yet God still redeemed the whole situation with the end result benefiting all involved: Two missionary teams were established. Paul was able to grow as a leader and did for Silas, Timothy, Titus, and others what Barnabas had done with and for him. Whereas Barnabas restored John Mark, mentoring him enough so he was later of service to Peter (Mark wrote Peter's version of the Gospel) and where even Paul came to "have need of him," as recorded in 2 Timothy 4.

A few conclusions are in order. This narrative alludes to:

- Creation: Paul and Barnabas did not appropriately understand competition and how it is designed for good purposes.

- The Fall: The Fall led to problems—stemming from Paul and Barnabas's prideful attitudes—and resulted in someone "winning" and someone else "losing" rather than understanding each other and each other's insights. If they would have appropriately appreciated and affirmed one another, a "win" could have been the result for everyone

- Redemption: First, redemption is needed. Second, God is not frustrated by human frailty as He ultimately redeems this situation. The result is not just one missionary team but two!

Biblical Narrative 2: Jesus in the Wilderness

The second biblical narrative and perhaps the most poignant example of the conflict (competition) between Christ and satan[4] occurred in the wilderness. Three times satan comes to Jesus, and each time he challenges (competes with) Him. The challenges were aimed at Jesus's theology, emotions, and physical cravings. Jesus was caught in the midst of a cosmic, eternal battle (competition). Some may use this as an argument against competition, stating how much anxiety and anguish it caused. Their point is well intentioned, and it does ring with a certain initial validity. Jesus did experience discomfort, He was immensely challenged (competition) and perhaps even distraught (caused by competition), yet His faithfulness (competing) exhibited a model and a hope for all of His followers. He demonstrated how to conquer (compete with) evil, how to persevere (compete), how to use the Scripture, and how important having an intimate knowledge of Scripture is as a prerequisite for successfully battling (competing) evil and the evil one. This narrative does not prove competition to be evil but rather demonstrates a model, a hope, and, even

---

[4] It is interesting to note the name satan actually means "adversary"! Not capitalizing *satan* is intentional.

more profound, it strikingly illuminates the necessity of God's plan and rationale for competition.

Unless we know evil, we cannot know good. Unless there is a competitor, there can be no measuring device (competition) to reveal progress, growth, or significance. To me, this is a most significant aspect of competition. We can only really and fully know God by knowing evil, that is, by comprehending the opposite of God.[5] One can somewhat appreciate a beautiful piece of art just by looking at it, but part of the reason some pieces of art become "priceless" is because they are compared (competition) to others of lesser quality, and some items that are purported to be art are quickly dispatched to "junk" status when placed alongside (competition) true masterpieces.

Similarly, Jesus stands in stark contrast (competition) to satan. When compared (competition) to satan, Jesus is easily seen as being superior (competition), and the true value of competition becomes vitally clear through the wilderness temptation (competition) account.

iv. Divine Revelation and the Argument from Silence   It is sometimes argued that competition and sport are intrinsically/inherently evil, yet there is nothing in the Bible to support such a view. This book will take a deeper look at this "argument from silence." There are three perspectives from which the argument from silence will be considered: (a) a holy God; (b) a loving God; and (c) a logical God.

Argument from Silence 1: A Holy God

Competition is sometimes argued to be intrinsically/inherently evil, yet there is nothing in the Bible to support such a view. This "argument from silence" assumes a holy God would certainly and clearly communicate if competition was evil and not good. Furthermore, if competition was intrinsically evil, a holy God would have clearly stated competition to be unholy and commanded humankind to avoid it, just as He did when He commanded all to flee sexual sin (1 Corinthians 6:18), idolatry (1 Corinthians 10:14), foolish and harmful lusts (1 Timothy 6:3–11),

---

[5] I do not believe satan to be equal to God. He is more akin to angels such as Gabriel and Michael.

and youthful lusts (2 Timothy 2:22). In addition, if competition was inherently detrimental to humans, a holy God would have communicated
clear biblical laws and principles concerning it to ensure the ultimate goal
of holiness.

Another argument for competition not being considered evil
emerges from a holy God Who inspired and superintended over all biblical passages that positively reference sport—a subset of competition. Yet
in light of all these passages, some people still claim sports are evil. Their
argument is based upon the presupposition that there is not a full-blown,
didactic affirmation of sport, even in the face of how many times the Bible
references sport in positive ways.

At best, this argument from silence is a "draw." Because there is
neither a biblical affirmation nor condemnation of sport, the argument
from silence is not conclusive. Thus, although it is true that theological
justification for competition cannot be irrefutably argued from Scripture's
silence alone, the absence of its condemnation by a holy God is a powerful
addition to the other arguments offered in this section.

Argument from Silence 2: A Loving God

It is comforting to know a loving God pronounces a myriad of decrees
and mandates for the benefit of His people. He proves His love for
humankind through His laws and commands. He warns us to have nothing to do with evil because He wants "goodness and blessings" to come
to those He has created. If competition were intrinsically evil, if it were
hideously evil, a loving Father would clearly counsel and command His
people to flee from any involvement. Again, the argument of silence as
it relates to competition suggests that competition cannot be considered
inherently evil or else a loving God would have loved His people enough
to have commanded them to have no association with it.

Argument from Silence 3: A Logical God

Ultimately, the argument from silence is based upon the reasonableness
of a logical God. It makes no logical sense for a holy and loving God not
to clearly communicate competition to be intrinsically, inherently evil, if
it were in fact evil. Even cursory readings of the Scriptures provide easily understood condemnations of what is evil and what is good, and yet

competition is nowhere so condemned. A logical God provides direction on what to avoid, what to engage in, and how people are to do both. Because there are no such prescriptions, it is, therefore, logical to assume competition is not intrinsically or inherently evil.

Summary of the Argument from Silence

God did not didactically proclaim competition to be intrinsically evil. However, neither did He single it out and proclaim it good. Thus, those who use the argument from silence to condemn competition must admit the argument from silence is at best a draw. Neither argument can claim a victory solely on the strength of the argument from silence. However, when the entirety of the biblical evidence is weighed, there is considerable support for considering competition good.

For example, the argument that includes competition as being part of the Genesis "all was called good" creation narrative adds significant support for considering competition good. If competition was included in the "good" of creation, and because it was never specifically condemned, competition is biblically affirmed and cannot be considered intrinsically evil.

In addition, when the created-order affirmation is combined with all the positive ways sport (a subset of competition) is presented in the Holy Scriptures, the overwhelming evidence tips the balance of the argument from silence to the side of competition being biblically justified and defensible.

v. Divine Revelation—Summary   The totality of the biblical witness affirms competition as is seen by didactic teachings, narratives, and general wisdom literature. Furthermore, competition is nowhere denied or denigrated by Scripture but is rather affirmed, and its value is repeatedly shown through the Bible. Thus, competition can be affirmed as a positive force through the divine revelation of the Scriptures. Can the same be true of competition as found in natural/general revelation?

b. Natural Revelation   Natural revelation is defined as God revealing Himself through the created order of nature and the human experience. In what follows, I will propose many of the ways in which natural revelation also affirms the "goodness" and purpose for competition in the creation. There are many people who vehemently disagree with this, and so in addition to my assertions, I will also take on one classic example of the opposing view, voiced by Alfie Kohn in his book, *No Competition*. Kohn's overall premise is that competition is, at the least, counterproductive, and more likely, inherently evil. He offers cooperation as a solution and a higher moral option. I believe Kohn's arguments are well intentioned but fallacious on many counts. I counter his assertions with answers emerging from the natural revelation of God. First, a perusal of nature.

i. Natural Revelation 1: Nature   Anyone who has ever walked in a virgin forest is quickly awed by its grandeur. I live in the United States, in the state of Ohio. At one time Ohio had millions of acres of such awe-inspiring forests, but now the state struggles to maintain a mere 700 acres of remnant virgin woodlands. These unspoiled tracts are the healthiest of all woodlands. In these old-growth preserves, trees must grow taller than their competitors to compete for the sunlight and must put down deep roots to compete for water and soil nutrients. These naturally growing trees produce the world's most valued timber because the wood of these trees is stronger, straighter, less diseased, and less knotty than wood from non-virgin forests. Thus, it is easy to understand how competition aids in creating positive results. However, it must be made clear that although competition contributes to this, it is not totally responsible. There is also an element of cooperation in these virgin timberlands, which contributes to the overall health of the forest. An interwoven network of roots form a more secure anchor against erosion, and a phalanx of trees can better serve as a collective protective network against gale winds than when standing alone.

The point demonstrated by the natural revelation as found in virgin timberlands is that competition is an important, positive force and thus cannot be considered intrinsically evil. However, I do believe it can be enhanced when combined with cooperation. This concept is further seen in the following.

ii. Natural Revelation 2: The Animal Kingdom   The first subset of natural revelation is found with the animal kingdom. Kohn and others would argue for cooperation and against competition. These arguments emerge from the faulty assumption that theorizes different animal species intentionally work together. They cite such examples as lions hunting together, and baboons and gazelles working cooperatively to protect themselves from lion attacks. They believe baboons watch for danger (prowling lions) and then communicate to gazelles, which listen to the audible warnings provided by their primate partners. These make for interesting propositions, but such inaccurate and invalidated assumptions result in fallacious conclusions.

Can one assume lions knowingly cooperate to acquire a food supply? Can credulity be stretched to the point of assigning anthropomorphic qualities such as love or compassion to baboons who then cognitively signal their allies—the gazelles? Is it really logical to state gazelles believe the animal kingdom is truly cooperating as they are consumed by the lion? This scenario is nothing more than observing the learned behavior of semi-intelligent gazelles associating sounds made by agitated baboons with danger. To make such anthropomorphic collaborative assumptions about the animal world is ludicrous, and it leads to illogical conclusions.

To carry it even further, once the gazelle is down, the lion pride reverts to "let the big dog eat" philosophy, proving even an assumed cooperation among the lion kingdom has its limits. I find it extremely irrational to attribute any credence to Kohn's assertions of intentional collaborations among quasi-logical species, but do find his examples more than supportive of competition (see the next paragraph). At best, he could argue lions killing gazelles is a perversion of the created order (the Fall— see the following summary), but in order for this to be true, he would have to work from a theological faith foundation for which there is no evidence in his writings.

Contrary to Kohn's speculations about animal-world cooperation, I propose another affirmation for competition within the animal kingdom. It has to do with how wolf packs strengthen the overall health of elk herds by hunting down the weak and sickly members of the herd (similar for lions and gazelles?). Species competition, thus, is good, rather than evil.

Although this treatise is not designed to be the definitive statement about each and every scriptural support for competition, nor the final authority on natural revelation's affirmation, these few rationales provide enough of a basis to undergird this assertion: Competition was part of God's plan and has good and proper roles within the created order. Moreover, these arguments leave no room for claiming cooperation to be the

only good in creation's interactions, nor can it be asserted that cooperation is the better of the two. However, I will affirm cooperation is a positive force in nature but not to the exclusion of competition. I will outline
my belief that both competition and cooperation are positive forces.

A counterargument is sometimes raised: "Okay. I'll grant you, competition has a useful purpose in the animal kingdom now, after the Fall,
but in the original created order, animals didn't hunt and devour each
other and the 'lion laid down with the lamb.'" This argument has certain validity and has to be admitted as one logical possibility, but even if
true, there are two remaining unresolved issues. First, there is no proof
for assuming pre-Fall animals were any different from post-Fall animals.
Second, regardless of the Fall, competition within the animal kingdom
does result in positive outcomes.

iii. Natural Revelation 3: The Human Experience   Insights from natural
revelation are also found in the created order and through common human
experiences, but these insights are often misinterpreted unless evaluated
through the lens of biblical theology and logic. A case in point is found
in the book *No Competition,* by Alfie Kohn. Kohn cites research done by
Mark A. May and Leonard Doob in 1937 that concludes: Human beings
by original nature strive for goals, but striving with others (cooperation)
or against others (competition) are learned forms of behavior (24, 25). He
indicates neither can be proved to be more genetically basic, fundamental,
or primordial (25). Kohn's overall thesis is competition is evil and cooperation is good. However, this conclusion and the data he uses to support his
conclusion do not prove competition to be evil, nor does it prove cooperation to be more ethical than competition. Furthermore, it never considers
the positive results of synchronization when competition and cooperation
are fused. Yet, there is much to be learned from the human experience and
much to be learned from a careful analysis of Kohn's thesis—albeit, lessons
Kohn did not intend.

Human Experience Case 1

One specific case Kohn cites as an attack upon competition entails a
boy who is embarrassed in a math class by his lack of knowing how to
compute fractions. According to Kohn, the boy's inadequacy in math
led to a public embarrassment, which had the potential to scar him for

life. Is this really an appropriate example of competition? I would suggest that rather than being descriptive of competition, it appears to be a clear case of child abuse—at least in how it is presented as happening. However, if taken in the best sense, assuming a well-intentioned and experienced teacher using competition to motivate learning, other clarifying insights emerge.

First, a certain level of embarrassment can be an appropriate motivator within a warm, supportive environment that challenges (competition) students to excel. Experiencing some embarrassment is far better than accepting mediocrity or worse, the alternative of allowing students not to care about their progress, learning, or growth. It must be asked: Is it a better solution to accept any answer on exams so as not to embarrass the student? Surely not! Moreover, to accept no standards for academic learning or no intellectual growth in students in the name of being kind or by trying to establish cooperation as a higher moral methodology is the height of lunacy. Furthermore, if this boy allows this experience to scar or ruin his life, it is not the fault of competition; rather, it is his fault for not allowing competition to motivate him to learn fractions.

Second, this example should be seen for exactly what it is: a theory that states human worth is based upon ability, accomplishment, and peer approval rather than upon the fact God created each individual in His image, which alone gives a person worth. Students steeped in a theology affirming their basic worth will not see competition as an enemy or something to be feared but rather as something to be welcomed and embraced. We achieve because we are created in the image of the Ultimate Achiever. Our worth is in Who created us, not in what we create.

Third, Kohn recognizes (though does not admit) that the end of this argument (cooperation is the goal) would ruin education because the end result is what is called cheating. Think carefully about the difference between cooperation and cheating. There is a very fine line between the two. Again, I ask, think it through. The end result of Kohn's argument would result in the elimination of all exams and standards. Are we really ready for this? Would you ever fly in a plane or have surgery performed on your brain by people who had never been held to any standards, even if it meant the risk of their being embarrassed? It is absolute lunacy to support an academic environment that warmly embraces any answer or winsomely accepts any effort no matter how wrong or lazy these endeavors are. Truth matters, right answers matter, hard work should be rewarded, and laziness or apathy corrected.

The following question must be asked of anyone who is troubled by the assertion articulated in the last paragraph about the necessity for a fixed truth and ultimate authority. To anyone who believes truth is not fixed but relative, I ask: *"Why are you at odds with ultimate truth?"* The answer to that question inevitably is: "Because there is no such thing as ultimate truth." However, such a response is itself an ultimate truth statement, and thus, it disproves the very rationale for saying a belief in ultimate truth is wrong. This leaves only two options: (a) Either there is ultimate truth (thus my statement is valid) or (b) one cannot state my argument in favor of ultimate truth is wrong (and thus again, my statement is valid). Either way my statement must be accepted, and the whole concept of truth being relative is disproved. Interestingly enough, even this discourse is an example of competition and demonstrates its value. It is an example of how a competition of ideas ensures rationale thinking and brings clarity!

Human Experience Case 2

Another human experience argument made by Kohn has to do with the Zuni culture. He states that Zunis are not competitive and bases this upon how the Zunis administrate a foot race. He assumes Zunis prohibit previous winners of a 4-mile foot race from running in future races based upon their noncompetitive mores and principles. Kohn states this prohibition proves Zunis are not competitive.

Two obvious questions arise. *First question:* Is not a race that declares a winner in itself competitive? *Second question:* Does disqualifying a previous winner to allow for other winners not in itself assume competition? Why else would the winner not be allowed to run (compete) unless there were competitive people involved who were "competing" for a chance at winning!

Human Experience Case 3

Kohn claims not all cultures are competitive. This again stretches common sense to the level of incredulity. Do not men within all cultures woo (competition) their wives and women seek to gain the attention (competition) of a future husband? Do not people in all cultures vie (competition) for jobs, houses, and political office? Not only do all cultures have competition, but competition is also an intrinsic part of every person's life in every one of those cultures. Even something as simple as a couple discussing (competition) where to go out for dinner demonstrates the commonness of competition within the human experience in every culture. It is interesting to note that these examples of competition all have positive results: (a) wives feel loved and appreciated; (b) employers get the best workers; (c) government is better when the better candidate is selected; and (d) couples choose a culinary establishment that pleases their palate.

Human Experience Case 4

Kohn further argues competition is not good because it is a perversion of something that is good: cooperation. I believe this argument suffers from a classic logical fallacy. Kohn's contention that cooperation is superior to competition is easily shown to be fallaciously absurd (*argumentum absurdum*) by the following points.

People do cooperate and often for good purposes, but they also cooperate for evil purposes, such as to cooperatively engage in criminal activity or cooperatively facilitate evils such as slavery, abortion, pornography, child abuse, pollution, nuclear war, and genocide. Thus, it cannot be concluded that cooperation is intrinsically good whereas competition is inherently evil, nor does it follow that cooperation is free from the effects of the Fall any more than competition is.

It is clear the misuse of either competition or cooperation cannot be used as a rationalization to dismiss either as being evil. Properly assessed, both are intended for, and can be utilized for, good, even though sometimes both are used for evil. Yet it is a non sequitur (it does not follow) to state because they are sometimes misappropriated, competition and cooperation are intrinsically, inherently evil.

More to the point in disproving Kohn's conclusion, competition—especially in its pristine created essence and even in its somewhat deteriorated "fallen" but redeemed form—serves an important role for the betterment of humankind and the entirety of the created order. Moreover, when an orthodox theology is appropriately applied, a best case scenario is achieved. When the proper balance and interaction of competition and cooperation are achieved, a truly magnificent power results as the following portrayal illustrates.

Human Experience Case 5

Imagine the race is on to provide a cure for diabetes. Two medical laboratories know the first to achieve such a cure will reap a very lucrative financial and positional reward. Both make this research the highest priority of their companies, assembling the best possible team of experts and providing them with all the equipment, resources, and support they need to "beat out" their competitors. All due pressure is applied to all involved, including incentives for progress and reprimands for delays. This scenario makes obvious how competition can positively motivate corporations and individuals to accomplish a socially redeemable goal.

There is, however, one obvious defect when competition is the only approach to solving the dilemma. It lacks what might be gained through having the two firms cooperate. Might this prove Kohn's postulation correct? His argument centers on cooperation being a better solution because the two research firms more quickly and efficiently achieve the goal of solving the problem of diabetes. Yet, this conjecture is proved to be premature when seen through a more thorough thought process.

Continuing with the diabetic cure scenario, assume the two medical firms decide cooperation is more effective and efficient and combine their research teams, laboratories, and resources. Ideas are debated (interestingly, even this cooperation is based upon a competition of ideas) and stories of successes and failures are shared as everyone unites into one cooperative unit. Energy and excitement are high. A week or two later a very subtle shift occurs. All involved realize progress has slowed and possibly even stalled. The malaise, though almost imperceptible at first, becomes undeniable. Some researchers begin to accept the inevitable (there really isn't a cure to be found, no matter how much we cooperate) or even more profound, a sense of complacency settles in among all the workers. This complacency is born of a confidence bred from the belief the best minds and resources in the world are cooperating, and thus, the answer will soon arrive. In essence, the intensity born and facilitated by competition has been diminished, if not eliminated, by the agreement to cooperate. The unintended consequence of cooperation (which was intended for good) is, in the end, evil. In the end, cooperation resulted in retarding the cure for diabetes.

Therefore, the bottom line is: Without cooperation valuable time, knowledge, and effort are lost or even wasted, and without competition the critical drive and motivation to succeed is forfeited. What is needed is a combination of cooperation and competition. Cooperation and competition are best when symbiotically enmeshed. They are at their worst when operating in isolation one from the other.

Human Experience—Summary

In other areas of the human experience, Kohn states there is much lacking in the research of competition and cooperation but believes enough has been done to confirm competition can be learned, and thus, competition is not inevitable. However, this seems to be a self-defeating argument because cooperation can also be learned and does not mean cooperation is inevitably good or even better than competition, nor does it mean competition is inherently evil. Simply put, both competition and cooperation must receive the same critique; both should be considered and evaluated from the same perspective. Furthermore, nowhere does he ever consider the positive synergy of the interaction of the two.

Although it is important enough to dispel many of Kohn's subpoints to demonstrate a superior philosophy and logic in support of competition, I choose not to engage each of his postulations because it would be too laborious and does not meet the basic purpose for which I write. Yet, I believe I have sufficiently dealt with enough of his overall argument, including some of his key assertions, to clearly and decisively refute his belief about competition being inherently evil. I do believe his strongest point has to do with cooperation, and this must receive proper appreciation, but I still contend I have made a stronger argument for why competition is a positive force and, moreover, maintain competition can reach its fullest potential when appropriately combined with cooperation. Even more profound, I believe competition assumes cooperation, for how can two teams compete unless they simultaneously cooperate?

Kohn's proposals all fail to prove their intended conclusion. Human experience does not prove cooperation to be superior to competition, nor does it prove competition is intrinsically evil.

iv. Relevancy of Revelation to Local Church Sports Outreach   A recent trend has developed in local church sports outreach ministries. This trend has attempted to deemphasize and even eliminate competition in church leagues, especially in church youth sports. I understand the motivation behind this de-emphasis. There is nothing wrong with the motivations, but there is something insidiously wrong with the basis for and the results of this de-emphasis on competition.

The leading intellect on the concept of self-image and sport is Lowrie McCown, founder and director of 360 Sports. McCown believes no learning can take place when competition is removed from the academic experience. He believes unless there is competition, students have no motivation for learning. When there is "no child left behind," no child has any reason to strive to get ahead or excel. Similarly, when every child gets a trophy because "every child is a winner," children quickly learn not to exert any undue energy in their sport. The unintended consequence of deemphasizing competition is a generation of unmotivated people who have been taught they get something for nothing! Anyone interested in going deeper on these topics should definitely read McCown's materials, including his book *Focus on Sport in Ministry* or contacting him at www.360sports.org.

Rather than doing away with competition, local church sports outreach ministries have the unique opportunity to engage youth and adults alike in biblically based, theologically sound, and Christ-centered competition. It cannot be too strongly stated: Local church sports outreach ministries have been strategically positioned by God to influence all future generations and cultures about competition. The future of competitive sport depends upon the local church; it depends upon local church sports ministers who understand the theology of competition and know how to communicate it to all they influence. *This is no little responsibility. This is no inconsequential responsibility.*

There is much to learn about competition from the natural revelation.

v. Summary of Natural Revelation   The preceding arguments affirm natural revelation's support for competition being a positive force and playing a vital role for good in the created order. Kohn's arguments from nature, which he believes prove competition to be (a) evil, (b) avoided, and (c) not inevitable, have been sufficiently dismissed. Not only have his arguments about competition being evil been effectively countered, but more importantly I have also explained how natural revelation substantiates competition to be a viable and positive force within the created order. I agree with Kohn's assertion that cooperation is also a positive force. Moreover, I believe the ideal would be a synthesis of the two. One without the other lessens the potency and effectiveness of both. To argue with me on this only serves to prove my point that competition (arguing is a competition of ideas) is good.

Furthermore, I believe both competition and cooperation have been created good, but both have been contaminated by the Fall and, therefore, the following discussion in section B will explain why not even the synthesis of competition and cooperation accomplishes the utopian answer needed for the created realm.

2. The Fall and Its Impact on Competition—Theological Foundation 2

How can you go wrong with a game that rewards a man for running home? Yet the game of baseball experienced a real low in 1919 when members of the Chicago White Sox collaborated with criminals and gamblers to willingly lose the World Series to a clearly inferior team. In their defense, many were simply trying to provide for their families because their owner, Charles Comiskey, through his own avarice, greatly underpaid them. Yet both the players who cheated, and Comiskey through his greed, provide examples of how the Fall negatively impacts sport and competition.

The impact of the Fall can be found in any generation and in all sporting endeavors:

- Contemporary Tour de France bicyclers use banned substances.
- Corrupt leaders of a communistic country lie about the age of their Olympic athletes.
- European football (soccer) supporters riot and even kill rival fans.
- Sports pages in local papers often read more like a jurisprudence section, listing a litany of athlete crimes and arrests.

Does this mean sports are evil? Can followers of Christ participate in such a culture and maintain their relationship with Christ with a clear conscience? Can local churches operate sports ministries?

In previous sections I have established that competition was created good, yet it, along with the entire created order, was undeniably impacted for the worse when "sin" entered the world. That initial sin is what theologians term *the Fall*. Through the Fall, mankind corrupted the entirety of creation, including competition and athletics, and as a result much evil has occurred throughout the history of athletics, including cheating, drug abuse, intentional maiming of human bodies, and even death. A perspective brought about by a comparative analysis from another area of life proves insightful.

Just as competition is part of the created order, so are the realms of science and industry. Science analyzed the need and desire of humans to travel and worked with industry to create one answer to this need, the automobile. This mode of transportation (cars) is amoral, meaning, a car has no morality in itself, yet a car can be used in moral ways. Driving a pregnant mother to a hospital to deliver a child and delivering food to the hungry or medicine to the sick are all examples of moral uses for a car. However, cars can also be used for immoral purposes, such as enabling gang members to carry out drive-by shootings, terrorists to accomplish suicide bombings, or couples to engage in adulterous activity. The immoral misuse of an automobile cannot be used to condemn all cars, nor can it be used to condemn either the realms of science or industry for their creation and production. Likewise, competition cannot be condemned because it is sometimes used in immoral ways or for immoral purposes.

In essence, competition and sport are neither moral (always good) nor immoral (always bad) but rather amoral (lacking intrinsic morality). The moral factor in sports and competition is the person competing in sports. Yes, the Fall has enabled the potential for an immoral misuse of competition, but it cannot erase the created purpose for potential moral use and good of competition. It is because both potentials exist—the potential for good or evil—that the third part of the *Theological rubric: Redemption* is necessary. The concept of redemption will be addressed in a following section.

a. The Fall: Its Relevancy for Local Church Sports Ministry
Most local churches see the huge potential for using sport to attract people to their church and into a personal relationship with Christ. However,

they are greatly disappointed when the negative implications of the Fall begin to emerge in their sports outreaches. These negative implications include altercations in adult sports, hostile parents at youth league games, and angry players spewing verbal profanities. Many church members question the validity of sports outreach when they observe such behaviors. When compared to sedate Sunday school classes or vacation Bible schools, sports outreach is often blamed for "bringing out the worst in people" and, thus, inappropriately deemed "evil." A relevant metaphor helps provide insight:

Indoor plumbing has been a huge blessing to anyone fortunate enough to afford it. Taken for granted in many cultures, this innovative system is not foolproof, and sometimes the plumbing system springs a leak. Such a leak can spread water everywhere, causing much damage. Yet, even when such damage occurs, homeowners never ask to have the system removed—only repaired. Similarly, sports are like the pipes and competition is like the water. When the pipes and joints are sealed and strong, things work fine, but when water pressure surges through the pipes, it is sure to expose the weakest spot in the system.

Likewise, competition finds the weakest link in an athlete's life, but just as a homeowner repairs, maintains, and strengthens a plumbing system, a local church is wise to maintain and strengthen its sports outreach so it can refine the athlete's life and character. In fact, *I believe, sports outreach ministries are better positioned, indeed better suited, to develop the spiritual life of people than any other ministry at the church's disposal.* Why? Because most ministries in the church don't apply pressure to anyone's life, and pressure is needed to reveal the spiritual weaknesses of each individual. Sport relevantly applies the appropriate pressure for the development of true spiritual character.

This is a key point to fully appreciating the strength of sports outreach ministry. Sport provides the church with rare opportunities, perhaps its only opportunity, to fully address the character issues of all who participate. The Fall's negative implications should be welcomed in a local church sports outreach because it is pressure that reveals the inner character of each player and thus provides the opportunity for the church to accomplish its mandate to "go and make disciples." Sports outreach provides the church with a most unique and highly successful way for people to come to know Christ (evangelism) and to develop Christ-like character (discipleship).

Therefore, local church members can rejoice when they walk by a soccer field full of young people and hear a few heated and perhaps profane words being uttered. They should rejoice because they know the sports outreach ministry is doing its job of reaching people far from Christ and rescuing them from the damning effects of the Fall!

3. Redemption—Theological Foundation 3 Two types of redemptions are necessary with the first leading to, and serving as, the catalyst for the second.

The first redemptive activity focuses on redeeming the person of sport. The evangelical community uses different terminologies to describe this personal redemption, including *salvation, being born again,* and/or *entering into a personal relationship with Jesus.* Regardless of the term, it describes God calling people to spiritual life and their acceptance of God's offer of a new spiritual and eternal life. This is a necessary prerequisite to accomplishing the second aspect of redemption.

The second part of redeeming activity focuses upon the Church redeeming the world and culture of sport. This includes both creating God-honoring alternatives for such activities as sports leagues, teams, tournaments, and activities, as well as training individual competitors how to participate in sport for God-honoring purposes, in God-honoring ways, and at God-honoring times.[6]

It must be unequivocally stated, there is a definite biblical standard for both the organization of and participation in sport, and it is incumbent upon anyone who confesses Christ to be Lord and Savior of their life to know (a) what is and isn't biblical and (b) to live out the heart, mind, and actions of Christ in their sporting participation. The overarching principles and more specific actions of Christ-like attitudes and activities will be discussed in detail in a subsequent Christmanship chapter, which

---

[6] Once again, I recommend Lowrie McCown for any serious discussion of sport, faith, and culture. In my opinion, Lowrie is the clearest thinking person on these concepts I have encountered. He understands culture, in particular, sport culture, and how Christians can impact culture. He is a foundational culture shaper for both the world of sports ministry and the world of sport in general. Refer to the previous footnote for contact information.

will further explain the principle of redeeming (a) the individual sports person and (b) the culture and organization of the sporting world.

So yes, there can be redeemed, biblically based, and Christ-honoring participation in sport, yet because of the Fall, true perfection may only be found in a future consummation. It is the responsibility of the Church (those redeemed by God) to be about the God-ordained task of bringing redemption to the world of sport and recreation. Redemption includes sharing the love of Christ with athletes who compete (redeeming individual people) and also participating in the competitive athletic world in Christ-honoring ways (redeeming the world of competitive sport).

4. Consummation—Theological Foundation 4   Many may believe the first three points of this theological rubric for competition and sport to be highly controversial (Creation—Fall—Redemption). The fourth part of the rubric—Consummation—may be even more so because it asks two questions. Will there be sport in the afterlife? Will we compete in our heavenly existence? The short answer is, yes, I believe there will be at least competition if not sport, and although the concept of heavenly sport is intriguing, I'm content to leave this discussion for a later time (probably during our eternal sojourn) because I believe our earthly time can be much more profitably used to concentrate on how to get the first three aspects of the rubric right in our current existence.

The reason that the concept of heavenly competition and sport is troubling to most is because they start with a presupposition that assumes competition and sport are intrinsically evil, and this presupposition doesn't square with the fact that heaven is totally void of evil. I agree heaven is devoid of evil but do not agree competition is evil. That is why I have labored to prove competition is not intrinsically, inherently evil. If it were, it could not be found in eternity in any fashion, but if it is not inherently evil then there is the possibility of heavenly competition and sport. However, it must be understood that just because it has been proved competition is not evil does not automatically mean heaven will include competition. Furthermore, and once more, in my opinion, we should focus more on the here and now and trust God with the heavenly future.

Thus, in the interim, my recommendation is to leave this for a heavenly discussion. If we do discover there is competition and/or sport in heaven, we can fully participate, enjoy, and worship God in our sporting competitions; if there isn't any such activity in heaven, then we can sit around and discuss with God why competition isn't in heaven. Of course, if competition is not in heaven and we are having such a debate (competition of ideas), the discussion will not be taking place in heaven but in the other alternative! Can you imagine any existence, heavenly or not, devoid of any discussion? Draw your own conclusions!

B. Summary of the Theological Foundations of Competition and Their Relevance for Local Church Sports Outreach Ministry

The bottom line: The discussion on whether or not there will be competition and sport in heaven is not all that relevant to local church sports outreach ministry. It really won't have much of an impact on any missional sport outreach a local church engages in, but I've included it for the purpose of being comprehensive and to provide local church sports ministers a handle on how to talk about it, should someone raise the question in postgame devotions or personal dialogues.

Beyond this, it's important to recognize even though the church has the correct purpose for engaging in sports (redeeming both the individual sports person and the world of sports) and attempts to engage in sport in a God-honoring way (Christmanship rather than gamesmanship or sportsmanship), there will inevitably be times of failure due to the Fall. At these times confession must be made and grace given. A forgiving grace must be extended to those who fail, as those who fail confess their failings (sin) and all seek to be reconciled to God, others, and self. A local church sports minister is wise to remember that perfection will not occur on earth and adjust expectations accordingly and, more importantly, anticipate the problems so as to minimize their negative effects. A church league will never truly experience perfection on earth. Only in the final consummation will there be the possibility of perfected competition.

We've completed the second stop on our journey. This brief theological overview has established that competition is a God-ordained part of the created order, and although created good, it is now negatively impacted by the Fall and in need of redemption. This leads to the next task: to determine if sport and athletics, being subcategories of competition, can be justified biblically. The train ride will continue in Chapter 3 as I seek to establish biblical principles for sport and athletics.

CHAPTER 3

BIBLICAL PRINCIPLES FOR DETERMINING CHRIST-HONORING SPORT

This chapter will build upon the premise established in Chapter 2 that competition is theologically sound by outlining the biblical foundation for sport and athletics. This is done by going one step further in creating a template based upon five biblical principles for determining which sports are biblically defensible and which ones are not.

REVIEW

Our journey began in Chapter 1 by determining a philosophical discussion of sport, which included a lengthy description and definition of competition, sport, athletics, and games. It also presented a seminal way of perceiving the synthesis of the **Progressive Intensity Levels (PIL)** (Graph 2 on page I-1) of competition with the **Internal and External Influences on Competition (IMIC and EMIC)** (Graphs 5-6 on pages I-1 and I-2) and how this impacts competitors' sporting experiences.

Chapter 2 encapsulated a basic theological rubric (Creation, Fall, Redemption, and Consummation, see Graph 10 on page I-4), which was used to help, define, and articulate biblically based theological principles that support competition. It also determined how competition should be viewed and critiqued. All of this provides a helpful foundation for ensuing discussions, but the focus of this treatise will concentrate on the third aspect of the rubric—redeeming sport and the sports person.

What is discussed in this chapter is necessary because it is not logical to conclude sport to be biblically defensible just because a theological foundation for competition has been established. As Chapter 1 explained, the two are not synonymous. A separate biblical basis for sport and athletics must be established. To that end, the following criteria (below) and explanatory graphs (Graph 11 on page I-4 and Graph 12 on page I-5).[1]

I. BIBLICAL PRINCIPLES FOR DETERMINING CHRIST-HONORING SPORTS

J.R.R. Tolkien believed the truths about the gospel and God were prevalent in every culture and revealed in their mythology. Similarly, I believe every culture has known and experienced the very close relationship between

---

[1] What follows is a rubric that has been formed over my years of teaching theology of competition and sports ethics courses to sports outreach ministry students. I am indebted to my students who have debated these concepts with me through the years and have been so helpful in shaping them. Of course, all errors of thinking, logic, or theology are my own and not the responsibility of my students. This material has previously appeared in a somewhat altered form in a training manual I co-wrote with a team of international sports ministers in Egypt during the summer of 2006. Although it was first published there, I had created this during the previous decades. Interestingly enough, even the idea of the pyramid preceded the time in Egypt but did seem to be sovereignly prepared for our collaboration in Egypt. It was offered to the ISC community free of charge to be used to support local church sports outreach throughout the world.

sport and religion. Christianity is no different—except Christianity is real and not mythological.

The ancient Greeks held Olympic Games to honor their mythological gods, including the god of the Olympic Games: Zeus. Ancient Greek athletes prayed to Zeus for athletic success, and ancient Greek temples were built next door to the stadiums and arenas. This serves as a certain kind of model for sport and spirituality connections. The sport and faith connection has been experienced by athletes throughout the millennia and in virtually every culture and country around the world.

With a Tolkien perspective in mind, Christians would do well to thoughtfully consider a biblically based worldview of sport and faith and determine whether or not sport is compatible with Christian theology. As mentioned before, a separate biblical basis for sport and athletics must be established—one that is distinct and different from theological truths that justify competition. To that end, the following criteria and explanatory graphs are offered.

Principle 1—All Things Created by and for God: *All Things Are Created Good*

This concept—"All things God created are good"—has already been articulated in the section on theology in Chapter 2. It is used here to also undergird a biblical foundation for the subcategories of competition: sports and athletics. Nothing is added here; rather, it is listed as the most significant principle not only for the general category of establishing a biblical defense for competition, but also for the subcategories of sport and athletics. Its profundity should not be overlooked or under-appreciated due to the brevity given to it here. All God created is good, including His creation of an order from which sport evolved. This is different from stating that God created sport. Humankind invented sport, but God created a "good order" from which sport (and a myriad of other human activity: music, art, drama, science, etc.) emerges and all is "good."

Principle 2—Stewardship: Maximize God-Given Talents: *Being a Good Steward of All God Entrusts to You*

Stewardship is the second principle from which a biblical defense of sport is based. The stewardship principle is foundational for providing a mandate for both the utilization of a person's gifts and talents and for their specific use in glorifying God. This principle is established in the Pentateuch and verified in the teachings of Christ.

Old Testament—Pentateuch

An example of the Pentateuch principle can be found in Exodus 31:2–5. It illustrates how people are endowed by God with certain gifts and how they are to use them for God's honor:

> See, I have called by name Bezalel . . . and I have filled him with the Spirit of God, in wisdom, in understanding, in knowledge, and in all manner of workmanship, to design artistic works, to work in gold, in silver, in bronze, in cutting jewels for setting, in carving wood and to work in all manner of workmanship.

This is a short section of a longer passage that goes on to describe other people and their gifts for the temple work. It establishes a transferable biblical concept that communicates God endows all people with gifts they are to "steward" for His honor and worship. This principle can be applied to other disciplines such as athletics and sport, as it provides a basis for the true sense of Christian vocation.

New Testament

Stewardship is also taught and affirmed throughout the New Testament gospels and epistles but especially in Jesus's parable about the talents found in Matthew 25. Here it is clear each person who receives a gift or talent from God is to use it in ways deemed acceptable to the Lord. All gifts including "workmanship" of woodworking—and by extension, sport—should be offered to God as an offering. To be gifted in athletics by God and not to "steward" the gift of athleticism would be to, as Eric Liddell believed, "to hold God in contempt."

Principle 3—"The Body is a Temple of the Holy Spirit": *Physical Fitness and Keeping the Earthly Body Fit*

The biblical concept of physical fitness, particularly as taught by the Apostle Paul, provides yet a further biblical principle that justifies Christian participation in sport. This includes, among many others, three passages found in the Corinthian correspondence (1 Corinthians 3:16 and 6:19; 2 Corinthians 6:16) concerning the value of the human body and its proper and improper ways of utilization. However, there is one verse that is frequently cited to denigrate physical exercise. It is a most important but sometimes misunderstood and misinterpreted verse concerning bodily exercise: 1 Timothy 4:8. Some interpret this verse as condemning all sport and athletics. Others believe it downplays the importance of bodily exercise. Still others state the verse dismisses sport as inconsequential. Yet, when understood within the overall context of the passage, and also within the overall Pauline theology of sport and the body, it becomes clear this verse is actually very supportive of fitness and the discipline of athletics. Still, after reading 1 Timothy 4:8, many athletes ask the following question:

> *How can I as an athlete justify my sporting endeavors when 1 Timothy 4:8 reads: "exercise is of little value"?*

Yes, 1 Timothy 4:8 is often translated to say physical exercise (and, by implication, sports and athletics) is of little value, and sadly this verse is often used to deter people from engaging in physical activity such as sports and athletics. Yet to use this verse to condemn or even criticize athletics demonstrates a lack of understanding of how to interpret the Bible (hermeneutics), including a classical error of basing one's interpretation on a poor translation. All good biblical interpretation begins with a translation faithful to the orthodox traditions of hermeneutics. To that end, the following discussion begins with establishing the best possible translation of this verse. It continues with an exegesis of the verse and its context, including the requisite implications and applications the passage suggests. The result provides a reasonable assessment for athletes with regard to their involvement in athletics and whether or not their "physical exercise profiteth little." Taken in its entirety, the following discussion helps to substantiate the third principle for establishing a biblical defense for sport and athletics. It begins with an overview of the context in which 1 Timothy 4.8 8 is found.

A. Context
Paul wrote two letters to his protégé, Timothy, whom he had assigned as the leader (bishop) of the Ephesian church. The first epistle written

to Timothy outlined directives for how the Ephesian church was to be organized, how leaders were to be chosen and developed, as well as how individual church members were to attain "godliness." In this specific passage, 1 Timothy 4.6–10 Paul is outlining obstacles to the spiritual growth necessary for attaining godliness. Verses 7 and 8 were given as a model to help overcome such obstacles. The specific model the Holy Spirit inspired Paul to articulate was an athletic one! The significance of this must not be overlooked or undervalued. Paul was inspired to urge first-century Ephesian Christians to pursue godliness as an athlete pursued physical prowess. By extension, the model proposed to those in the early church is applicable for believers in all subsequent generations.

B. Which Translation

The athletic model of 1 Timothy 4:7 and 4:8 is easier to comprehend in the original Greek than how it is often translated into English, such as the King James Version's (KJV): "physical exercise profiteth little." Verses 4:7 and 4:8 are rooted by three Greek words, each used twice. The first, *gymnasia,* is translated "exercise" and is found in both verses. It comes from the root word *gymnazo* (gymnasium), which means to exercise or train as would an athlete. In 4:7, this word is in the imperative, directing the Ephesians to engage in rigorous exercise and be diligent in their pursuit of godliness. In 4:8, the same word for exercise is used when comparing athletic endeavors to seeking to attain godliness.

The second word, also found in both verses, is *eusebeian*—translated as "devoutness" or "godliness." The implication of 4:7 is the Ephesian believers were to train (*gymnazo*) for this godliness (*eusebeian*) with the same dedication as athletes who trained for the arena.

The third Greek word *ophelimos*—translated "beneficial"—is found only in 4:8 but used twice to bring clarity to the overall message of the passage. It states the purpose of all exercising and training: a "beneficial" end. Training for the physical (*somatike*—"bodily") is beneficial for a few things (*oligon*), but training for godliness is beneficial for all things (*panta*).

So, how have the various renditions of these verses been translated with regard to the value of physical exercise? The following examples are representatives of the three categories of traditional renderings:

- Little value (profiteth little—KJV)
- Less value (limited—Philips)
- Some value (NIV)

There is an obvious disparity among these three. The first translation makes a negative evaluation: Physical activity should not be engaged in because it has little intrinsic value. This suggests bodily exercise and athletics are negative or even sinful. At the very least, they are held in low regard. The second view, while a step in the right direction, does not hold physical activity with the same high esteem generally affirmed throughout the Bible, nor does it fit with the basic context and message of this passage. The first translation assumes physical exercise is evil, and the second translation errs by not fully appreciating the intrinsic value of physical endeavors. Both should be rejected in favor of the third option.

The third translation does the best job of comprehending the immediate context while also affirming the entire biblical perspective on sport. It appropriately renders a textual option affirming physical activity and its intrinsic value. Yet, it does so without erring in ascribing physical exercise a higher value than is biblically prescribed. The first two options are antithetical to the context, but the third is congruent with it. So, the proper translation should be "of some value," not of "little" or "limited value." It could be argued there is only a slight difference between "limited value" and "some value," but the latter is preferred because it states an affirmative whereas the former emphasizes the negative.

The significance of this point is made even more poignant when one realizes that although the Apostle Paul was the human writer of the epistles to his "son in the faith," the true author of the Epistle was the Holy Spirit, who intended the letter and its lessons to be a model for all future generations. He inspired Paul to specifically use an athletic term within an athletic motif and context to communicate both the implicit lesson—physical activity is beneficial for some things—along with the explicit lesson—godliness is beneficial for all things.

Therefore, when context is considered, this verse cannot be interpreted to indicate the realm of sports and athletics is to be avoided, thought poorly of, or even more disturbing, devoid of virtue. The true message of this passage is a direct command to be actively, regularly, and sincerely working hard to develop godliness, emulating athletes who work to better themselves physically. If 4:7 were eliminated, then 4:8 would be translated quite differently. The problem of removing 4:8 from its context, especially 4:7, becomes apparent. A completely antithetical interpretation is made when the verse is lifted from its context. It becomes even more apparent when isolated from the rest of the Bible.[2]

So, a proper translation as found in the NIV and ESV ensures a proper hermeneutic (biblical interpretation) and provides a solid foundation from which to base the following exegesis. Properly understood and rendered, the verse should read: "bodily training is of some value" (ESV); "training your body helps you in some ways" (New Century Bible); or "workouts in the gymnasium are useful" (The Message).

C. Biblical *a Priori*[3]

A second basic underlying principle of biblical interpretation is to allow Scripture to interpret itself by comparing and using other relevant Scriptures to shed light on the passage in question. As it relates to sport and athletics, the overwhelming biblical evidence concerning sport is positive and thus would support the translation: "bodily training is of some value."

---

[2] Translators and interpreters need to be wary of assigning too much significance to a word's etymological root. Just because the origin of a word was based in sports doesn't necessarily mean it always connotes or references its sporting root. For example, a judge who says to a three-time repeat criminal "three strikes and you're out" is not making a specific reference to baseball. Although the phrase has an athletic origin, its meaning has evolved and acquired a significance beyond sport. That's what makes translating this particular verse in its context so important. The context assumes the choice of a sporting word is intentionally related to its original sporting meaning because the entire passage is based upon the sporting motif. Thus, its sports etymology is intentional and is a key to understanding the spiritual meaning of the teaching. It is used in such a way as to communicate about physical exercise in comparison to spiritual exercise. The significance of this "in context" translation is clear: The sporting meaning is not without purpose or just a meaningless metaphor. It is foundational to translating and interpreting this passage accurately.

[3] Biblical *a prioris* aid Christians in their attempt to interpret the Scripture by looking at what the entire Bible has to say about a particular subject or ethical dilemma. In this case, the biblical *a priori* overwhelmingly values sport, athletics, and physical activities as being biblically based and Christ honoring.

What does the Bible state about athletics? First and perhaps foremost, the Scripture never condemns sport, athletics, or physical activity. Second, every time the Bible mentions or references athletics, it does so in a positive light. The most profound example of this is the Holy Spirit inspiring the Apostle Paul to use an athletic metaphor to summarize his life.[4] It is inconceivable to believe God would inspire such a metaphor to describe the life of the most important, the most spiritually influential, person within the entire New Testament outside of Christ Himself or perhaps Barnabas, if the metaphor was intrinsically or inherently evil.[5] Suffice it to say, athletics are treated favorably in Scripture.

Even more profound, however, is not so much what this verse is not saying as what it is saying. It places an intrinsic value upon physical activity by clearly stating it is of some value. This statement is in agreement with the overall biblical view of sport and its perspective of the human body as found in the Corinthian correspondence and elsewhere.[6]

To summarize then, this brief overview of the biblical *a priori* on sport and athletics supports the third option of interpretation: "some value." The first option of interpretation—"little value"—does an injustice to the overall biblical view (biblical *a priori*) of physical activity and sport. The second interpretation—"less or limited value"—is a step in the right direction but still communicates the negative rather than the positive and thus doesn't square with the overall message of the Bible. The best interpretation, by far, is the third option because it is congruent with the rest of Scripture. The third option emphasizes the positives of physical activity while accurately upholding God's intent to maintain spiritual activity as the highest, all-encompassing value.

So once again, rather than interpreting this verse as a support for denigrating athletics, this passage is in complete agreement with the rest of Scripture. It actually lifts athletic training and physical exercise up as great examples of a most beneficial model for spiritual growth! Followers of Christ are encouraged to approach their spirituality as would

---

[4] 2 Timothy 4:6–8.

[5] Consult both Stuart Weir's *What the Book Says about Sport* and my own writings on the theology of competition found in the other chapters of this book for further discussion on biblical support for sport.

[6] See my unpublished article "The Pauline Theology of the Human Body."

athletes their sporting endeavors: consistently, energetically, and under the direction of a knowledgeable trainer. Certainly, Paul places spiritual development as the highest priority in a Christian's life, but any interpretation attempting to use this passage to state athletics as invaluable demonstrates a revealing bias and a true lack of how to approach and interpret the whole of Scripture.

D. Biblical Comparison

A third aid in interpreting this passage comes from the biblical technique of comparison. A good example of how to establish the meaning of a verse through the technique of comparison is Luke 14:26. Jesus's teaching about hating one's family members, at first blush, seems harsh and even unbiblical. Indeed, at face value, it is. However, when understood through the lens of biblical comparison, Jesus's command for His followers to "hate" their parents and siblings makes sense. He wasn't saying His followers were to conjure up passionate negative emotions or engage in hurtful actions toward family members. Rather, He was teaching one's love for God should be so passionate it would seem, by comparison, the person hated his or her family. Furthermore, Jesus demonstratively loved His family, and He taught that loving one's family was imperative. Similarly, Paul uses the same teaching technique: comparison. By comparison, Paul wrote Spiritual activity is beneficial for all things, whereas physical activity is beneficial for a few things. This is quite different from saying it is of no value or "profiteth nothing."

E. Summary of Biblical Interpretation of 1 Timothy 4:8

After a careful analysis, the true essence of this passage emerges: 1 Timothy 4:8 affirms physical exercise. However, this passage cannot be used to suggest physical activity should be the highest priority or noblest virtue of a believer. Physical exercise is beneficial for some things, but godliness is beneficial for all things. The strongest criticism anyone wishing to denigrate athletic endeavors can offer from this verse would be to use it as a safeguard to keep athletics and sports in check. This appropriate caution would help to maintain a proper perspective about sporting activities by insisting physical activity be kept in its rightful place as being important but never superseding spiritual endeavors. Furthermore, and perhaps even more profoundly, efforts to attain godliness can be enhanced if they emulate athletic training! For example, a consistent and fervent training program supervised under the watchful eye of a qualified "coach" will greatly advance one's pursuit of godliness.

Thus, once again for emphasis, this passage cannot be used to denigrate sport or to discourage participation in athletics by stating the Bible condemns sporting endeavors. The biblical perspective is clear: Physical activities are of some value, but spiritual activities are to be valued above all others. Of course this then begs the question: Can physical activities be separated from spiritual endeavors? Or perhaps more to the point: Can people worship God through their physical activities? This frequently asked question will be addressed in the FAQ chapter: Chapter 8.

F. Final Analysis of the Third Principle for Determining Biblically Defensible Sport

Sport can be deemed biblically defensible because nowhere does the Bible specifically denounce or denigrate sport and, moreover, where it does reference sport, sport is presented in positive, favorable ways. Therefore, Christian athletes and coaches can engage in athletic pursuits with a complete confidence their endeavors and activities are fully supported by Scripture.

The fourth principle for determining biblically defensible sport follows.

Principle 4—Use of Sporting Metaphors: *Positive Biblical References to Sport*

The significance of Paul's positive use of sporting metaphor is twofold: (a) Its very existence within Holy Spirit–inspired Scripture justifies sporting endeavors, and (b) it serves as a model for how athletics can be used for spiritual purposes. Together, these two points make a strong argument in establishing a biblical basis for sport. The following is but a short selection of three key sections of Scripture taken from the many biblical sporting passages. The first will be mentioned here and outlined in Principle 5; the second is a review of a previously discussed passage; and a third will be added here.

1 Corinthians 9

Not only does this passage use the sporting metaphor of running to communicate a spiritual message, but it also serves as a model and example of what Paul states in 1 Corinthians 9:19–27. In this passage he is inspired to exhort the Corinthian Christians to "become all things to all people" (v. 22). He then proceeds over the next few verses to demonstrate what he has just articulated: He uses sport as a teaching tool as if to model the use of "all things" (sport) to reach "all people" (athletes). The analogies of boxing and running would have been relevant to first-century Corinthians because Corinth was the center for ancient Greek athletics. This section of the Corinthian correspondence is the best example of Paul stating the principle: "become all things to all people that by all means I might save some" (v. 23); and then applying the principle: "do you not know that in a race . . ." (v. 24). Together they support the argument for a biblical defense of sport.[7]

2 Timothy 4:6–8

As highlighted in a previous section, a most convincing argument for justifying athletics is the fact that Paul always used sports in a positive context, including the fact that the Holy Spirit inspired Paul to use them to summarize his life. Would the Holy Spirit lead Paul—perhaps the most important person of the New Testament outside of the Lord Jesus Himself—to use a metaphor that was intrinsically evil to summarize his life? Out of all the possibilities the Holy Spirit could have inspired Paul to use—marriage, family, parenting, agriculture, nature, etc.—God chose sport to honor his faithful disciple! This passage raises sporting metaphor to new heights of significance and in so doing makes an unassailable case for the biblical justification of sport.

Hebrews 11:1–12:2

Traditionally called the "Faith Chapter," Hebrews 11:1–12:2 is perhaps the best of all New Testament sporting motif passages. The Holy Spirit inspired the writer of Hebrews to pen a most beautiful, inspirational, and

---

[7] The fifth principle for determining biblically defensible sport (which follows this fourth principle) entails a more in-depth discussion of this passage.

profound passage.[8] From the imagery of a stadium packed with the cheering saints to the specific admonishments to lay aside the weights that hinder athletic efforts, it is a perfect description of the games, activities, and religious rituals of the ancient Olympics and provides a unique window into the ancient athletic culture. Best of all, the Holy Spirit teaches timeless spiritual truths through the sporting analogies.[9] Twenty-first-century disciples of Christ would be at a great loss without this wonderful word picture and its timeless lessons of faith. It too adds its weight and helps to legitimate biblical support for sport.

Objections

Some have raised an important objection. They argue the use of athletic metaphor in Scripture does not necessarily equate with biblical support for sport. The argument is as follows: If the only requirement for being biblically sanctioned is to be included in Holy Writ, then activities such as prostitution, murder, theft, and many other immoralities are also biblically defensible.

This argument may have a certain validity but is nonetheless fallacious because its premises are not based on truth. The main difference is that prostitution and murder are clearly condemned throughout the Bible. Sport never is. Thus, this argument is found wanting. However, war is a closer analogy.

Those who would seek to undermine the principle of biblical sporting metaphors being used to support sport would be better served by comparing scriptural athletic passages with those dealing with war. War is controversial. Some within the Christian kingdom view it as completely and totally evil; others believe in certain situations it can be biblically

---

[8] I believe the Apostle Paul to be the human author of Hebrews. Historically, copies of the letter to the Hebrews were always found with the Pauline corpus and rational answers for linguistic and textual objections are plentiful. Moreover, the strongest argument in favor of Paul remains unanswered: He is the only New Testament–era author capable of writing Hebrews 11:1–12:2! Obviously, this is hotly disputed among scholars, but the question of authorship does not change the validity of including this passage as a support for the biblical defensibility of sport.

[9] See my unpublished articles on specific athletics-based passages and words for a more in-depth description and explanation.

justified. Its relevance to the topic is related to whether or not God can use questionable endeavors such as war as legitimate teaching tools. The real question of those objecting to biblical references of an activity being biblically justifiable is well understood: Just because something is used to teach spiritual lessons does not make the lesson object biblically defensible. Yet, this argument does not take into account the arguments outlined here.

If one verse could be cited that explicitly condemns sport or athletics, if there was even one biblical use of sport that portrayed sport as being evil, then the objections of the anti-sport contingent would be far more convincing. As it stands, biblical narratives of sport always hold sport in high regard, use sport to illustrate spiritual truths, and never does the Bible condemn sport or even give any warnings about involvement with sport. Together, these rationales make a strong case for the fourth principle for the biblical defense of sport.

Principle 5—Evangelism, Discipleship, the Great Commission, and the Great Commandments: *The Use of Sport and Competition for Evangelism and Discipleship*

It is often stated: Sport and athletics are currently the most strategic and effective evangelistic and discipling methodology currently available to the church. The current use of sports for outreach by churches, church plants, mission boards, schools, and para-ministries is unprecedented and growing every year. The fifth principle is thus based upon both the Great Commission found in Matthew 28:18–20 to use sports to attract people to the gospel (evangelism) and also the Great Commandments as found in Matthew 22:37 to use sport to train people in their love of God and people (discipleship). Obviously, neither of these passages mentions sport directly, but both are used here to establish the biblical commands of evangelism and discipleship, which sports outreach ministry seeks to accomplish.

Rodger Oswald, one of sports ministry's pioneers, has fleshed this concept out by outlining a basic 4-step rationale justifying the biblically based methodology of sports ministry, which has as its underlying principle God's loving redemption of humankind.[10]

---

[10] Rodger Oswald is a professor, author, and recognized worldwide expert in local church sport. In addition he founded and for many years led Church Sports International (CSI)—www. csi.org. Rodger currently serves as CSRM's staff Emeritus and

Oswald's first step recognizes God to be a God of redemption. The Gospel writer Luke was inspired by the Holy Spirit to record: "For the Son of Man has come to seek and save that which was lost" (Luke 19:10). This is further verified by another inspired Gospel writer, Matthew: ". . . go ye therefore, and teach all nations, baptizing them in the name of the Father, and of the Son, and of the Holy Ghost" (Matthew 20:19).

The second step demonstrates God's desire to involve His people in the redemption effort. This is affirmed by yet another divinely inspired author in the correspondence of Paul to the Corinthians: " . . . and [God] hath given us to the ministry of reconciliation . . . now then we are ambassadors for Christ" (2 Corinthians 5:17–20). This partnership in gospel ministry is shared by people who serve as God's ambassadors. This partnership is confirmed and verified by scores of other verses.

So the first two stops along this progression make it clear that local church bodies attempting to reach their communities for Christ are obeying the biblical mandate. The question for them was not should they reach people for Christ, but rather, how should they do it. It is to this Oswald offers step three.

The third step is also found in Paul's letters to the Corinthians: "I have become all things to all men, so that I might reach some" (1 Corinthians 9:19–23). This passage indicates a biblical principle of freedom in methodology as it pertains to reaching people for Christ. Paul states "though I be free . . . yet . . . I made myself servant to all"; "unto the Jews I became as a Jew" and "to the weak I became weak"; so "that I might by all means save some." This passage makes it abundantly clear that the church has a lot of leeway when it comes to choosing a methodology to reach the lost. This leeway could well include sport.

The fourth step is articulated in the ensuing verses of 1 Corinthians 9. As Oswald insightfully points out, God is a God of diversity as is evidenced in his being, character, creation, and commands to His creation (1993, 6, 7). Furthermore, I believe 1 Corinthians 9:24–27, which immediately follows

---

teaches this basic outline where ever he goes. It continues to be a strong foundation for understanding the biblical basis for sport. It should be understood that although this fifth principle is really Rodger's and I am indebted to Oswald for his wise insights. My summarizing of them is not nearly as eloquent, nor should he be blamed for any misuse or misguided notions I am guilty of. History may reveal Oswald to be the most theologically and philosophically influential person of the Sports Outreach Movement.

the passage just discussed, demonstrates a living example of what Paul was trying to communicate and Oswald teaches. Having just stated "all means" can be used, Paul models this principle by using a sporting metaphor that was relevant and understood by those he was writing to. He wrote athletic metaphors to those who lived in Corinth, the city that housed the Greek athletic office and served as the home base for two of the four prestigious "crown games."

To summarize, Oswald's rationale was based upon the biblical mandate for the church to use any means to work out its evangelistic efforts.

Caution Relating to Principle 5

Even though Principle 5 is a strong support for establishing a theological basis for sport, it must be understood that this support is based in pragmatism (what works) rather than being based on a theological foundation (what's right or orthodox). By itself, such pragmatism could not substantiate or justify sport as being biblically defensible. If sport was condemned in the Scripture, then the use of it for spiritual purposes would be sinful, even if it facilitated and enhanced the church's evangelism and/or discipleship efforts. If there were no other biblical justifications, then the methodology of using competition and sport for spiritual purposes would be highly suspect. Every human endeavor, even evangelistic methods, must be rooted in, and based upon, theology—not solely in pragmatics. Any activity, even when evangelistically based, would be condemned if found to be antithetical to orthodox Christian teaching. The Christian church community should certainly condemn the use of ancient pagan religion's methods, such as "temple prostitutes," even if this methodology successfully accomplished certain goals of the church like growth, visibility, or outreach. It would do so based upon the lack of biblical or theological support and specific biblical condemnations of such relationships and sexual activity. Similarly, pragmatic-, sport-, or athletics-based evangelism should be condemned if it does not have theological support. However, this is not the case with sport as has just been outlined in the five principles for biblically defensible sport. Sport clearly has biblical support.

II. SUMMARY OF BIBLICAL PRINCIPLES

This is a brief summary of the biblical defense for sport and athletics. Although brief, it provides a cogent overview for a biblically based, theological defense of sport. However, even if sport can be generally defended biblically, it would be fallacious to assume each and every sport, and each and every action within sport, is thus automatically defended scripturally. The next step in our journey for constructing a biblical defense for sport and athletics is to assemble a template that can determine what would make a particular sport biblically defensible and a worthy pursuit for a Christian's participation. The real question is: Can it be assumed, because competition is theologically supported and sport, in general, is biblically defensible, that all sport is thus biblically defensible? Logically, the answer is no. The next chapter creates a template for determining which individual sports may or may not "make the cut."[11]

---

[11] This template has the same genesis and evaluative process (my classes/my students) as previous sections of this book (Chapter 3, footnote 1). It too was offered to and used by the ISC Egyptian manual writing team. The same caveats mentioned in Chapter 3, footnote 1 apply here.

CHAPTER 4

A TEMPLATE FOR DETERMINING BIBLICALLY DEFENSIBLE SPORTS

This chapter will establish a template for determining which individual sports are compatible with a Christian worldview and explains the six requisite mandates for biblically defensible sports. In addition it outlines which sports are biblically justifiable and which ones are not.

I. A TEMPLATE FOR DETERMINING BIBLICALLY DEFENSIBLE SPORTS

At the risk of alienating those wishing for a simplistic and quick answer to their sport and faith questions, the journey continues for determining which sports can be biblically justified and how to compete in Christ-honoring ways. My efforts are purposeful, although admittedly laborious. One of the objectives of this lengthy foray is to provide a rubric to enable Christian competitors to make biblically informed decisions regarding any future sporting dilemma.

Chapter 3 outlined the five biblical principles that established sports to be, in general, biblically defensible. This chapter takes the next step in the process. It determines which individual sports are compatible with a Christian worldview and which ones are not.

Graph 12 on page I-5 outlines six criteria necessary for an individual sport to be biblically defensible: (a) It must have a redemptive purpose or goal; (b) the governing rules must ensure biblical principles; (c) the governing rules must be enforced properly and fairly by officials, referees, and umpires; (d) both the administrative management and the on-field coaching must adhere to the biblical principles and governing rules; (e) participants must strive to compete according to the governing rules of the sport which are based upon biblical principles; and (f) spectators (including parents of athletes) must strive to conduct themselves within the biblical principles and governing rules of the sport, and in addition encourage participants rather than taunt or denigrate them. This template is designed to guide the discussion on how to determine if a particular sport is, or is not, biblically defensible. It touches on but is not intended to be a definitive statement about each and every action within sports. A much more detailed explanation of specific sports-related actions will be addressed when Christmanship is discussed. What follows is a more detailed expression of this rubric.

A. Sport Must Have a Redemptive Purpose or Goal in Order to Be Biblically Justifiable

Biblically Based Redemptive Purpose (BBRP)

In this context the term "redemptive" is defined in a nonpersonal way. It is broader in scope than to describe the spiritual redemption of a person or the soul of a person. Rather, it defines the process for making the world of sport profitable (not necessarily financially profitable) and enjoyable for all involved. Although sport may be a tool or catalytic activity used by God to lead someone into a personal relationship with Him, that is not the primary way the word "redemptive" is used in this discussion. *Redemptive Purposes* or goals can include teachable moments, lessons for life, opportunities for individual or group growth, entertainment, recreation, health, fun, accomplishment, etc. What is not acceptable, from a biblical perspective would be sporting activity specifically designed with evil intent or for harmful results. Any athletic endeavors intentionally intended to bring about physical, emotional, spiritual, or relational harm to people, despoil or misuse the environment, blaspheme Jesus, or glorify any mythological god or religion other than Christianity would be antithetical to a biblical framework. Certainly anything enhancing biblical concepts such as joy, fulfillment, and witness would qualify as being redemptive.

A *Biblically Based Redemptive Purpose* (*BBRP*) is based upon scriptural commands for every activity to be done to the glory of God as found in passages such as 1 Corinthians 10:31 and Colossians 3:17, 23.

B. Governing Rules Must Ensure Biblical Principles
Biblically Based Rules (BBR)

Even a cursory perusal of scripture reveals that the Bible does not attempt to be a comprehensive ethics textbook. It would be utterly impossible for any book to contain all rules and all interpretations of rules needed for people to successfully live ethically astute and morally appropriate lives. Yet the Bible is brilliantly comprehensive in providing a set of standards (commands, laws, statutes) from which ethical principles can be ascertained and together these biblical rules and principles can address any ethical decision and guide all moral actions.

Thus, though it is difficult, nay well impossible, to find a biblical command directly intended to govern sport, it is uncanny how relevant biblical principles are when applied to sporting activity. Although not one of the Ten Commandments addresses sport, biblical principles such as love for one's neighbor or honesty offer clear ethical parameters for sporting endeavors. Once biblical principles for ethics are properly understood, it becomes fairly easy to determine moral behavior for sport.

To summarize, not only must there be a redemptive goal or purpose for sport and an avoidance of intentional evil or harm, but in addition sport must be governed by *Biblically Based Rules* (*BBR*) that are based upon biblical commands and principles. These include love and compassion for all participants codified in:

- ☺ Assurances of equal opportunity for sporting success, including never rewarding any success that comes from cheating or competing unfairly
  - Based on the biblical doctrines of fairness, respect, and honesty
- ☺ Protection of each person's human body from any undue or intentional physical harm and not rewarding any action, activity, training, conditioning, or medical procedures that would intentionally do damage to life or limb
  - Based on the biblical doctrines of the sanctity of human life and caring for the human body, which is the "temple of the Holy Spirit"
- ☺ Rewarding an athlete for living out the "Fruits of the Spirit"
  - Based upon the biblical expectations for a Spirit-filled life
- ☺ Enabling participants to honor God in all aspects of their play and competition including when, where, and how the contests are conducted
  - Based upon the Ten Commandments, decrees concerning
    - Appropriately worshipping and honoring the one true God
    - Appropriately honoring the Lord's Day
    - Appropriately honoring life, property, and integrity of others

Of course, this brief overview and outline of the *Biblically Based Rules* suffers from a lack of depth and breadth but lays the foundation for the further definitions and clarity discussed at length in ensuing chapters. However, this highlighted outline does establish a biblically based philosophy from which Christian athletic competitors can begin to formulate and evaluate the specific sports they compete in, as well as the specific actions called for in their sport.

C. Governing Rules Must Be Properly Enforced by Game Officials

Biblically Based Rule Enforcement (BBRE)

Even if each and every rule for a sport were to be based upon *Biblically Based Rules,* they would be nothing more than mere suggestions unless they were enforced and perpetrators were penalized. Furthermore, the penalties must be enacted regardless of whether or not the rules were intentionally broken. Even unintentional breaking of the rules must be enforced. This then assumes, and more importantly demands, sporting activities to be (a) supervised by, (b) all rules enforced by, and (c) every infraction penalized by those who officiate the games, such as referees, umpires, or officials.

Biblically Based Rule Enforcement (BBRE) assumes the role of being a sports official to be a high and honorable calling. This calling is to be taken seriously by those who bear the burden of enforcing the letter and spirit of the sport and by those whom they officiate. Officials should by highly honored and praised when they effectively fulfill their role, and just as importantly, they should be held accountable when they don't.[1]

D. Both the Administrative Management and the On-Field Coaching Must Adhere to the Biblical Principles and Governing Rules

Biblically Based Management and Coaching (BBMC)

Even if a sport has a redeeming value and *Biblically Based Rules* are enforced, a sport would still not be biblically defensible if those who organize, coach, manage, and otherwise supervise the athletic endeavors don't fulfill their role in teaching and administrating the activities in biblically based ways. Furthermore, each member of one's own team as well as coaches and competitors on other teams must be honored and treated with the kind of respect and love individuals created in the image of God deserve. All coaching and management personnel are responsible for creating a healthy, honoring atmosphere for their athletes to compete in and maintain an ethos that fosters the highest competitive ideals—Christmanship.

E. Participants Must Always Compete within the Biblical Principles and Governing Rules

Biblically Based Competing (BBC)

Athletes also have a role to fulfill in ensuring a sport to be biblically defensible. Similar to coaches and managers, athletes must compete in the ethic of Christmanship with their own team members, but also toward co-competitors from other teams. To fully comprehend this, a pause

---

[1] This topic is highly controversial and is discussed at length in the Christmanship chapter.

in this discussion is needed, allowing an illustrative metaphor to aid in summarizing and comprehending these concepts.

1. Explanatory Analogy   Even if (a) General Motors or Honda creates an automobile in a biblically defensible way and (b) the driving of such vehicles is "policed" by the authorities and (c) drivers are taught (coached/managed) how to navigate a car correctly, individual drivers can still use the car for evil purposes such as drive-by shootings, illegal drug distribution, or to intentionally run over "an enemy." The corresponding ethic becomes clear: Even though cars are designed for good and the use of them is supervised, those driving them must use them in righteous and loving ways in order for cars to be deemed truly good. Similarly, athletes must compete biblically in order for sport to be biblically defensible. However, there is still one more step on this rubric.

F. Spectators Must Always Conduct Themselves within the Biblical Principles and Governing Rules; in Addition They Should Encourage Rather Than Denigrate Sports Participants and Officials

Biblically Based Spectating and Cheering (BBSC)

The responsibility for ensuring a biblically defensible sports endeavor is not solely incumbent on those administrating, officiating, and participating in athletic activities but also for all who are spectators and supporters of the activity. It is indeed sad to reflect upon the misery caused by fans and supporters to athletes and even to each other.

Non-biblical activity by nonparticipants can include any of the following:

- The production, circulation, and administration of injurious drugs and other so-called "performance enhancements"
- Hate-filled invectives and "taunting"
- Gambling on sporting events or activities
- Intentional physical injury, violence, or even deaths perpetrated on any competitor, official, or opposing fans

Biblically Based Spectating and Cheering (BBSC) assumes fans and supporters who love, honor, and respect all athletes, even those on other teams or from other communities and countries. It demands attitudes and actions founded on biblical commands and principles.

1. Parents of Athletes A special statement must be made concerning one specific group of spectators: *parents of athletes*. Certainly the majority of parents enjoy their child's athletic endeavors without incident, but there is a growing problem of overzealous parents applying unhealthy amounts of pressure on their children and undue criticism on game officials, league directors, and coaches. Suffice it to say, parents play a key role in creating a positive, redemptive atmosphere in youth sports. An entire sporting event could be done in Christ-honoring ways by everyone on the field, and yet an overbearing parent can turn the whole endeavor into a very negative experience for all involved.[2]

Although certainly the bulk of what is required remains the responsibility of those who compete and administrate competition, in order for sports to be biblically defensible, fans also play a role in truly making athletic endeavors Christ honoring.

G. Summary of Biblically Defensible Template

For a particular sporting activity to be biblically defensible, it must meet the six standards outlined here. However, a specific sport cannot be considered non-biblically defensible because a particular referee, coach, player, or spectator does not adhere to the principles outlined here.

The point of distinction is *sport versus a sporting activity*. Typically, if a *sport* meets the first criteria of having a *Redemptive Purpose*, then it cannot be judged to be biblically indefensible, even if an individual coach, player, or fan acts in non-biblical ways. However, a specific *sporting activity*, game, league, or organization can be considered non-biblical even if the *sport* meets the *Biblically Based Template for Sport (BBTS)*. The *sporting activity* of individuals not competing in biblical ways would be considered non-biblical but the *sport* itself would still be biblically defensible.

---

[2] For parents serious about ensuring a positive environment for their children, I would recommend a set of fictional children's stories written by Tim Conrad: *The Sapphire Lake* series. These delightful sports-based novels are written to engage pre-adolescents and yet insightfully empower parents of athletes with biblical principles and suggestions for making the youth sports experience a positive for everyone. These books can be ordered either through Uncharted Waters or CSRM at www.csrm.org.

This principle is articulated in the following section on biblically defensible sports.

To Recap . . .

So far our journey toward a full understanding and execution of Christmanship has:

- ☺ Chapter 1—Defined a philosophical foundation for competition
- ☺ Chapter 2—Revealed a theological foundation for competition
- ☺ Chapter 3—Outlined a Biblically based foundation for Christian sport
- ☺ Chapter 4—Has so far established:
  - A template for determining which individual sports are compatible with a Christian worldview, and
  - Criteria from which to judge which specific sports and athletic events are consistent with biblical principles.

These biblical principles will now be used to determine which specific sports can and which ones cannot be justified biblically.

II. BIBLICALLY DEFENSIBLE SPORTS

Dozing commuters can be observed on most any urban train. These experienced travelers have an uncanny ability to sleep soundly until the very moment they reach their destination or until something of interest occurs. I'm sure at least a few of the passengers on our journey toward Christmanship, a biblical basis for sport, have yawned their way through some of what has been thus far discussed but are now awake so as not to miss the next stop or two. We've finally arrived at the station most people have an interest in: "Is my sport biblically defensible?" and "Are my actions within my sport biblically defensible?" So, it is indeed time to wake up so as not to miss the excitement.

Most people believe athletic endeavors are positive activities and yet even those who value sport sometimes find it difficult to justify certain sports such as boxing or possibly football or hockey. These, among other sports, are often condemned due to their brutal nature and/or episodic violence. Other critics have difficulty justifying the tens of millions of dollars paid to an athlete for hitting, kicking, shooting, or throwing a ball when "millions of people are starving and we can't even pay our teachers a decent wage." What follows is an attempt to apply the aforementioned paradigm for determining what is, and what is not, a biblically defensible sport.

A. *Redemptive Purposes (BBRP)* Make All the Difference

If cinematic pirates such as Johnny Depp or Errol Flynn are "swash-buckling" with sharpened swords on the deck of a ship, it is called a battle, and their purpose is to kill or at least maim one's enemy. Although sword battles (competition) might be justified through a "just war theory" with the "good person" seeking to defeat the "bad person" in the midst of a war zone, even this justification realizes the tragedy of death, injury, or dismemberment. However, such activity could never be justified as a biblically defensible sport because it does not meet the requirement of having a *Biblically Based Redemptive Purpose (BBRP)* nor would it satisfy the requisite demands of having *Biblically Based Rules (BBR)* that ensure safety to life and limb. However, if Flynn and Depp were to cover the ends of their swords with safety shields and electronic sensors; don protective body gear; and compete in the Olympic Games, their weapons become "epees," their assassins are called "fencers," and both are cheered on to victory. Fencing meets the criteria for participating in a biblically defensible sport whereas sword fighting does not.

This illustration shows how the exact same activity—sword dueling—can be either redemptive or destructive. When the first requirement from the template explained earlier in this chapter—*Redemptive Purpose*—is applied to sword fighting, this competitive activity can be biblically defensible and honorably taken part in because it meets the criteria of having a redemptive value and is administrated, coached *(BBMC)*, and participated in *(BBC)* according to rules and behaviors in accordance with biblical principles.

Logically this opens the door for almost any sport, yet should not be confused as license for every manifestation of every sport, as the next point explains.

B. Governing Rules *(BBR)* Ensure Biblical Principles

The general concepts of American football, boxing, and hockey are biblically defensible, but not every specific manifestation of these sports can be so justified. For example, there is a huge difference between "prizefighting" and amateur boxing. There is a significant distinction between the National Football League and a recreational flag football league.

The purpose of prizefighting is to physically beat an opponent into submission. The objective is to batter the opposing boxer until either a technical knockout (TKO) or, even better, literally knocking a co-competitor into unconsciousness. The ultimate goal of professional boxing is to physically incapacitate another human being. Thus, prizefighting does not meet the standards as set forth in the *Biblically Based Template for Sport (BBTS)*. It does not provide for the safety and health of the boxers and thus violates the second criteria of the *BBTS—Biblically Based Rules (BBR)*. It also stretches the first criteria of *Biblically Based Redemptive Purpose (BBRP)* beyond reason. Some might argue otherwise, but such logic borders on incredulity. To argue a prizefighter's *Redemptive Purpose* for brutally beating another woman is to provide financially for her family is insanity at best! Moreover, to state a boxer has a "God-given gift" to pummel another human being borders on blasphemy. However, it is possible to create an environment in which boxing (or any other "fighting" sport) could be biblically justifiable.

If the rules (the *BBR*, the second *BBTS* requirement) for boxing are adapted to meet both the *Redemptive Purpose* and the *Biblically Based Rules* to provide protection for the boxer, then boxing can meet the *BBTS* requirements. The *Redemptive Purpose* would be similar to other sports—enjoyment, physical fitness and health, stewardship of talent, and to honor God while challenging a co-competitor. The rules and format would also have to be adapted. Protective body gear would be required, and governing rules such as no blows above the neck or below the belt would meet the *Biblically Based Rules* requirements. To meet the *BBR* demands, how the contest is decided would be changed. To be biblically defensible, a "win" would change from being a savage attempt to "knock out" and "bloody" the other boxer to a point system awarding boxers for landing various kinds of punches in "safe zones" on a fellow boxer's body.

Battle sports can meet the bare minimums of *BBTS* expectations and would thus be biblically defensible. However, boxers would still need to consider stewardship issues such as whether this endeavor is the best use of their time, resources, and talents. Only they can truly answer this question.

C. Rules Must Be Enforced *(BBRE)*

The rules for ice hockey have been designed to create a fast-paced game and have allowed for a certain level of necessary physical contact among players. Officially the rules do not sanction actions that unduly cause bodily injury. High sticking, slashing, and even fighting are all illegal and usually punished by various levels of penalties. Yet, it is clear the National Hockey League (NHL) fosters fighting by not adequately enforcing its prohibition. Fighting would disappear if players were banished from the league along with coaches and team owners who won't discipline their own players. At the very least, fighting would be greatly curtailed if the officials of the game would eject any player who fights.

Thus, as it currently exists, any level of ice hockey that does not deal decisively with fighting would not meet the third or fourth *BBST* standards: *Biblically Based Rule Enforcement (BBRE)* and *Biblically Based Management and Coaching (BBMC)*. It might also be impacted by the fifth *BBST* standard: *Biblically Based Competing (BBC)*.[3]

One argument often raised in defense of allowing fighting in hockey is it sanctions an "acceptable" alternative for players to personally police "dirty" players. The argument made states: "If fighting wasn't allowed, then the players would resort to clubbing each other with their sticks and this would cause far worse physical injuries to occur." The obvious reply is high-sticking is already not allowed but perhaps higher penalties would need to be levied for such behavior—such as, if you intentionally injure a player and the injured player has to miss games due to the injury, the offending player would miss the same amount of games plus an additional, escalating number of games. For example: Player A hits player B with his stick (either intentionally or unintentionally) and a resultant injury causes the wounded player to miss five games. Player A, who caused the injury, would serve a five-game suspension to correspond with the games player B missed.

---

[3] An interesting caveat to this discussion is an individual hockey player could be biblically justified in fighting in the midst of a hockey game. For more on this consult Chapter 6.

In addition, player A would be suspended for one additional game for a first offense. A second offense would result in an additional 3-game suspension, a third offense would garner a 10-game suspension, and a fourth would result in a full season suspension.

The rationale is obvious: League leadership is to create a safe environment for its players. The game of ice hockey is a wonderful combination of athleticism, stamina, strength, strategy, and teamwork, but unless there are rules and those rules are enforced and penalized, it cannot be biblically defensible. If the rules were seriously enforced, it would certainly meet all *BBST* standards and be biblically defensible.

An interesting caveat to this discussion about fighting and violence is that an individual hockey player could be biblically justified in fighting in the midst of a hockey game if he did so in aid of a teammate who is being attacked. This concept will be discussed in greater detail in Chapter 6.

D. Biblically Based Management and Coaching Is Essential *(BBMC)*

In the sport of baseball there is a difference between "pitching inside" and intentionally hitting a batter with a ball hurled at speeds in excess of 90 miles per hour! Sometimes the athlete chooses to intentionally hit the opposing batter.[4] This action is often followed by the opposing field manager ordering his pitcher to intentionally hit a subsequent batter on the other team. These actions are usually dealt with by the umpires, who often eject the guilty pitchers and managers, thus fulfilling their roles *(BBRE)* in maintaining an environment which meets *BBTS* standards. This demonstrates how an athletic contest can quickly slip into activity that could call its validity into question. Yet, the entire sport of baseball cannot be deemed unbiblical just because a couple of participants don't adhere to the overall *BBTS* mandates. So, baseball is biblically defensible because it meets the first three mandates: (a) *Redemptive Purpose*; (b) *Biblically Based Rules*; and (c) *Biblically Based Rule Enforcement*. The only thing in this

---

[4] To explain this action to those who have never watched the game of baseball, it must be understood there are times in which the batter has bested the pitcher in previous "at bats." Thus, occasionally the pitcher retaliates by hitting the batter with a pitched ball.

scenario not biblically defensible is the athlete or coach who competes in non–Christ-like ways, with non–Christ-like actions or attitudes.

E. How the Game Is Played and Coached Makes All the Difference *(BBC)*

It should be fairly clear by now: Almost any sport can meet the *BBST* standards if a *Redeeming Purpose* is present and all governing rules meet the *Biblically Based Rules* criteria, especially those ensuring the safety of all involved. However, some sports are more conducive to creating a positive and safe environment than others. The more physical the sport, the greater the likelihood athletes will be unable to compete in Christ-honoring ways. Graph 13 on page I-5 illustrates various levels of physicality found within sport.

It is reasonable to believe a bit of anger might surface from the person on the receiving end of a bone-rattling tackle in American football or body check in hockey, but the problem has developed into something more insidious. There is a widely held belief that it is well within the ethic of *collision* sports to attempt to purposely injure a co-competitor as long as it is done within the rules of the game and not the result of a "cheap" or illegal action. This view of ethics and morality is based upon postmodern humanistic relativism, not upon Biblical Rules and Principles. It threatens sports such as American football or rugby with the accusation of not meeting the fourth level of the *BBTS* criteria—*Biblically Based Competing (BBC)*.

Sports that require acts of physically colliding with other athletes are not necessarily ruled out of bounds of the *BBTS,* but the room for error is minuscule and gets smaller the more physical the sport. For example the game of American football relies heavily upon strength and aggressiveness. Neither is inherently evil but if uncontrolled is problematic to the ethic of Christmanship. Nontackle American-style football (either flag or tag) has much less "baggage" associated with it than does tackle-based football. A few of the ethical temptations inherent with tackle football include (a) performance-enhancing drugs to add strength, endurance, and quickness; (b) injuries intentionally caused by savage brutality; (c) 90 percent of all NFL games are played on the Lord's Day; and (d) giving way to emotional outburst of anger caused by the physical nature of the game.[5]

---

[5] These temptations are discussed in Chapter 6.

Can the sport of American football meet the *BBTS* standards? Yes, it can, but not as currently organized and played. Literally hundreds of thousands of injuries are incurred by those participating in this sport each year. Many of these result in paralysis and other lifelong physical impairments. In an era in which the life expectancy of professional football players is significantly shorter than the average American male, the NFL has been sued by former players for not taking more significant actions to protect the physical well-being of the players! These facts alone beg for a change in the way the game is played and approached. It needs to be reformed in such ways so as to protect those who compete and not tempt any player to risk their physical health by taking dangerous drugs or to risk their spiritual health by having to compete on the Lord's Day.

F. Spectators and Fans Have a Responsibility as Well (BBSC)

It would not make sense to ban any sport because of unruly fans, but some American high schools have taken the drastic actions of banning spectators from viewing scholastic athletic contests. This drastic action is due to repeated violence perpetrated by those attending the games. There are many youth leagues who have adopted "no parent" zones around athletic facilities due to the verbal and physical abuse engaged in by berserk adults. Attacks upon umpires, officials, coaches, and players are unfortunately too prevalent. Some of these attacks have even resulted in injuries and deaths.

By now, it should be apparent sports fans bear the responsibility for meeting the *BBST* requirements. Viewing athletic and sporting events is a privilege, not a right, and all spectators need to refrain from negative behavior and, in addition, participate in positive and encouraging cheering.

III. WHAT SPORTS ARE IN? WHAT SPORTS ARE OUT?

I believe with appropriate changes of rules and the way the rules are enforced, managed, coached, played, and watched, the vast majority of sports meet the *BBST* standards and the following articulates my assessment.

A. Non-Biblical Sports

One sport that would not meet the standards is **prizefighting boxing** due to its lack of having an overwhelming *Redemptive Purpose* and its governance not meeting the *Biblically Based Rules* for sport. Boxing in general could be biblically defensible provided the necessary environment is created, but not prizefighting as it is currently organized.

B. Sports Needing Changes to Be Fully Biblically Defensible

Sports on the border of not meeting the standards are **almost any organized sport** played on the Lord's Day[6]; **American football** and, to a lesser extent, **rugby,** due to their valuing violent brutality; **ice hockey** for condoning fighting; and **any sport not taking a hard stand on performance-enhancing drugs.**

C. Sports Meeting Most of the *BBTS* Standards

Sports such as **baseball, lacrosse, basketball,** or **field hockey** should not be deemed unbiblical because of willful human actions of athletes or coaches who do not adhere to *BBTS* standards. Neither should sports such as **football (soccer)** be determined to be unbiblical because spectators become unruly. All **net sports** and all **track and field** athletics would still meet *BBTS* standards even though some participants might take performance-enhancing drugs. However, such individual sports people can and should be deemed unbiblical in their participation if their actions or attitudes lie outside of the Christmanship ethic. Those specific actions are discussed in Chapter 6.

---

[6] The issues of the Lord's Day are thoroughly dealt with in Chapter 7. Or, interested readers can access the paper I presented at the University of York St. John's Symposium titled "Who was Right—Eric Liddell or Jonathon Edwards."

CHAPTER 5

HISTORICAL MODELS

History maketh a young man to be old, without either wrinkles or grey hairs; privileging him with the experience of age, without either the infirmities or inconveniences thereof. Without history a man's soul is purblind, seeing only the things which almost touch his eyes.
Thomas Fuller (*Heroes*, p. xiii)

I. HISTORICAL MODELS OF FAITH AND SPORT INTEGRATION

Introduction to the Fourfold Paradigm

This chapter will summarize three historic periods in which competitors have attempted to integrate their faith with their sport.[1] It will do so by describing the efforts made in each era and by analyzing these efforts through my fourfold faith–sport integration paradigm of "accommodation, capitulation, redemption and rejection" (Graph 16, Sport Faith Integration on page I-7). This paradigm represents four classic approaches athletes take when attempting to integrate faith and sport. It captures the essence of how coaches and athletes attempt to remain faithful to, and live out, their faith in and through their athletic endeavors. I will describe how this faith integration is manifested in each of the following three historical eras and what lessons can be learned by contemporary Christian competitors.

The first chronological era to be considered is the ancient athletics of the Greco-Roman world. It includes not only the ancient Greek and Roman perspectives but also how first-century Hebrews and Christians perceived and/or interacted with athletics. The second period is the Muscular Christian Era of the late nineteenth and early twentieth centuries. The final overview will focus on the Sports Outreach Movement of the late twentieth and early twenty-first centuries.[2]

A. First-Century Faith and Sport Integration

History is often helpful in bringing clarity to modern-day situations. Specifically, much can be learned about *faith and sport integration* from four

---

[1] The three time periods I have chosen to concentrate on are the ones I am most familiar with. There certainly has been competition and sport throughout history and throughout all cultures, much of which I am not qualified to discuss. Even though I can't authoritatively comment on the jousting contests of medieval Europe, Mayan ball games, or ancient African footraces, I believe this fourfold paradigm would fit them or any historical or cultural setting. I leave these issues to those more knowledgeable than me.

[2] I have taken the liberty to establish names for the last two historical epochs. They cannot be intelligently discussed until named and defined. I am open to better or more descriptive terms, but I believe Muscular Christianity was a philosophy ascribed to by athletes during a certain era of time and, at the time I am writing this footnote, I believe "movement" to most aptly describe those involved in sports outreach. I will leave it to future analysts and historians to put an ending date on this movement and perhaps a more suitable moniker.

different ethnic and cultural groups of the first century AD. Each group had its own distinctive philosophy and each suggests a unique way to respond when the demands of faith and sport collide. These four approaches provide models for ensuing generations of athletes to contemplate.

For centuries, ancient Greek athletics produced as exemplary a humanistically based model as could be expected. Yet their attempt to *"accommodate"* religion into sport and virtue into their athletes (rather than the other way around) demonstrates they often valued sport more than religion.[3] Conversely, ancient Rome *"capitulated"* any true sense of virtue in their sports culture. Pragmatic and utilitarian at its core, sport in Rome was used for battle preparation and to mollify the restless masses. It thus devolved into a decadent hedonism. Moreover, whereas Greek temples were built in conjunction with athletic facilities, the Romans built theirs separately. By comparison, ancient Hebrews only built religious facilities, never athletic edifices, as their culture evidenced a third option, which generally eschewed athletics. By and large, the Jewish culture *"rejected"* sport and all *faith and sport integration* or participation.[4]

All three cultures have at least one positive element to contribute to the faith–sport integration discussion but fail to deliver the cogent model of vitality accomplished by a worldview of a yet-to-be-articulated fourth option—*"redemption."* *"Redemption"* can be ascertained from the Bible in general and in specific from the life and writings of the Apostle Paul. This *"redemption"* philosophy serves as the ultimate model for followers of Christ.

Two warnings are in order. One error often made by those commenting on ancient Greek athletics—particularly the ancient Olympics—is to simplistically lump a thousand years of Olympiads into a summarizing sentence or two. This dilemma is present for me, as well, as I try to boil down the essence of ancient Greek athletics for the purposes of understanding the *faith–sport integration paradigm*. Furthermore, I recognize each of these four ancient historical approaches to *faith–sport integration* falls short of complete

---

[3] Although the ancient Greeks and Romans were not Christian, they were religious. How they integrated their religion and sport is what is focused on here. Even though their spiritual beliefs are not Christo-centric they can still be informative to contemporary Christians attempting faith–sport integration.

[4] One exception to this would be Herod the Great, who built some relatively inauspicious athletic facilities and organized a few athletic festivals during his reign. However, although ethnically a Jew, Herod never exhibited any evidence indicating he had any strong allegiance to a Jewish faith or spirituality.

compliance to the demands of the paradigm (Graph 16, Sport Faith Integration on page I-7). For example, it may be true that a few ancient Greek athletes were sincere in competing "in the image of Zeus," but by and large, sport was their first priority and they only *accommodated* religion when and where expedient. Undoubtedly throughout the ancient Olympiad millennium some may have been genuine in their religious affections towards Zeus, Hera, Poseidon, or other gods. Furthermore, Greek athletes may have given the outward appearance that they practiced sport and faith as a syncretistic whole, yet I maintain most esteemed athletics more than religion. Similarly, exceptions could be found in all four ancient groups where individual examples don't fit the overall general stereotype. Nonetheless, I believe each of the four cultures generally represents and illustrates the overall fourfold paradigm, and each exemplifies the general category well enough to draw conclusions, suggest lessons to be learned, and models to be emulated.

What follows, then, is a look into the history of ancient athletics, the sporting context in which the New Testament was written, and a four-part definition of the *faith–sport integration paradigm: capitulation; accommodation; redemption; and rejection.* The chapter starts with the threefold basis found in the ancient triumvirate of the classical Greek, decadent Roman, and eschewing Hebrew models and adds an evolving early Christian perspective as found in the life and letters of Paul (Graph 15, Comparative Religious Views on page I-6). I will apply one aspect of the fourfold *faith–sport integration paradigm* to each ancient historic model and proceed to further develop and explain each of them in the later sections concerning the nineteenth-century Muscular Christianity Era and the twentieth-century Sports Outreach movement.

1. First Century: Hellenism—Athletics as a High Humanistic Ideal

Accommodation

Egypt, Mexico, and other cultures have had certain levels of athletics, play, and games, but Greece is unsurpassed in its athletic sophistication and grandeur.[5] Ancient Greek athletic philosophies were so powerful they

---

[5] Any good book on ancient Greek athletics would help one understand the Hellenistic philosophy of sport. I've included many that have influenced and informed me in the Bibliography section found at the end of this book. I would call special attention to three authors I have found most insightful and helpful: H. A. Harris, E. N. Gardiner and the archaeological works of Oscar Broneer.

continue to influence twenty-first-century sport through its specific traditions and concepts, which include the following:

- Sports academies
- Trainers and coaches
- Sports facilities that are still built upon the same principles and shapes as in ancient Greece
- The Olympic Games themselves

Greek games and competitions had their beginnings mainly in military endeavors, but eventually evolved into an overall training for citizenship in Greek society. The exercises and practices were called "gymnastics" while the competitions that developed were termed "athletics." The gymnastics became part of a comprehensive educational system, which included mental, physical, and spiritual training. The Greeks believed the most virtuous man was a well-rounded man, which made him complete in every way. Their term *kalokagathia* described the highest ideal of "the beauty of goodness and the goodness of beauty." This was the goal of the ancient academies—to produce men of virtue, strength, and character.

Athletic training began as early as age 7 and lasted for most boys until at least 14 years of age. For many the training would continue until age 18, and some underwent special, extended training as part of the group called the *epheboi*. These additional two years of strenuous training were often in preparation for the military. Most men's training in the academy did not end with school, however, for they often continued to exercise well into middle age and beyond. Aristotle even records an insightful interlude of his mentor Plato, wrestling with a student.[6] Interestingly, athletes trained to music! It was thought music would prevent them from becoming too brutal, and athletics would ensure them from becoming too effeminate.

The Greeks were extremely competitive, infatuated with the human body, and committed to overall excellence and virtue of the human soul. The second part of this equation clashed with Roman views whereas the first part offended Jewish sensibilities. Hellenistic culture approached athletics in a dramatically different way than did its Roman and Hebrew

---

[6] H. A. Harris, *Greek Athletes of the Ancient World* (London: Oxford University Press, 1930), p. 117.

counterparts. For the Greek, athletics fulfilled many functions: (a) as memorials for fallen heroes; (b) to honor pagan gods; (c) to develop virtue in the athlete; and (d) to provide individual athletes with an "arena" to fulfill their gifts. The Greeks highly prized the human body and sought to glorify and protect the bodies of their athletes.

Greek games were for the participants—not for those who watched. Although spectators were not uncommon at most Greek athletic festivals, fan accommodations were usually "Spartan."[7] Although non-athletes highly valued the heroic efforts of their athletes, the games were not designed with spectators in mind. Though not every Greek athlete or Greek festival remained true to the high ideals espoused for athletics—because athletics were held in higher esteem than religion—Hellenistic athletics remained ethically superior to what was to follow in Rome.[8]

2. First Century: Roman Sports—Athletics as Decadence and Decline

Capitulation

In direct opposition to Greek sports, ancient Roman athletics were all about the spectator. Huge facilities were built to handle large crowds. The Coliseum had room for up to 60,000 and, by some estimates, the Circus Maximus accommodated nearly 400,000! Romans cared little about individual athletes who battled for their lives in gladiatorial battles. The gladiators were dispensable as they were not valued for any other purpose than to provide entertainment and ghastly, brutal exhilaration to a very depraved society. Violence and savagery were highly valued. No self-respecting Roman would be found watching Greek athletes running and jumping sans clothing. They craved bloodshed and violence. Untold atrocities experienced by the conquering Roman military developed a "bloodlust" amongst its legions of soldiers; no simple foot race could satisfy. Virtue was not valued. Raw, brutal force and, most importantly, bloody battles, were demanded.

E. N. Gardiner succinctly states "the Romans of the Republic despised athletics."[9] Though they may have despised athletics, they still

---

[7]One story from antiquity relates how one Ancient Greek was so angry with one of his slaves that he "forced" the slave to attend the ancient Olympic Games!

[8]Graph 15 on page I-6 outlines and compares the Greek, Roman, and Jewish perspectives on sport.

[9]E. N. Gardiner, *Athletics of the Ancient World* (London: Oxford University Press, 1930), p. 117.

thoroughly enjoyed strenuous exercise, for they were quite active in pursuits such as hunting, riding, and swimming—all valued for their vigorous attributes. I believe disdain for Greek athletics originated from at least six causal factors.

1. The typical Roman predilection toward practicality and pragmatism drove them away from what they considered to be frivolous enterprises such as athletics. The Romans had developed a rather grisly and grim view of life, which grew out of their experiences of war. Exercise could be a means to better health or strength, but it was certainly not to be an end in itself. To spend all of one's effort training to be an athlete was deemed a waste of time.

2. A second reason Romans could not entirely value exercise and athletics was that it was unthinkable for a high-born Roman to submit to the demands of a trainer, who often was a man of no important family or position.

3. As if the pragmatic passions of the Romans would not have been enough to preclude any leanings toward full-time athletics, a third fact made Greek athletics unpalatable to the Roman: Greeks performed their exercises despicably nude. To appear naked in public was the most revolting aspect of Greek athletics and ensured complete disdain from any sensible Roman.

4. In addition to these issues, the fourth causal factor had to do with Rome having no political or military rivals and thus no one to compete with. Whereas each Greek city was a rival of all the other Greek cities and athletic competitions played a vital role in the balance of power, Rome simply crushed its victims by brute, military force and thus had no need of any other way of competing. This may also have led to the fifth reason why Rome never fully appreciated the Greek athletics.

5. Rome had been so brutalized by the ravages of war that its sensitivities had been dulled, and thus, it was much more intrigued by the gore of gladiatorial battles than the finesse of athletics. They had a certain blood thirst, which the comparatively tame Grecian games could not satisfy. They wanted entertainment, not athleticism.

6. There was one last reason the pragmatic Romans held Grecian athletics in contempt: All the attention Greeks gave to athletics had never helped Greece withstand the power of Rome. As Gardiner points out, even the Roman word *ludi* represented their view that athletic games were "ludicrous"—

nothing more than entertainment.[10] For the Roman it was a complete *capitulation* of religion to the preeminence of satisfying visceral lusts.

3. First Century: Jewish Culture—Athletics as Frivolity

Rejection

A third group of people living in the first century were Hebrews. They agreed with many of the Roman criticisms of Greek athletics but also held disparaging views of first-century Roman athletics. Jews disdained Greco-Roman athletics due to theological beliefs and pragmatic realities. Theological concerns rooted in the Mosaic Law, especially the Ten Commandments, included:

- Athletic festivals dedicated to pagan gods
  - Complete with all the pagan rituals, parades, religious sacrifices, vows, offerings, and prayers to pagan gods
- Statues honoring victorious athletes
  - Violating beliefs concerning idolatry and graven images
- Glorification of athletes rather than God
- Deification of athletes and emperors
- Hellenistic ideals that placed too high a value upon the body and not enough on the spirit
- Blatant lack of modesty displayed by naked Greek athletes
- Rome's barbaric craving of brutal bloodletting

In addition to these theological concerns, the basic pragmatic issue of simple survival must be added. Being a subjugated nation and race, Jews could ill afford participation in leisure activities. Ever-prevalent poverty rendered athletics, at best, frivolous. Efforts to feed, clothe, and house themselves precluded athletic participation.

One cannot make too much of the survival issue, however, for, although it was certainly a deterrent to underclass Jews of the first century, wealthy Jews did not take part in athletics either, believing them to be of relative unimportance. This exemplified the third area in which the Jews

---

[10] Ibid., p. 119.

collided with the Greco-Roman philosophy: a priority of eternal over temporal. In their worldview, they were to pursue issues of weightier consequence.

An even greater survival issue, albeit different for those Christian Hebrews of the first century AD, was forced participation in gladiatorial-based athletic spectacles in which they were the victims of the brutal deaths in Coliseum "festivals."

These are just a few of the reasons why I believe it was unusual for first-century Jews to be involved in athletics. Although the veracity of Jewish objections to sport participation cannot be dismissed, it must be understood that Jewish involvement in sport was certainly curtailed but not unheard of.

a. Indications of Jewish Involvement in Sport First-century Jews were split into two major groups of people: those of the *diaspora* and those living in or near Jerusalem. Those living throughout the Roman Empire were more influenced by Roman and Hellenistic cultures and more likely to participate in Greco-Roman athletic activities than their Judean counterparts. At the very least, it must be assumed the *diaspora* Jews had more exposure to the sports culture and were more likely to succumb to its influences. In addition, there are accounts of Jewish involvement in athletics, even as athletes, as evidenced by the four following considerations.

1. H. A. Harris cites historical and archaeological data of Jewish association with athletics. These include athletic pictures in the Jewish catacombs at Rome and a letter from the emperor Claudius to Alexandrian Jews concerning their participation in athletics.[11] These historical evidences, along with other references, indicate Jewish involvement in athletics—at least by those living in a Hellenized setting.

2. Again, it is naive to believe Jews living a great distance from Jerusalem would not have been tremendously affected by a long-term exposure to Hellenic culture.

3. Any enlightened Jew realized the obvious theological short-comings of condemning sports and athletics as a whole. They could comprehend nothing was intrinsically evil with athletics in the same way there is nothing inherently evil with music. Each is without morality in and of itself and thus considered amoral. Therefore, any wise

---

[11]H. A. Harris, *Greek Athletes and Athletics* (Bloomington: Indiana University Press, 1966), p. 133.

Jew could make a case for participation in athletics being, at the worst, amoral. Moreover, many positives were associated with the high ideals of Greek athletics.

4. Of deeper saliency, however, are the life and writings of Paul himself. Even a casual reader of the Pauline corpus understands Paul was well acquainted with the athletics of his day. His coherent and profound usages of technical athletic terms are apparent as is his inspired and ingenious ability to insightfully use sporting motifs to communicate deep spiritual truths. All give credence to the real possibility that Paul was a personal participant and/or observer of the athletics of his day. Paul did not just know about athletics. He exhibits an intimate, firsthand knowledge. I am in full agreement with H. A. Harris when he observes "St. Paul knew his athletics, while Epictetus did not."[12] One cannot read the words of Paul without recognizing his informed comprehensions, which could only come from a firsthand experience. These writings go far beyond a mere use of athletic terms, which long ago lost their association with sport, such as modern-day sayings: "take a rain check" or "three strikes and you're out."[13] The significance of this is more fully realized upon the recognition no one was more dedicated to Judaism than Paul as is recorded in the Acts of the Apostles. It is the person and writings of Paul that provide the segue from the third, ancient-world historical model of *rejection* to the fourth historical perspective: athletics as vocation—*Redemption*.[14]

---

[12] Ibid., p. 131. Having personally done field research throughout Greece along the missionary paths of Paul and having thoroughly researched this topic overall, I am absolutely convinced Paul and his missionary mates were fully cognizant of the athletic activities in many of the Greek cities, and it is all but certain Paul would have at least witnessed one athletic gathering—the Isthmian Festival in AD 51. This opinion is further articulated and can be found at the end of this book in the Appendices on first-century athletics and the Apostle Paul's interactions and involvements in athletics.

[13] I address Pfitzner's argument in his "Agon Motif" about how the "agon" had become separated from its athletic moorings in my Appendices on first-century athletics and the Apostle Paul. His argument is well founded for the occasional "one-off" word in some passages, which has most certainly become detached from its etymological, athletic roots, but its strains credulity to extrapolate and misapply this argument to long, highly descriptive passages that include athletic words, concepts, architecture, statuary, and history.

[14] Graph 15 on page I-6 outlines, compares, and summarizes the first three worldviews. They will serve as the beginning for the remaining discussion, providing keen insights into our contemporary situation.

4. First Century: An Evolving Pauline Christian Culture—Athletics as Vocation

Redemption

A fourth philosophy—evolving in conjunction with Christianity—was ushered in by the Apostle Paul in the middle of the first century AD. This philosophy would not be fully unpacked for nearly 2,000 years but nonetheless provided the foundation for both the Muscular Christian Era and the Sports Outreach Movement. For the most part, the closest these early Christians came to participating in athletics was as persecuted victims in the Coliseum. Yet, there is much evidence to substantiate Paul was well acquainted with both the classical Greek and the brutal Roman athletics of the day. His experiences with Greek athletics as a young lad in the gymnasium at Tarsus and his adult observations of Greek-styled games, especially in Corinth and environs, provided a solid foundation for him.[15] The Roman-styled athletic decadence he knew, especially in Rome and Ephesus, enabled him to recognize the need for a spiritual basis for a *faith–sport integration*. Paul's biblical passages using sporting metaphor and athletic principles were most certainly inspired by the Holy Spirit, but just as certainly, emerged out of his personal experiences with the athletics he encountered throughout Greece, Asia Minor, and perhaps, beyond.

It is one thing to state that Paul had a wealth of athletic experience and interest from which to draw upon; it is quite another to stretch belief to state Paul ever attempted to articulate a well-defined theology of competition and sport. Nonetheless, even a casual reader of Paul's letters understands he holds athletics in high regard. Paul had no reservation in revealing God's truth through sporting metaphors. This is made even more forceful by the fact his writings are the very Words of God Himself! It logically follows that the Bible never communicates sport to be intrinsically evil! Yes, it is true Paul never delineated an organized biblical

---

[15] That Paul received training in the gymnasium at Tarsus is, I believe, justifiable speculation but remains speculation nonetheless. His observation of the Corinthian, Isthmian, and perhaps Nemean games and athletic activities is more believable. It must also be understood that while I maintain Paul was well acquainted with first-century athletics, it is quite a different thing to say he was fully immersed in the sports culture. Again, refer to the Appendix on first-century athletics and Paul.

basis for sport, yet it would be impossible to claim he condemned them or even discouraged participation in them. He understood and modeled how sport was to be *redeemed.*

5. First Century: Summary of First-Century Faith–Sport Historical Models   The Greek perspective represents the highest ideals of a secular culture and perspective. Although the goals and purposes were designed to produce virtue within competitors, the entire culture was fraught with inherent problems because it was based upon pagan religion and humanistic ideals. I link it with *accommodation* because most of those participating in Greek sports held athletics as a higher priority than religion and only accommodated religion when deemed necessary or advantageous. It could be compared to contemporary "sportsmanship" ideals that shift according to, and along with, the larger culture. Humanistic-based philosophies always reflect culture more than directing or transforming culture. Thus, as Hellenism gave way to Rome, the Greek ideals "devolved" into Roman decadence and perversity. The highest value in Roman competition was to survive—to win, at all costs. This might best be compared to the contemporary sporting creed or philosophy termed *gamesmanship.* This is why I link it to the concept of *capitulation,* which completely subordinates anything religious to the demands and priorities of sport or, more disturbing, dismisses religion altogether.

The historical Jewish perspective offers some help to this continuing downward spiral when it calls focus to be placed upon the eternal, true God. I link it with the concept of *rejection* because, for the most part, Jews rejected any participation within sport. Yet even a rejection of athletics falls short of a true understanding of a theistically based view of competition and sport. This view was in its infancy of development through the experiences and writing of the Apostle Paul. Thus, I link this embryonic philosophy with the concept of *redemption.*

Each of these themes and philosophies become more fully developed in the next two sections of this treatise. The Muscular Christian Era of the late nineteenth century takes the next step, and all are ultimately fulfilled in my "Christmanship" ethic of the late twentieth and early twenty-first century during the Sports Outreach Movement. Christmanship is more fully articulated later in this work.

B. Muscular Christianity Era

Different scholars give slightly different time periods for what has been deemed the Muscular Christian Era. Ladd and Mathisen claim 1860–1900[16] whereas Clifford Putney believes it ran for another 20 years or so.[17] A closer look suggests it began as early as the 1820s and was still somewhat in vogue 100 years later, as evidenced by Eric Liddell in 1924 and beyond. I believe the Muscular Christian Era can best be comprehended as a "bell curve." Its genesis was the early 1800s. It peaked during the 1880s and was in declension by the 1920s. Regardless of the exact dates, the philosophy of Muscular Christianity was preeminent for a period of approximately 100 years and greatly influenced the general culture and countless individuals.

The foremost authority on British Muscular Christianity is Stuart Weir of Oxfordshire, England.[18] Weir is quick to point out there are clear distinctions between the American and British versions of what is commonly called Muscular Christianity.[19] There is much merit in Weir's assessment. I believe, however, that Weir doesn't go far enough in distinguishing only two variations. I believe there to be four basic manifestations

---

[16] See their excellent work *Muscular Christianity, Evangelical Protestants and the Development of American Sport.*

[17] *Muscular Christianity, Manhood and Sports in Protestant America, 1880–1920.*

[18] I have termed the time period from approximately 1950 through the present day (2014) as the Sports Outreach Movement. The last 70 years have produced a groundswell of churches, para-ministries and individuals who seek to integrate their faith with sport and use the methodology of sport and recreation to "reach out" to those outside the Christian faith and church. In the final analysis, the Sports Outreach Movement may prove to also have followed a bell curve, as its roots existed in the lives of individual athletes and coaches during the first half of the twentieth century, grew to prominence through the second half of the century, and then in the early twenty-first century seemed to enter into what Ladd and Matheson hinted at in the final chapter of their book: a "future disengagement." See the last chapter of this book for my thoughts on the Sports Outreach Movement's future and legacy.

[19] Besides being one of only a handful of experts on the Muscular Christian era, Weir is a prolific writer and editor. He served as one of the directors of Christians in Sport, based in Oxford, England, and in 2006 initiated Verite' Sports—an international sports ministry. A quick Google will reveal a dozen or more books by Weir—the most significant is *What the Book Says about Sport.* No true exposition on either the Muscular Christian Era or Sports Outreach Movement is complete without consulting Mr. Weir.

of Muscular Christianity: (a) Classical/British; (b) YMCA/United States; (c) Evangelical/International; and (d) Olympic/French-European.[20] These various expressions need to be further defined and explained, but it must be realized that Muscular Christianity was both a Western manifestation of a larger social phenomena as well as a catalyst to an emerging and larger movement.

The larger context from which Muscular Christianity emerged was:

- A society experiencing increasingly more leisure time

- Rising feminism that threatened traditional male roles, endeavors, and, most importantly, male self-esteem and identity

- An increasing stream of wealth among the growing middle class, which provided the resources for recreational equipment, travel, and leisure time

Muscular Christianity was a catalyst for social and spiritual change in providing the answers to many questions of young males concerning vocation, gender, purpose, and identity. Related movements such as muscular Judaism were greatly inspired and shaped by Muscular Christianity but have been far less documented. For example, Eric Liddell is often equated with Muscular Christianity whereas Harold Abrams is not seen through the lens of Muscular Judaism. Even the extremely well-researched and, for the most part, accurate Academy Award–winning movie *Chariots of Fire* refers to Liddell as a Muscular Christian but never refers to Abrams as a Muscular Jew.[21] Regardless, Muscular Christianity was a major force for those integrating faith and sport during this era.

---

[20] I associate the four expressions Classical, Evangelical, YMCA, and Olympic with geographic locales: Britain, International, America, and France/European because I believe these were the regions that most shaped and gave expression to a particular variation of Muscular Christianity. Any attempt to categorize broad spectrums such as these must be taken as being generally true rather than true in each specific case.

[21] I am not of aware of much documentation about how other faith traditions interacted with the sports world. This may show my own naivety and my cultural "bubble," but I believe at the very least, if this information exists, it is not widely known. It is certainly not widely discussed. I would suspect similar parallel movements and experiences to Muscular Christianity could be found in faith communities such as Judaism, Islam, Eastern religions, and other Christian spin-offs such as Mormonism, but currently I am unaware of any information.

What follows is an overview of the four expressions of Muscular Christianity and how similar they are to the Ancient World Quadrangle of Greek, Roman, Jewish, and Christian perspectives of sport. These four concepts will then be applied and compared to the fourfold *faith–sport integration paradigm* in an effort to develop models for sports people of the Sports Outreach Movement attempting to synthesize their faith and sport.

Muscular Christianity: British—The Roots of Muscular Christianity: Arnoldian Theory

Redemption

Economics are intricately intertwined with athletics and sport. Professional sports have both a positive and negative association with money. Cold, hard realities of economics relegated sport to the ultra-rich for millennia as only the wealthy could afford "leisure." Only as the Industrial Revolution brought about a true middle class did sport reach the masses. As a result, having a need for a theology of leisure, sport, and athletics was not required until men like the headmaster of Rugby School—Thomas Arnold—and others began to incorporate athletics into the school system and sports began to subsequently flow into the broader culture.[22] Thus, the roots of the Muscular Christian Era are found in the early 1800s as sport became part of a school's curriculum and leisure time became more and more part of the fabric of society.

In addition, ancient Greek philosophies influenced men like Headmaster Arnold as he sought to mold the entire "tri-part man" by training students in body, mind, and spirit. First, Arnold strengthened Rugby School's already strong academic pursuits to *inform* the intellect of his

---

[22]It is sometimes thought Arnold's school got its name from the sport of rugby, and the school only taught the sport of rugby. In reality, Rugby was and has always been a most-respected educational institution whose name has become synonymous with the sport after it was first played by students there. There are also varied thoughts concerning Arnold's direct or indirect support for and utilization of sport at Rugby. At the very least it must be recognized the Muscular Christian ethos began and flourished under his leadership. I'll leave the debate as to whether or not he was the direct or indirect catalyst for school sport to others more informed in this area. For my purposes, and from my research of documents and site visits at Rugby, Repton, and other English schools, it is well-documented that Rugby School was recognized as a hub for the development of the Muscular Christian culture.

young men. Second, and perhaps most importantly to him, Arnold also sought and received Anglican ordination so as to *reform and transform* his students spiritually. Third, Arnold supported physical activities as a methodology to *form* a physical robustness in his students. He believed, most naively, as did most of the day, that physical activity would naturally produce a certain spiritual character and virtue within his protégés.[23]

Arnold was both a catalyst for the holistic approach to education as well as being a product of the overall culture of early nineteenth-century Britain. Rugby School's "heyday" was from approximately 1820–1850 and became a prime example of *redeeming* athletics. During this time period, the movement of young men seeking a "robust faith" eventually emerged, manifested in the formation of groups like the YMCA, organized in 1844 by George Williams and 11 others.[24]

Certain segments of this British Muscular Christian expression were indeed overtly evangelical theologically, evangelistically motivated in purpose, and personally pietistic in practice, yet there was a much wider and larger sense in which the British form of Muscular Christianity was much more secular. Many young men who thought of themselves as "Muscular Christians" emphasized the muscular part and equated the Christian part with being, as Gilbert and Sullivan penned in one light opera of that era: "he is an English Man"—as opposed to being a "heathen" or someone from another country or religious culture. The main emphasis for the British version of Muscular Christianity eventually was on the physical side more so than the Christian side. Certainly, the early focus of men like George Williams and his YMCA associates was more on the Christian part of the Muscular Christian concept than on the muscular, but this was the "minority report" for England. Eventually, the Y embraced both parts equally as this Anglo breeding ground for the emerging movement gave birth to other strains of Muscular Christianity. In its roots however, Anglo Muscular Christian philosophy was conceived to truly integrate faith and sport to *redeem* both the person of sport and the world of sport.

---

[23] I personally subscribe to the theory that sport develops character in youth and reveals the character of adults.

[24] See vignettes of both Arnold and Williams in my "Surrounded by Witnesses," which provide a fuller picture of these men, the cultural milieu of their day, and their impact on Muscular Christianity.

1. Muscular Christianity: YMCA/United States

Accommodation

The first YMCA formed in the United States was in Boston in 1851.[25] However, the New York YMCA became the undisputed leader of the movement, especially through the vision and efforts of Scotch-Irish immigrant Robert Ross McBurney. McBurney was the key strategist for the Y from the 1860s through his death in 1899. McBurney was a contemporary of other well-known persons in the movement such as Dwight L. Moody. Moody, Billy Sunday, and others became known as "evangelists," but in their formative years were initially trained by and ministered through the YMCA.[26] In fact, Moody and Sunday often stated the Y did more to prepare them for ministry than anything else. Such was the early YMCA in America: thoroughly Christian, devotedly pietistic, profoundly evangelical, and actively evangelistic. Yet typical "secular creep" occurred because the physical side of the "triangle" was easier to emphasize than were the intellectual and spiritual. Building and maintaining facilities often took precedence over establishing and nurturing spiritual relationships. Concerns about the health of budgets superseded concerns about the spiritual welfare of individual members. The change did not occur overnight, but did insidiously change the YMCA by shifting its moorings first from evangelistic, to evangelical, and then to the more inclusive ecumenical, all the while moving more and more toward secularized *accommodation*. The legacy of this shift results in most twenty-first-century Ys advocating the philosophy of promoting "healthy bodies and minds" in an environment of Christian values. Currently, this environment usually consists of nothing more than four words seen on YMCA literature, billboards, and building walls: responsibility, respect, caring, and honesty. Furthermore it is clearly evidenced by a decided movement away from being called the Young Men's Christian Association or YMCA, to simply a much more secular terminology: "the Y." Although there is never just one single cause

---

[25] Montreal was the first in North America, forming a few months earlier than Boston, and it played a huge role in shaping American Muscular Christianity as it produced the inventor of basketball James Naismith.

[26] McBurney, Moody, and Sunday are more broadly discussed in my unpublished "Surrounded by Witnesses."

for the secularization of an organization, at least part of the reason this *accommodation* occurred was because many of those committed to evangelical Christianity could not reconcile their sport with their faith—including some of the main leaders of the YMCA.

2. Muscular Christianity: Evangelical/International

Rejection

Part of my reasoning for identifying the American/YMCA version of Muscular Christianity with the *accommodation* motif stems from the fact many of the true evangelicals of that day left the YMCA organization and, in so doing, *rejected* the realm of sport. Moody left the YMCA and became an international evangelist. Billy Sunday quit playing major league baseball to become the heir of Moody's crusade ministry, and although not an American, Eric Liddell left athletic competitions at the height of his prowess and became a missionary in China. In addition, C. T. Studd left the world of cricket for the mission field in China with the "Cambridge Seven" and lived the rest of his life as a missionary in Africa. These four are the most prominent examples of evangelical Muscular Christians who *rejected* athletics for what they perceived to be a higher calling. They embodied a much more evangelical and evangelistic Muscular Christianity for a while, but I believe all struggled with the culture of sport and recreation because they could not reconcile their faith with their sport. Thus, they chose "religion" over sport.

Sunday left professional baseball initially over Lord's Day issues but also because of the rampant "vices" that surrounded the game, such as gambling, alcohol, and vulgarity. Moody had always emphasized the spiritual over the physical, at best using sport and recreation as a tool for reaching people for Christ. He even moved away from using recreation as a tool during his many years as an evangelist. However, later in life Moody was greatly influenced by Kynaston and C. T. Studd's use of their athletic "platforms" as Muscular Christians. This resulted in his fully embracing evangelism through athletics and recreation as evidenced by the organized "Muscular Christian" activities at his Northfield Conferences. Yet, Moody never developed a true theology of competition and sport. At best he viewed athletics as nothing more than a pragmatic aid in reaching people for Christ. When "push came to shove," he joined Sunday in rejecting athletics.

Progressive Intensity Levels of Competition

Professional Sport

Varsity Sport

Recreational Sport

Athletics

Games

Playful Games

Play

Graph 2

External Influences on Competition

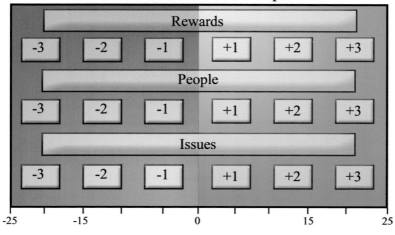

Rewards

| -3 | -2 | -1 | +1 | +2 | +3 |

People

| -3 | -2 | -1 | +1 | +2 | +3 |

Issues

| -3 | -2 | -1 | +1 | +2 | +3 |

-25   -15   0   15   25

Graph 5

Internal Influences on Competition

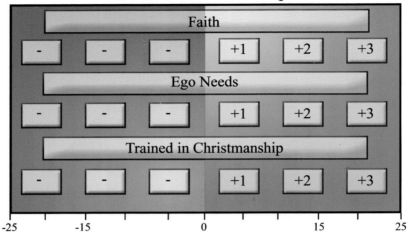

Graph 6

Volatility Scale

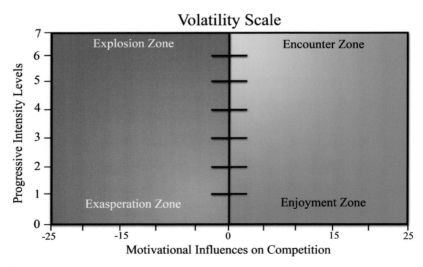

Graph 7

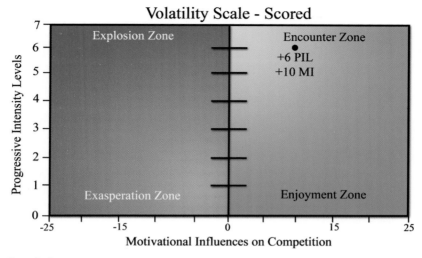

Graph 8

Graph 9

Theological Rubric

Creation	Fall	Redemption	Consummation
God said: It was good	Serpent Said: Thou Shalt Die	Jesus said: I have made all things new	Revelation says: There will be new heaven & earth
All competition was created good	Mankind corrupted competition	Jesus redeems competition	Competition will be made pure
All competition is Biblically defensible	Humanistic competition is not Biblically defensible	Christ redeemed competition is Biblically defensible	All competition will be made new

Graph 10

Defending Sports Pyramid

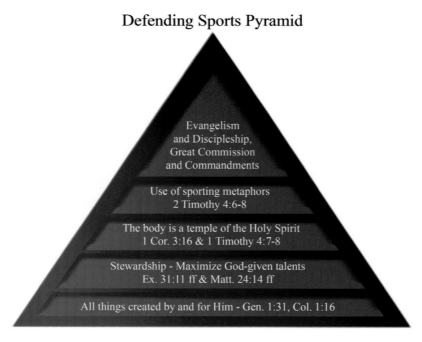

Evangelism
and Discipleship,
Great Commission
and Commandments

Use of sporting metaphors
2 Timothy 4:6-8

The body is a temple of the Holy Spirit
1 Cor. 3:16 & 1 Timothy 4:7-8

Stewardship - Maximize God-given talents
Ex. 31:11 ff & Matt. 24:14 ff

All things created by and for Him - Gen. 1:31, Col. 1:16

Graph 11

Template for
Biblically Defensible Sports

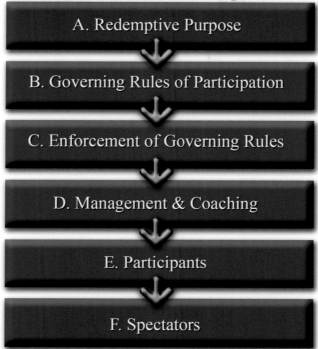

A. Redemptive Purpose

B. Governing Rules of Participation

C. Enforcement of Governing Rules

D. Management & Coaching

E. Participants

F. Spectators

Graph 12

Physicality in Sport

No Contact	Minimal Contact	Contact	Collision
All Net Sports	Baseball	Basketball	American Football
Golf	Fencing	Football (Soccer)	Rugby
Bowling	Volleyball	Lacrosse	Ice Hockey
Track & Field	Ultimate Frisbee	Wrestling	Boxing

Graph 13

Sports That Meet BBTS Standards

Meets BBTS Standards	Borderline Standards	Does Not Meet BBTS Standards
All Net Sports	American Football	Prize-Fighting
All Track & Field Sports	Rugby	
Baseball	Ice Hockey	
Basketball	Boxing	
Football (Soccer)	Wrestling	
Lacrosse	Fighting Sports	
Field Hockey	All Sports on the Lord's Day	
Most Winter Sports		

Graph 14

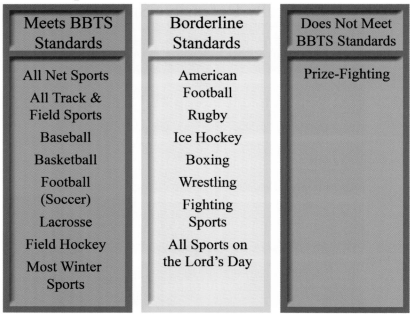

Comparison of Greek, Roman and Jewish Views of Sport

Concept	Greek	Roman	Jewish
Civic/Religious Goal	Freedom	Right	Righteousness
Personal Concern	Beauty/Focus on the Body	Power/Focus on the Government	Nakedness and Disgrace
Virtue	Wisdom/Focus on the Mind	Pleasure/Focus on Self	Obedience/Focus on God
Rewards	Internal	External	Eternal
Who Games Were For	The Athletes	The Fans	No One
The Athlete	Held in Esteem	For Fan's Enjoyment	Viewed as Frivolous

Graph 15

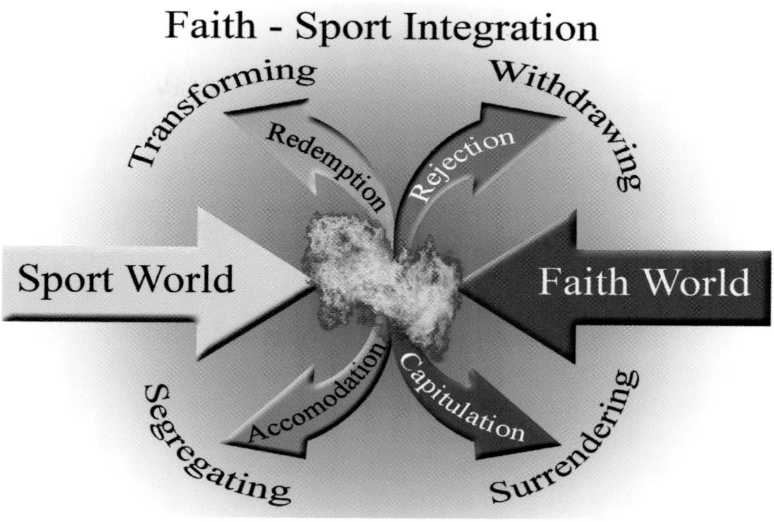

Faith - Sport Integration

Transforming

Withdrawing

Redemption

Rejection

Sport World

Faith World

Segregating

Accomodation

Capitulation

Surrendering

Graph 16

Honor Code for Determining Biblically Based Sports

Honors Christ

Honors the Redemptive Purpose

Honors the Temple of the Holy Spirit

Honors the Lord's Day

Honors the Family

Honors Organizational Principles

Graph 17

The evangelical root of Muscular Christianity continued and persevered throughout the world and was carried on organizationally through the YMCA by men like John R. Mott and in athletics and missions through men like C.T. Studd and his "Cambridge Seven." Later men, such as Eric Liddell, who continued to stay physically active, were clear to place the emphasis decidedly upon the Christian side of Muscular Christianity. Most embodied "manly pursuits" such as athletics and rigorous, even life-threatening mission work but *rejected* athletics whenever there was a perceived conflict between faith and sport. Their theology of sport was simple but naive. They separated their spiritual life from their athletic life. The spiritual was believed to be of higher value and if ever there was a conflict they simply dismissed athletic involvement. It almost seems they had a nagging, latent doubt about the theological validity of sport and athletics. Certainly, they never developed any definitive theology for competition and athletics.[27]

This Platonic dualism illustrates the necessity of a theology of competition and sport. The sport–faith dilemma need not be relegated to an "all or nothing" solution. A definitive theological framework is needed, one that can articulate and differentiate between specific sporting actions, times, and attitudes that are not congruous with biblical endeavors and those that are. More importantly it is imperative to develop a distinction between non-biblical activities within sport and the belief that sport itself is innately evil. Unethical acts within sport can and should be *rejected*, but sport itself can be biblically justified and need not be *rejected*. I belabored this theological foundation in the first four chapters of this treatise, and I outline specific sporting attitudes, motives, and actions in great detail in the following chapter. There is much to be learned from those Muscular Christian pioneers of the late nineteenth and early twentieth centuries but a complete *rejection* of sports is not one of them.

3. Muscular Christianity: Olympic-Secular/French-European

Capitulation

A unique strain of Muscular Christianity developed from a most unusual source, that I call "The Three Thoms of Muscular Christianity." Thomas

---

[27] The closest may have been Eric Liddell, who did seem to understand a latent sense of being able to worship while running, but even he eventually surrendered to the prevailing notion of the day to "make his life count" for more than athletics by turning to the Chinese mission field.

Arnold—headmaster—had a student by the name of Thomas Hughes. Hughes became a leading thinker and recognized author in the mid- to late 1800s. Hughes incorporated all the philosophies and theologies he had learned from his mentor at Rugby—Thomas Arnold—into his most enduring fictional character, Tom Brown.[28] These Tom Brown novels were the catalyst for the creation of a modern athletic movement as they inspired one reader—Baron Pierre De Coubertin—to breathe new life into the ancient Olympic Game concept.

The good baron never pretended to embrace the religious or spiritual overtones of the "Three Thoms" (Arnold, Hughes, and Brown) or the overall Muscular Christian philosophy. Rather, De Coubertin believed sport, in itself, had the power to bring about personal and societal change. He was a confirmed humanistic skeptic who renounced his Roman Catholic upbringing and yet could never rid himself of speaking, thinking, or operating in spiritual concepts. This is observed in the "spirit" of his neo-Olympic Games right down to the athlete's pledge (creed) and his "belief" athletics were a "higher power" that could "heal the wounds" of the nations and bring about an "international peace" through the "brotherhood of man." Many share this belief today and continue to attempt to use sport as a way to develop virtue in individuals and to bridge culture and ideology in nations. They seek to do this from an intentionally designed secular basis. The religious roots and essence had been *capitulated* in favor of a completely secular approach to the Muscular Christian philosophies.

4. Muscular Christianity: A Fifth Option Emerges

Syncretization

Even though I have just done so, it is too much of a stretch to assign men such as Sunday or Liddell into only one of these categories just to make the paradigm work. I stand by these as limited examples but believe they beg for a fifth category. Although it is true that Liddell did

---

[28]The two Tom Brown novels (*Tom Brown— School Days* and *Tom Brown at Oxford*) are still widely available today and were even turned into a late 1990s PBS movie. As was mentioned in a previous footnote, there is some debate as to Arnold's direct or indirect influence upon the development of Muscular Christianity, but there is little doubt as to Hughes's influence through his writings and life. It is safe to say Hughes was greatly influenced by Arnold and, subsequently, De Coubertin by Hughes.

reject the world stage of the Olympics in favor of Christian missions, and it is also true Billy Sunday walked away from professional baseball for crusade work, it would be too far a stretch to state they believed sport to be intrinsically evil. Liddell organized athletics for the children of the Japanese prison camp he and they were incarcerated in during World War II, and he informally raced against some of the world's greatest sprinters when they came to visit him in China. Sunday used his "platform" as a former pro athlete to attract people to his crusades and in addition he would do publicity events in a baseball uniform with the likes of actor Douglas Fairbanks. Moody used athletic competition to great advantage for the college students who attended his summer Northfield Conferences and was often found leading spiritual meetings on camping trips.

For these men and others, it only made sense to reject sport when they deemed it conflicted with their theological beliefs, and yet, when and where appropriate, they participated in and used athletics for redemptive purposes. Their examples pave the way for creating a fifth alternative: *syncretization.* This will be explored more in the discussion of the Sports Outreach Movement, which articulates how contemporary competitors must stay involved in their athletic vocations and activities and yet be guided in these endeavors to reject certain unbiblical attitudes, actions, relationships, and times of participation.

5. Muscular Christianity: Summary of the Muscular Christian Era

I believe there is room to "tweak and critique" my fourfold description and categorization of the past two century's interactions with faith–sport conflicts. Yet, I believe I have sufficiently established the fact that Christians of the past two centuries responded in much the same way as have the sporting Christians throughout history. The four Muscular Christian expressions help to define and illustrate the *faith– sport integration paradigm.* I also maintain their responses—especially those of *rejection* and *accommodation*—are a result of not having, nor understanding, a biblically based theology of competition and sport.

C. Sports Outreach Movement

In 2007 I was invited to make a symposium presentation titled "Who was Right? Eric Liddell or Jonathon Edwards: Lord's Day Issues." The invitation came from the Sport and Spirituality Centre of York St. John University of York, England.[29] Although I had suggested a Lord's Day theme, at the time I wondered if the invitation was extended to an American because of the potential difficulty a "Brit" might experience in discussing the religious views of two fellow British Isle citizens—particularly since one was still alive and remained a very prominent member of the wider British athletic family! I took the chance; as the saying goes, "A fool rushes in" . . . and I guess I'm still foolish as I now attempt to discuss the current landscape of the *faith–sport integration paradigm,* which includes friends, colleagues, partners, and fellow believers.[30]

I contend that the Sports Outreach Movement began in the years following the worldwide economic depression of the 1930s, caught fire in the decade following the end of World War II, and possibly peaked at the turn of the millennium.[31] Although church-based sports ministries have been around for much longer, the world of para-sport ministries was initiated in 1954, when the Fellowship of Christian Athletes (FCA) was organized.[32] Athletes in Action began a few years later and by 1980 I estimated that more than 200 para-sport ministries were operating in America alone.[33]

A common opinion is the local church lagged behind this new wave of para-sports ministries, and yet historical data confirm

---

[29] This centre was short lived and no longer exists at York St. Johns, although it was revived by my colleague Dr. Andrew Parker at the University of Gloucester in 2009.

[30] Refer to the Preface of this book, which contains my more in-depth comments about this concern.

[31] I say possibly because it may grow and become more influential in the near or distant future, which is currently unknown, but as already indicated, I predict it will appear in history as a bell-shaped curve, peaking in the years 1980–2000 and slowly declining over the next few decades.

[32] These groups are often called para-church but are referred to here as para-ministries. Theologically all believers make up the church and, thus, I have determined to differentiate between ministries based in local churches and para-ministries organized outside a local church. In addition, I recognize the YMCA can be considered the oldest para-sports ministry in the world (formed June 6, 1844), but for the most part it has rejected its evangelical heritage and its evangelistic outreaches. Thus, it is fair to say the advent of FCA and the others that followed helped initiate the sports outreach movement in 1954.

[33] There is no quality research data to determine the total number, and it continues to be a "moving target" as new ministries are started every year and some cease to exist.

individual churches have utilized sports and recreation for gospel outreach for hundreds of years.[34] The Southern Baptist Convention published its first book on church recreation in 1937, and a church basketball league, consisting of 50 teams, was established in Cleveland, Ohio, within 10 years of the game's 1891–1892 creation! Yet, even with this history, there certainly has been a concentrated proliferation of local church sports outreach since the 1970s, and this trend inspired a 1990s groundswell by a dozen or so para-ministries, which emerged to serve this burgeoning local church sports ministry phenomenon.

One such example was founded in 1992 by Rodger Oswald: Church Sports International (CSI). Its mission is to *"create a vision for sports ministry in the local church, equip the church to carry out that vision, and to come alongside in order to implement the vision"*; www.csi.org (accessed September 11, 2009).[35] A second example is the association of Church Sports and Recreation Ministers (CSRM). An informal association began in the late 1980s with official incorporation in 1995. CSRM is international in scope and exists to *"equip local churches to change lives through sport outreach."*[36] Christians in Sport (CIS), an umbrella Sports Ministry in the United Kingdom, hired Bryan Mason as its local church liaison in 1995, and Mason served in that role until hired as the European director of CSRM in 2004. Mason personally witnessed the growth of church sports outreach ministry as is evidenced by the fact that he personally visited and encouraged hundreds of U.K. churches to utilize sport or recreation in some form of ministry. Since 2010 Mason has been developing a sports outreach resource for churches called Higher Sports. A fourth evidence is Upward Basketball. Upward began serving churches in 1995, and although at the time of writing this, Upward is numerically declining somewhat, it has served as many as 4,000 churches a year. It provides local congregations with

---

[34] See my doctoral dissertation's chapter on history, which relates numerous churches and denominations that used sports for evangelism, discipleship, fellowship, and other related ministry opportunities.

[35] This quote comes directly from CSI's website; www.csrm.org (accessed September 11, 2009).

[36] This quote comes directly from CSRM's website, www.csrm.org. Disclaimer: I served as the executive director of CSRM when I wrote this treatise.

"basketball leagues in a box."[37] The training, support, and resources provided by Upward enables local congregations a very practical and feasible way to reach out to their community even if they don't have a comprehensive sports outreach program or staff.

The list goes on. Suffice it to say these peripheral support ministries, businesses, and organizations would not exist if there wasn't a growing local church sports outreach ministry community.[38]

Yet still another indicator demonstrating the emergence of the Sports Outreach Movement is the growth of sports ministry coursework and majors in the academic world. The formal arm of training began with the Master's College in the mid-1990s and an increasing number of Bible colleges, universities, and seminaries are preparing future sports ministers as well as training those currently in the field. The CSRM website lists the most current list of undergraduate programs in the United States and Canada.[39] In addition, according to the CRSM website, as of September 2009, two concentrations in sports ministry were accredited in 2004 and 2008, one of which continues: the University of Gloucester. In addition there are two 1-year programs offered at schools in the United Kingdom, and master's-level tutorial-based course work in sports ministry was initiated in South Africa in the summer of 2005 at the South African Theological Seminary.[40] Most recently, the

---

[37] The number of churches Upward serves is a moving target, as it is a rapidly growing organization. The "basketball league in a box" is not meant as a disparaging comment but rather descriptive of Upward's brilliant design and support system. Upward has refined its resource to such a degree that local churches are able to effectively administrate youth basketball leagues with the equipment shipped to them "in a box" by Upward. This equipment insures a solid, albeit a noncompetitive, youth basketball ministry, especially when combined with the high-quality training Upward provides local church leaders.

[38] Again, my doctoral dissertation would be a helpful resource as it outlines the growth of this industry.

[39] There were 10 listed at the time of writing.

[40] Disclaimer: I have been a professor at Malone University and had the privilege of guiding its program from its inception until 2012. I believe what is reported here to be true and factual, but my biases undoubtedly come through. At the current time, no University offers a doctoral program for Sports Ministry, although I am aware of two students who earned a D. Min. with a sports outreach concentration: myself at Ashland Seminary and

Agon[41] Institute of Sports Ministry was founded in 2013 in conjunction with various seminaries and universities. The *Agon* provides both a master's-level concentration and a recognized certification in sports ministry and founded by CSRM and UW.[42]

Informal training has also proliferated. Each local church with a sports ministry and most para-sports ministries have their own "in-house" training tracks. CSRM took the informal training to the next level by establishing the world's only known sports ministry certification. The CSRM certification began in 1998, and all in-house training tracks came into existence within the past few decades.

So the Sport Outreach Movement has grown and proliferated over the last 70–80 years, but how has it influenced and impacted the *faith–sport integration paradigm*? At the risk of offending many friends, colleagues, and partners, I offer the following assessment. The category is listed and briefly explained, and then I list the groups I believe best exemplify the category.

1. Redemption—Those who are attempting to redeem the individuals within sport as well as impacting the broader community by attempting to redeem the wider culture of sport—*most local churches and para-sports ministries.*

2. Rejection—Those who reject competition and create environments in which play occurs but not competition. This is done because they have a working theology that competition is evil—*Upward and any local church, sports ministry, and/or camp which eliminates competition or walks away from competitive sport and athletics.* (This may be changing, however, as the Upward leadership is refining their program to include a graduated level of competition within their sports leagues and a new "Upward Stars" program.)[43]

Aaron Treadway at Liberty University, and two who received honorary sports outreach doctorates: myself—D. Div. from Briercrest Seminary—and Steve Conner from Azusa Pacific University. The most current list of academic sports outreach programs is maintained by CSRM on its website: www.csrm.org.

[41] *Agon* is the Greek New Testament word for the athletic struggle and experience.

[42] Disclaimer: I was one of the founders of the *Agon*, and CSRM (of which I serve as the executive director) was one of the two founding sports ministries.

[43] Caz McCaslin's (the founder and CEO of Upward) own description of this can be accessed through the recording of his presentation at the CSRM Academic Symposium

3. Accommodation—Those who turn a blind eye to what occurs within their athletic department. They claim to run Christian athletic departments and may even require all coaches and staff to sign statements declaring their personal commitment to Christ, yet never hold their coaches accountable for their athletes' spiritual development and fire coaches who aren't successful at winning games, conferences, and/or national titles. They further accommodate their Christian theological principles by allowing and supporting athletic endeavors (meetings, practices, scouting, recruiting, and even games) to occur on the Lord's Day and high holy days such as Good Friday—*many local churches, universities, high schools.*

4. Capitulation—Those who have completely left their evangelical roots, such as the YMCA. I'm sure a case could be made for an individual branch of a YMCA and the even more probable likelihood specific YMCA staff members could be found who are true to the original evangelical and evangelistic goals and ideals of the Y. Unfortunately, it is far more likely the Y has, at best, an ethic rooted in basic humanistic philosophies.[44] Otherwise, a prerequisite of the Sports Outreach Movement is to be evangelical to the point of being evangelistic and biblical; thus, no recent sports ministry or organization has completely left the faith. I do think, however, the potential for *capitulation* lies in ministries such as 360 Sports, Coaches 4 Life, Quantum Sports, and other similar ministries. This potential stems from a methodology that "cloaks" the gospel in "secular

---

of 2010—www.csrm.org. It is possible Upward's theological perspective of competition is evolving as they have entered the world of competitive sport with their Upward Stars program and other endeavors. I commend such endeavors.

[44] As a disclaimer, I served on the staff of an urban YMCA two different times. The two tenures were separated by a 15-year period. Even I was amazed at how much the same metro YMCA had changed in those intervening 15 years. During the first tenure, many staff did not consider themselves Christians, nor did they pretend to believe they did anything that could be defined as a ministry. Nonetheless, there remained a remnant of staff members who believed they had a vocational ministry at the Y and sincerely attempted to not only operate their facility and programming in Christian ways, but more importantly actively encouraged Y participants to consider a personal relationship with Christ. Today, yet another decade later, this shift away from Christian ministry is even more pronounced although the current Danville, Illinois, YMCA director, Mike Brown, lives out the original goals and ethic of the YMCA's founders.

speak" so as to be acceptable to those athletic directors and coaches who are not necessarily committed to Christ or with those who are personally faithful to Christ but coach in secular environments. The motivations of these ministries are pure and well intentioned. The long-term outcome won't be known for decades to come.[45] The state of the modern-day Y would not only shock George Williams, Robert McBurney, and John R. Mott, but sadly, I'm also sure they would be broken-hearted to see their legacy today. None of the sports outreach movement ministries, including the founders/leaders of 360 Sports Coaches 4 Life and Quantum Sport desire a similar destiny for what they have established. As long as they remain involved in the leadership of these ministries, the focus will stay true to the priority of evangelism and evangelical theological foundations. Their legacy may be different—*YMCA and potentially others.*

II. SUMMARY OF HISTORICAL FAITH AND SPORT INTEGRATION

It should now be clear from this study: Historical attempts to integrate faith with sport fall into one of four classic categories: *redemption, rejection, accommodation,* or *capitulation.* When these responses are considered in light of this chapter, it becomes obvious two responses (*capitulation* and *accommodation)* should always be avoided by serious followers of Christ. *Capitulation* demonstrates sport to be the primary priority of one's life as the sporting person has willingly chosen sport over faith, thus leaving a relationship with Christ behind in their pursuit of "worldly gain." This specifically breaks the Lord's command to "have no other God." *Accommodation* reveals a person in constant conflict, bearing the continual guilt

---

[45] I truly consider Lowrie McCown of 360 Sports, Wade Salem of Coaches 4 Life, and Ken Youngson as dear brothers. They are without question strong evangelicals and are creatively attempting to engage sports people for gospel purposes. In particular, Ken Youngson has a huge and strategic vision for how Quantum Sport can reach all of New Zealand for Christ. My statements here reflect my assessment of historic models more than current specific endeavors. Yet it is true many ministries with strong evangelical roots ended up very secular decades after shifts in approach occurred—the very shifts these three ministries made at the turn of the twenty-first century. I've shared these thoughts with these men, and all are keenly aware of the risk and also of the huge potential to redeem both the people of sport as well as the culture of sport through their chosen methodologies.

of wanting faith to be primary but realizing it often is not. Though desiring to remain in a warm relationship with Jesus, those who accommodate their faith often succumb to the temptations and enticements of sport and very often end up *capitulating* their faith altogether. This breaches the biblical principle of "whatever is not done in faith is sin."

The other two categories, *rejection* and *redemption,* are compatible with a Christian ethic and worldview but need further consideration and clarification.

The third category, *rejection,* stems from a strong, but sometimes misguided, desire to zealously keep faith in Christ as the primary commitment in life. All who walk away from sport when they believe it contradicts or negatively impacts their relationship with Jesus are to be commended for their dedication to spiritual priorities, but they must be admonished to give careful consideration of a thorough contemplation of a biblically based theology of competition before rejecting any involvement in sport. Sport and competition can well fit within a Christian worldview and, moreover, athletes can learn how to *redeem* both their personal participation in sport as well as the sporting culture in general. More significantly, they will find by remaining in sport that they are best able to fulfill their "holy vocation." Certainly, orthodox theology has very specific proscriptions and there may well be times Christian sports people should "reject" sport when participation in it violates clear biblical commands. However, rejection should not necessarily be the first option when conflict occurs. My main counsel to the conflicted Christian sports person is to sincerely work through the principles outlined in the first four chapters of this treatise before summarily dismissing any involvement in sport. The conflict may just be used of God to bring about transformation within the Christian sports person as well as serving as the catalyst for the redemption of the situation in conflict through the Christian sports person.

To be more specific, there is a big difference in an athlete who walks away from a sport when instructed to inject steroids as opposed to simply refusing to partake in such illegal and immoral behavior. Often, rejection of particular actions within sport is the appropriate response, but the goal should be to remain within the sport for the purpose of fulfilling God's call and to bring *redemption* to the sports person and sporting culture. It must be realized, however, that decisions to not *accommodate* may lead to being suspended, fired, or released as a player or a coach, but being rejected is different from choosing *rejection.*

Thus, I believe the lessons of historical attempts at the faith–sport integration can be categorized into two expressions:

- Secular Expression
  - Sport no faith (Capitulation)
  - Sport over faith (Accommodation)
- Religious Expression
  - Faith no sport (Rejection)
  - Faith over sport (Redemption—of both the individual sports person and the sports world)

The significance of this is the theme of the next chapter—Christmanship—which proscribes how individual sports persons can remain in and redeem sport. More profoundly, it outlines how they can worship in and through their sporting endeavors.

CHAPTER 6

CHRISTMANSHIP— A CONTEMPORARY ETHIC OF COMPETITION

This chapter will feature the author's motif of Christmanship, which outlines a biblically based guideline for determining individual participation in, and specific actions within, sport and athletics.

I. THE DILEMMA

Countless athletes have articulated a common dilemma: They struggle with their sport becoming their "God." To participate in sport, especially at varsity, collegiate, and professional levels (see Chapter 1's discussion of the *Progressive Intensity Levels–PIL* of competition), one must expect rigorous training and time-consuming commitments. Often, the commitment to sport's demands collides with other priorities in life, such as family, school, and spiritual development. This demand of one's efforts tends to be all-consuming—an all-or-nothing, either/or dilemma. Either be totally driven by athletic training and its demands or be totally consumed with a pursuit of Christ. At least this is how it seems to many athletes caught in this dilemma. Here are just a few of the decisions all world-class athletes and most varsity athletes and coaches will navigate:

- Time—stewardship concerns about how many hours of my week should be consumed with training, conditioning, and preparation for sport
- Schedules—conflicts between sporting endeavors, church activities, and family commitments
- Relationships—conflicts between family, friends, and team commitments
- School—conflicts between sport participation and academics
- Vocation—is sport a valid career or should it be avocational?

The first five chapters have painstakingly answered the first part of this dilemma by showing competition and sports to be theologically sound and biblically defensible in a general, overarching sense. They also established theological support for the vast majority of specific sports and sporting activities. What is still lacking is a definitive set of standards and prescriptions for Christ-honoring competing for individual sports people. Such is the essence of this chapter. The real question now becomes: "Since competition in general and my sport in particular are theologically sound and biblically defensible, what can I do to ensure I can honor God in all of my efforts within my sport?" To go a step further, "Within my sport, what specific actions and activities are proscribed according to a biblical ethic?"

II. THE ANSWER: CHRISTMANSHIP—A CONTEMPORARY CHRISTIAN ETHIC OF SPORT

I have often been asked to speak on the topic of "Would Jesus Tackle Bret Favre?" (or whoever is the all-pro quarterback at the time). Although perhaps an intriguing and clever seminar title, at best, it runs the risk of trivializing significant issues, and at worst, it could well be blasphemous. Yet for most Christian athletes, it rings like a clarion bell to their heartfelt emotions. Those sincerely seeking to follow Christ and compete in the image of Christ earnestly desire to know if and how they can compete in such a way as to honor Christ and be good stewards of all Christ has blessed them with.

Most competitors are caught up in and believe in the "win at all cost" philosophy of sports. Yet, at some point during their career, whether it is an amateur or professional career, an athlete stops and reflects upon the meaning of sports and her involvement in them. This chapter attempts to aid athletes as they contemplate the issues of sports and their participation. In particular, it is to help athletes to understand what a Christian ethic of competition is. It will initially consider sportsmanship and gamesmanship and their functions. It will then compare those with the new Christian ethic of competition: "Christmanship." Specific actions and attitudes recommended and affirmed by the Scripture and embodying the Christmanship ethic will follow. My heartfelt desire and prayer is for readers to be set free from just striving for victory, and all would experience an "overwhelming victory" in Jesus Christ our Lord. My experience in athletics has spanned five decades and includes both recreational and varsity playing opportunities and as a coach at every level from the sandlot to the collegiate ranks. My theological resume consists of three postgraduate degrees in theology, including two doctorates. This combination finds real release in the ideas articulated in this work.

A. Sportsmanship, Gamesmanship, or Christmanship[1]

Chances are, if you are an athlete, you are wearing something with the name NIKE on it. The decade of the 1980s saw Nike skyrocket as a major

---

[1] Sometimes there is a reaction to the word *Christmanship* on the basis of the gender of the term not being applicable to female competitors. I am in full support of the spirit of this concern and am willing to change the terminology from *Christmanship* to *Christpersonship* (or whatever is deemed acceptable) as long as the words *Sportsmanship* and *Gamesmanship* are also changed and held to the same standard.

supplier of sporting goods in America. The company chose its name well because Nike is a Greek word that means "conqueror." This stems from the mythological daughter of Zeus, a Greek goddess named Nike. Nike was the goddess of victory and was prominently featured in statuary and artwork surrounding ancient Greek athletics, particularly at the site of the original Olympics.

Common sense tells us that wearing a pair of shoes advertised by some famous athlete will not enable us to perform like him; however, wearing quality shoes and uniforms does help to bolster confidence and athletic performance. Athletes the world over want to win and often deeply believe in the motto of the late Vince Lombardi, "Winning isn't everything, it is the only thing." Thus, with a name like *Nike,* athletes and others are choosing to associate with a sporting goods company whose name means victory. The problem is there are always more losers than winners, and even the best athletes fail—even those wearing Nikes. What began for most athletes as a joy ends up being the source of frustration and bitterness. Professional baseball players fail to reach base safely three-quarters of the time. Even those who are inducted into the Hall of Fame have failed 70 percent of the time!

Is it possible to actually enjoy sports and competition? Do athletics have any redeeming value? What is success in sport? Is there a value in sports? Is it possible to not only attain a victory but more importantly to experience "overwhelming victory"?

1. Sportsmanship   The word *ship* means to send, bear, or transport. When used in the English language as a suffix, it denotes a bearing of a condition, character, office, or skill. The word *man* is the generic word used to describe the human race. Therefore, *manship* has the connotation of humankind bearing upon itself certain conditions, characteristics, offices, or skills. When *sports* is added to *manship*, it becomes "Sportsmanship," which is the definitive word to describe the characteristic skills and ethics "sportsmen" should bear upon themselves as they compete.

Thus, the word *Sportsmanship* has evolved in its meaning to describe appropriate, ethical behavior by participants in sport. It outlines acceptable ethics and morals of sport that would include having fun, playing fair, utilizing skills and abilities, and being a good loser or a good winner. However, these ethics are determined by the popular opinion of a society that has no permanent mooring to derive its ethics from. Morality is different for each culture, country, and religion, and it changes according to popular opinion. Thus, the "Sportsmanship" ethic has no final authority. It fluctuates with places, times, players, and coaches. One thing is consistent and does not change: the desire to win. Thus, the final authority or ethic of sport is to win. Therefore, the ethic of sport is not determined by the philosophy of Sportsmanship but rather by the pragmatism of Gamesmanship.

2. Gamesmanship It is assumed that twentieth-century sports ethics are founded upon the concept of Sportsmanship. Yet, as one contemplates modern-day sports, it is imperative to explore more than the surface of the sports culture in order to not become enslaved to its value system. Sportsmanship is an admirable goal; however, it is often conceived of quite differently by different people and associations. Even if there is an agreed-upon consensus of definition for Sportsmanship, it is very seldom adhered to. The thought of embodying Sportsmanship is usually overruled by a desire to win. Sportsmanship is rarely rewarded.

When people accept at face value worldviews on winning, they then become enslaved to the ethic of "win at all costs," and Sportsmanship is quickly forgotten. Winning is exalted as the ultimate accomplishment. To subdue and conquer an opponent is the pinnacle of success and fulfillment of sport.

Conversely, a loser is worth nothing; she is totally useless, inept, and thus can be taunted and trampled by her opponent. These attitudes and actions are hardly congruent with the essence of Sportsmanship. A definition of words is important to understanding any further discussion of the ethics of competition.

Although Sportsmanship espouses such things as fairness and fun, only winners are rewarded. Out of "Sportsmanship" a new ethic has *devolved*: Gamesmanship. Gamesmanship maintains that the highest ethic of sport is to win. To have fun is no longer the foundation of competitive ethics as only winning matters.

Because Gamesmanship has replaced Sportsmanship as a basis for determining competitive ethics in sports, athletes have received mixed messages as to what their attitudes and actions should be. What they hear and see communicated is win, regardless of the cost or means. Playing fair and having their coaches and others in authority commend them is contradictory.

Athletes are told to have fun, be coachable, and to respect authority. Then, they observe their coaches, school administrators, and booster club members yelling obscenities at umpires, referees, and opposing teams. Their coach states "all that matters is to give your best effort," yet the coach plays only the best athletes on the team. Kids receive the verbal communication to have fun, but what they observe is adults concerned only about winning.

Athletes are also confused about what is really fair. Coaches accuse one another of cheating and yet many times they also cheat. All of these coaches believe their actions are justifiable because they do not consider what they do to be cheating. They believe they are only "bending a rule" to benefit their own players or program. In essence they also base their morality on humanistic pragmatism. They do whatever it takes to win. They communicate by their actions that winning is much more important than any standard of morality. These coaches state they are concerned about their players, but in reality it is obvious their real priority is to win.

One of the saddest accounts of what the pressure to win does to a man is found in the autobiography of coach Tates Locke. Locke was the head basketball coach at four major universities. He began to cheat in earnest after losing time and again to other universities that had, in his opinion, won because they had cheated. In his book *Caught in the Net,* he relates his experience while coaching at Clemson University:

> At Clemson I lost touch with my values. Stuff was just laying [*sic*] there. Money came easy and so did the women. There were alumni wives who were quite open about their personal need for affection. I had never been a part of anything like this before. After I married Nancy and all through my years at West Point and Miami, I wouldn't even consider looking at another woman. It was the way I was brought up. But, my values changed almost overnight at Clemson. The pressures from losing in my first two or three years made me an easy target, I guess. I was drinking too much Scotch, popping too many pills. Life was moving too fast for this small town guy to handle. My values slipped and slipped and slipped and the people who got hurt were my family. We had some family problems . . . but those problems could be attributed to

basketball, not booze, pills and women. I was married to my job . . . Everybody says there is God, your family and your job. I loved my job first . . . If I can offer one bit of advice to a young coach today . . . it is that the individual must be willing to accept the unwritten code which already exists . . . Just go out and get the job done. If it is recruiting, then go out and recruit. Play the game by the same rules of the street. It is like in sales or anything else; somewhere down the line you are going to have to give out green stamps. You are going to have to cheat somewhere down the line but do it and don't talk about it. Take it from someone who cheated and got caught.[2]

By his own admission, Tates Locke relates he lost his moral basis for life, but this is not the saddest part of his story. It is not that his family suffered or his mental or physical health failed—all as direct results of his conscious decisions to cheat and turn his back on what he knew to be right. What is even more repulsive and odious is that even after he had been caught, fired, ridiculed, and it cost everyone involved great agony, he still does not admit that cheating, lying, and breaking the rules are wrong.

This is the epitome of "gamesmanship." Many coaches and athletes believe it is acceptable to lose not only your soul but also your marriage, health, and integrity to simply win a few more games. This belief system based upon humanistic relativism is not a new one, as demonstrated by the following quote:

The emphasis upon winning and the absence of a body of established amateur traditions permitted large outlays of money for football, the open recruitment of player talent, fierce training schedules, and clear cases of premeditated brutality. The eligibility problem, professionalism, deaths and serious injuries from football, and a lack of gentlemanly behavior, and the issue of whether to make football even more financially rewarding and respectable all contributed to a virtual state of

---

[2] Tates Locke and Bob Ibach, *Caught in the Net* (West Point, NY: Leisure Press, 1982), pp. 139, 172, 174.

anarchy among the nation's colleges. Consequently football became the subject of a vigorous nationwide debate which [*sic*] eventually involved college presidents, faculties, the press, and even the president of the United States . . . The spirit of American youth, as of the American man, is to "get there" by fair means or foul, and the lack of moral scruple which [*sic*] pervades the struggles of the business world meets with temptations equally irresistible in the miniature contest of the football field.[3]

This quote is not taken from the 2010 *New York Times* or *Chicago Tribune*. It was written in 1890, yes, 1890! So no, the problem is not a new one. The pressures to win at all cost have been negatively affecting those involved with athletics for years. These problems occur because of the aforementioned fluctuation of morals and values, which have their root in the current and popular philosophy of humanistic relativism. The major tenant of relativism is there is no ultimate or final authority, and therefore, everything is relative. Thus, people are set free to establish their own morality and do whatever they wish. They decide for themselves what is moral and right. How this affects sports and athletes is easily observed.

Because only winners are rewarded, athletes believe it is all right to cheat if cheating helps attain a win. All the great-sounding platitudes are forgotten. All that is important is to be victorious. However, the result of these actions based upon relativism is chaos. Teams, leagues, and institutions able to exert the necessary influence of power, money, prestige, and favors will increase their chances of winning and not be penalized for cheating even when caught. Those that cannot or will not cheat, or exert unprincipled influences, will compete at a great disadvantage. No longer will the best athlete or team always win. Rather, the athlete or team with the lowest set of morals will most often win.

Tragically, as a result of this cheating, the very essence of competition itself is then compromised and all victories are then hollow shells,

---

[3] Benjamin G. Rader, *American Sports* (Englewood Cliffs, NJ: Prentice Hall, 1983), pp. 134, 135.

lacking any real meaning or accomplishment. The competitors who chose to cheat to win, in the end, only cheat themselves because their victory is hollow and meaningless.

What began innocently enough as a code of ethics to rule unscrupulous competition among athletes has degenerated to a cesspool of immorality. Sportsmanship always descends to Gamesmanship.

For Christian athletes desiring to compete with the proper code of ethics, neither Sportsmanship nor Gamesmanship is totally satisfying. For these athletes, total fulfillment and satisfaction will only come by adhering to the concept of Christmanship. Christmanship for Christian athletes means these athletes are to bear upon themselves the characteristics and skill that would emulate Christ and be conformed to His image in the arena or competition.

3. Christmanship Christmanship embodies the best of Sportsmanship (fun, fairness, and being a good loser/winner, etc.) and the best of Gamesmanship (giving one's best effort to compete well and attempt to win) but it transcends and surpasses them both. It establishes and holds high the challenge for Christian athletes to compete as Christ would compete. For most athletes, however, this concept of Christmanship is probably nothing more than a nebulous idea. The concept must be further defined, explained, and outlined, and its practical aspects discussed, understood, and lived out.

None of the Ten Commandments are specific to sport. The Sermon on the Mount is decisively free of any mandates concerning sporting competition. There are no known accounts of Christ having competed in the leagues or competitions of his day, and thus, we must look at different Scriptures that reveal to us principles, foundations, and parameters from which the Christmanship ethic must be constructed. Such an ethic will provide for all involved in athletics the following specific actions and attitudes concerning competition. This will in turn give athletes a total fulfillment and satisfaction in their athletic endeavors. Their actions will not be based upon relativistic morals that change with the winds, nor will they find their root in the quagmire of pragmatism, but rather will be rooted in the authority of "God's will" as revealed through His Scriptures. It is through these concepts and principles found in Scripture that athletes will experience "overwhelming victory."

a. Remolding Our Minds   Before exploring the specific actions and attitudes required in a Christian ethic of competition, one must pause to give Jesus Christ a chance to remold our minds. The Apostle Paul mandates in Romans 12:2 to "let God remold our minds." This is never truer than in the realm of competition. Athletes must put aside all previously held beliefs concerning sports and allow God to begin afresh with one's mind. Most athletes have been coached and have competed in the ethics prevalent in our society and world. Those ethics are based upon the pragmatism of winning at all cost. Thus, to truly "let God remold our minds" a thoughtful and prayerful consideration is necessary concerning the following six areas. At first glance these specific actions and attitudes may not fit into previously held beliefs. But, upon further contemplation even the most fiercely competitive of all athletes will begin to understand true fulfillment will only come when Jesus Christ is allowed to come and shape one's very thinking. The six areas that need to be thought through again have to do with coaches, teammates, officials, opponents, competition itself, and success.

i. Teammates   At first thought, athletes might not think they have a problem with their own teammates. Athletes, it is assumed, are totally committed to their team. However, when athletes take a closer look at their motivation for competing, they may, in fact, find there are several motives for competing that have nothing to do with having a concern for the team one plays for.

Athletes rarely admit they compete not for the team's glory but for their own glory and for their own personal gratification. Athletes do not play for a team, school, or club solely for the benefit of that group. They play for their own glory and for their own particular satisfaction, fulfillment, thrill, and excitement. This is a subtle yet profound difference. If an individual is participating for his or her own gratification and is unwilling to submit to the team's needs, problems arise. Athletes must clarify their own motivations for competing by asking themselves the following questions:

- Why do I feel bad when I make a mistake? Is it because it reflects poorly on me (embarrassment) or because it hurts the team?
- When I make an out in baseball or miss a shot in basketball or football (soccer), is my first thought of how I hurt the team's

chances to win or about my own batting average or shooting percentage?

- Do I willingly sacrifice personal gain to enhance the team's chance to succeed?

- When I don't play to my fullest potential (don't run out a pop fly or other easy out in baseball or don't come to a game properly rested and prepared, etc.), do I consider I have let my teammates down?

- Why do I feel excited and good after playing a great game and yet the team lost?

Athletes would do well to understand the relevance of Philippians 2:2–4: "*Never act from motives of rivalry or personal vanity, but (in humility) think more of each other than you do of yourselves. None of you should think only of his own affairs, but should learn to see things from other people's point of view.*" This unselfish attitude should be applied to a team situation. The apostle Paul indicates that we must "*live together in harmony, live together in love.*"

As important as this biblical principle is, it must be balanced by another concept as described in the Gospel of John. Although it is true that athletes should be concerned about their teammates and the team's best interest, they should never feel guilty about their own enjoyment and enthusiasm of competing. In John 10:10 the apostle shares with us Christ came that we might have a fulfilled life. Therefore, we can be assured God rejoices when we compete to our fullest ability and thoroughly enjoy our participation in sports. After all, Christ is the one who created us and, therefore, knows us in the most intimate sense possible, and God as a loving father is quite happy when we experience exhilaration while competing.

The early Greek athletes probably understood this concept better than do our present-day competitors. They believed the "gods" had created them with certain abilities and gave them opportunities to utilize their gifts. Thus, those athletes viewed their competition as an act of worship. Eric Liddell's quote in the movie *Chariots of Fire* expressed this well. "I believe God made me for a purpose, for China, but He also made me fast, and when I run I feel His pleasure and to give it up would be to hold Him in contempt. To win is to honor Him."[4]

Therefore, Christian athletes should enjoy competing and know their competition pleases Christ, but they must always keep their personal gains, goals, and personal preferences in balance with the goals and needs of their team and teammates.

ii. Coaches   It's rare for players to express neutral opinions when it comes to their coach. Typically, players either love or resent their coach. Those that do resent their coaches do so even for things their coaches demand that are for the benefit of the athlete such as hustle, conditioning, and discipline. Most athletes do not understand what discipline really is. They believe discipline is punishment. However, discipline is not necessarily what athletes deserve when they do something wrong.

A common definition of discipline would be something like "training to act in accordance with rules or actions." Discipline connotes much more the idea of training than it does of punishment. It refers to the constraints it takes to train athletes in appropriate ways of conducting themselves. Wise athletes will submit themselves fully to knowledgeable coaches who care enough about their athletes to push them to excellence. Athletes should never resent rigorous training and discipline designed to empower them to excel. Rather, athletes should resent the coach who never pushes them to excel. Discipline coming from a caring, educated, and wise coach will be a positive force and will propel athletes to attain their greatest potential. This potential will only be reached, however, if the athletes willingly submit and fully apply themselves to it.

---

[4] The movie has Liddell making these statements to his sister, who in the movie was portrayed as desiring for Eric to stop his running and join her on the mission field. In reality, Jenny was Eric's biggest fan and fully supported his running. The plot of the movie used Jenny as a composite figure who represented the multitudes of people who condemned Liddell's running. It is doubtful Liddell ever uttered just these words in just this way or sequence. But after many hours of research including interviews with Lidell's family, friends and those who were with Liddell in the Japanese prisoner of war camp, I believe the *Chariots of Fire* quote accurately summarized his theology.

It is appropriate for athletes to desire the best possible coaching available. Athletes and their parents should shop around for the best possible youth league, high school, and collegiate coaches and programs. Rather than blindly enrolling in the local league and/or school, athletes should shop around and research the satisfaction levels and successes of the teams and leagues they are considering joining. Particular questions to be asked of a league, school, and coach are:

- What is the statement of purpose for your league, school, and/or coach?
- What is your philosophy/theology of competition and coaching?
- What policies do you have about team membership and/or cutting of players?
- What added expenses and/or fees are there to participate in sports?

Questions to Ask with Regard to Youth Leagues:

- Are the coaches in the leagues trained in the psychological, emotional, physiological, and theological aspects of coaching?
- What is the philosophy of playing time?
- What is the methodology of teaching styles?

Questions to Ask with Regard to Middle and High School Varsity Sports:

- What training and/or certifications are required of the coaching staff of the school with regard to the psychological, emotional, and physiological development of their athletes?
- What role does sport play in the overall educational process of the school?
- How many years is the current coach under contract for and does the school board intend to honor that contract?
- Does the coach plan on honoring his/her contract?

Questions to Ask with Regard to Collegiate Varsity Sports:

- What is the coach's philosophy and preferences or style of play?
- What are the financial considerations of attending the school?
- How long is the coach under contract, and does he/she plan to honor his/her commitment to that contact?
- What role does the coach intend for the athlete in his/her program (in what position, how many minutes or innings per game will the athlete play, etc.)?

There are times when athletes have no choice in who their coach is and will have to play for a coach who is intolerable for one reason or another. It is at this point Christian athletes have a unique opportunity to give evidence of their faith. Of course, Christian players should never obey a coach's demands to cheat or purposely injure an opposing player, but for the most part they should go beyond what their coach requires in terms of conscientious training and effort. Regardless of how a coach treats players, those players must always demonstrate respect for their coach. Moreover, in relating to a coach, Christian players must keep the goal of emulating Christ as their top priority. Christ will be glorified if athletes keep their priorities straight and seek Christmanship as opposed to personal gain.

There may come a time when a relationship between a coach and players deteriorates to a point of endangering the psychological, emotional or physical well-being of the athletes involved. At this juncture, athletes should determine a course of action only after much prayer and discussion with parents and other appropriate adults. Christian athletes should never take it upon themselves to challenge a coach's authority. Once again, Christmanship is the goal; the Christian athlete's course of action will be to glorify and emulate Christ. There may well come a time when a player must leave a team, but this should be done only after the player has made every effort possible to be reconciled with the coach. Except in extreme situations it should always be done at a natural termination point such as at the end of a season or semester. It must be done as amicably as possible as would reflect the athlete's faith in Christ.

The reasoning behind leaving amicably and at all times attempting to emulate Jesus Christ is to glorify Christ in all that one does. It is important for Christian athletes to be seen as having distinctively different values, attitudes, and lifestyles, not for their own glory but for the glory of Christ. Athletes never know when they may be able to lead other athletes on the team into a personal relationship with Christ or even lead their own coach into a relationship with Christ. These times often come through hard struggles between players and coaches. It is the athlete's responsibility to be faithful in the little things and know that God is about the business of making good things come out of bad situations. In the end following God's principles will be in your best interest.

iii. Officials   The third area in which athletes must "remold their minds" is how to appropriately view and interact with the officials who are involved in sport. Nowhere in athletics is there more verbal abuse or more frustrations vented than from athletes and coaches toward referees and umpires. Unfortunately, these groups of people hardly ever get along and only rarely do they work together as partners in working toward making sport a positive experience for all involved.

In order for there to be a positive experience, athletes and coaches must understand officials are not enemies but rather are facilitators of competitions.[5] An official's role is to facilitate leagues, games, competitions, and tournaments. In fact, one of the main reasons officials are needed is because athletes and coaches would cheat those they compete against! Officials include league directors and commissioners, referees, umpires, score keepers, tournament directors, and others. These people are needed to ensure competitions proceed in the fairest and safest way possible. Athletes must understand there would be no games, there would be no competitions, without officials.

Not only are officials to be regarded as facilitators of athletic competitions, but even more importantly, Christian competitors are to view officials as ***people***, people who are created in the image of God. Because Christ created these people and, furthermore, because Christ died for

---

[5] Of course, the reverse is also true. Officials must not view athletes and coaches as enemies either. Officials have just as much responsibility for creating a positive environment for enjoyable athletic experiences.

them, it is imperative for Christian athletes go out of their way to love them. Moreover, Christian athletes must explore how they can enhance officials' ability to better do their job.

This attitude is diametrically opposed to the most common ethic of most people who are involved in athletics today. Most competitors operate under the "win at all cost" concept concerning officials. They believe they are entitled to "work officials" so they may gain an advantage over an opponent. Most athletes in this day and age have been trained in how to "work an official." Coaches and trainers have taught their athletes how to gain an unfair advantage by using what they consider "techniques" to get an official to call things their way. Because of this, coaches often believe they have the right to yell, scream, threaten, intimidate, or even physically abuse an official in order to get a call changed or an event run to one's benefit. Christian athletes who operate under the Christmanship concept need to relate the command of Romans with regard to their interactions with officials. Rather than "work" an official, Christians must "seek to live at peace with all men" (Romans 12:9–12). Therefore, this passage in Romans mandates that a competitor's response to officials is to bless them, even if a player or coach feels an official is "persecuting" them. Again, their response must be to bless officials and to strive to live at peace with them.

The Apostle Paul did not recommend competitors to get along with others as long as the other person was willing. Rather, he said we are to live at peace with them "as much as it depends upon us." Christian athletes cannot assume responsibility for an official's actions toward them. They can only be responsible for their own actions toward the official. There is a key principle for confronting officials.

Key Principle—Confrontation Is to Be Based on Love

Living at peace with officials does not mean there are never to be any confrontations. Coaches may very well need to appropriately confront an official for reasons beyond attempting to gain an unfair advantage. There are occasions when it becomes necessary to motivate officials. Just as an athlete needs to be motivated by a well-meaning coach, there are times in which an athlete and/or coach may need to lovingly motivate an official to do a better job. Once again the model for the believer in Christ comes from the Scriptures. Christ always kept a person's integrity intact.

He demonstrated how confrontations can motivate those who were confronted to proper action or belief. A major key is the basis on which the confrontation stems. The Christian athlete's motivation needs to be based upon love for the official.

However, Christian competitors will often be accused of "working an official" by another means. Some may accuse a Christian athlete of using loving tactics to get along better with officials to gain an advantage. However, let there be no doubt that the motivation for loving an official is not to get preferential treatment, but rather to set an official free to get the play called correctly. No true competitor wants preferential treatment. A true athlete simply wants an equal opportunity to win the competition fairly. Do not be confused. Loving an official is not to be done to gain an unfair advantage but rather is to be done because officials are people who are created in the image of our Lord and Savior Jesus Christ, and they deserve our best efforts on their behalf. The goal is to love the official, love the opponent, and get a fairly officiated contest.

Keep in mind there were times in which Christ chose to remain silent when he was unjustly condemned. This indicates there are times to confront and there are times not to confront. The Scripture admonishes us "to be angry but sin not." If athletes cannot confront without sinning, then they must not confront at all. It is entirely appropriate to lovingly confront officials, leagues, associations, and institutions about injustices and unfair practices. In fact, it is not only consistent with the ethic of "Christmanship," but it is also mandatory! Still, one must confront in love and with living in peace in mind. These two principles then lead the Christian athlete to understand that the following actions are the way to confront these injustices.

Players in youth leagues, junior and senior high school, college, and even pros must realize they should rarely, if ever, have any confrontations with game officials. This is not their job or role. Those confrontations must be left up to coaches and athletic directors. Most coaches and athletic directors have avenues available to them through which they can explain their grievances. It is imperative they go through their given systems to address unfair practices. Except in extreme situations, athletes should remain silent in their interactions with officials other than complimenting and encouraging them.

It is interesting to note, when thinking about interacting with officials, what typically occurs in the world of competition. Many coaches and players start off a protest with a rather low-key approach. When they perceive the official is not hearing them, they increase the intensity, volume, and/or profaneness of their attempts to be heard. If their verbal attacks are regular and consistent, they are most often tuned out by the official or, even worse, the official is distracted from calling a fair game. Thus, once again, the coach must become even more demonstrative. They may even intimidate and physically assault an official. Sometimes these actions get immediate results. However, the results are always short-term gains. The long-term result is a lost relationship and most likely an official who may spite a coach or athlete who has previously intimidated them. Then, the cycle begins again. To experience overwhelming victory, athletes must love the officials and encourage them to get the call right.

There is one particular experience that demands coaches to lovingly confront officials: when players of either team are in danger of injury because officials are not protecting the competing players. If ever officials shirk their responsibility by not calling fouls or issuing red cards, then coaches must quickly (but still lovingly) confront the officials and demand they execute one of their primary roles: protect players.

iv. Opponents   Most amateur athletes have known the frustration of rushing out of work, jumping into their trusty automobile, and while speeding down the highway attempt to both put on their uniform and also eat a fast-food burger and fries. You can imagine their frustration upon arriving at a dusty softball field or a sweat-filled gymnasium only to find their opponent did not show up. What was an excited anticipation of a game now is nothing more than a frustration because he has no one to play. This illustration points out opponents are important, and athletes need to reconsider how they view these opponents.

Actually the word *opponent* is an inappropriate term to describe the players on the other team. Opponent conveys the idea competitors have enemies. There are no enemies when it comes to sports, only other competitors. Athletes must realize the people with whom they compete must be seen as "co-competitors." Without them, there would be no game or competition. These co-competitors must also be viewed as people created by God and for whom Christ came and died. Thus, they must be treated with utmost dignity and respect. They must never be cheated, purposely injured, intimidated, discouraged, or forced to compete in a manner that is damaging to them. Winning by anything other than one's own ability is not fulfilling. If athletes must cheat or harm their co-competitors to win, the win is not due to being a superior athlete or team. Rather, it is due to that athlete's having lower morals.

Co-competitors must also be encouraged to excel. Not only are they to be treated fairly and given an equal opportunity to win a contest, but they also must be encouraged to compete to their fullest. A scene in the movie *Chariots of Fire,* although fictional, exemplifies this concept very well. The sprinter known as the "Flying Scot"—Eric Liddell—was just about to compete in the 400 meter race in the Olympics when he was given a note by Jackson Schultz, an opponent from the American team. It read: "It says in the old book, 'He that honors me I will honor.'" Encouraging one's opponent sounds ludicrous until athletes examine their premise for competing.

If winning is the only goal then, of course, athletes can do anything to win, including cheating, injuring, intimidating, and discouraging their "opponent." However, if the goal is to compete against the best there is and to measure oneself against such competition, as well as to win, then true competitors wish for their co-competitors to push them to their full potential. Furthermore, for believers in Christ, the goal is to conform to the image of Christ ("Christmanship"). In the ethic of Christmanship, cheating, maiming, intimidating, and even discouraging is not appropriate, and winning is only important when it is the measuring device used by both competitors.

Beyond the attempts to encourage co-competitors, athletes must also strive to compete at their fullest potential, regardless of the score. If athletes do not compete to their fullest potential, they are making a statement their co-competitors are not worthy of their best effort. Furthermore, it does not challenge the co-competitor to improve. A true competitor will never insult a co-competitor by not giving his or her best effort.

However, there is a difference between competing with full intensity and humiliating an opponent. Ideally once athletes have an understanding of the full implication of competing in the image of Christ, they will place less emphasis on the score and outcome and will place more emphasis upon their own efforts. However, there are still some times when the score differential is so huge an opponent feels humiliated. It is at this time Christian athletes have to come to grips with what Christ would do. I believe two personal experiences can best help set our parameters for this discussion.

The first example comes from a time in which I was coaching basketball at the collegiate level. We were getting ready to play a Division II college, which had just finished playing a Division I college a few days earlier. The Division I college had annihilated the Division II college by 40 or more points. Not only did they win by such a huge margin, but the style in which they won had also infuriated the Division II coach. The Division I team applied full-court defensive pressure the entire game and never once let up on their intensity. This Division II coach asked my opinion, and I responded by saying I believed the coach of the Division I school did what was best for his own kids and his program. I said I believed at the level they compete in, they can never have a letdown. It was the following March when that same Division I squad was awarded a spot in the final 64-team tournament and won a number of ball games. They even beat a few of the upper-seeded teams. I suggested to the Division II coach a humiliating loss should have motivated his athletes to improve. After they improve, they should then decide whether or not to compete with Division I teams. They should choose their level and then work to be successful at that level.

Another experience came while coaching a junior high team. We had a 30-point lead at half-time and ended up winning by more than 50 points. At the end of the game I was confronted by a very humiliated and angry coach from the other team. Not only did he question my coaching tactics, but he also doubted my faith. As we began to discuss the elements of the game, I pointed out to him there was never a time during the game that I had my best five players on the floor at the same time. I also indicated to him that we did not full-court press, and in fact, we changed many of our defensive concepts once the score became lopsided. I explained to him we did not do all the things we normally did to win ball games. I did insist my athletes play hard and with full intensity, however.

It was because I was coaching at a Christian school that he believed my team should have shown mercy upon his team. I responded that I believed we were only required to do what would exemplify the image of Christ by the way we competed, which included competing defensively. I further communicated to him that I believed Christ is a God of compassion but not for only one team. I, as a coach, must have compassion for my own team as well as for a humiliated opponent. Thus, I must weigh in the balance the best interest of both teams. Sometimes this will result in large differentials in scores, but it should never give license to willingly humiliate an opponent. The best solution to this problem is to schedule teams of similar abilities.

Although some of the issues surrounding one's co-competitor are rather complex, I believe they can best be dealt with in the context of asking the question, "What would Christ do in this situation and how would He compete?" The issues become clearer when athletes contemplate the meaning of competition itself. Competition is a measuring stick. Just as I want my car's oil to be measured by an accurate stick, I, as a competitor, want to measure myself against proper and accurate competition.

v. Competition   There are people who wish to dispose of all competition. They believe competition is harmful, wrong, and even repugnant to God! They also believe competition is innately evil, but is it? Can competition be acceptable within a Christian ethic? The answer is unequivocal. Not only is competition compatible with the Christian ethic, but it is also part of God's design for the world. Competition is part and parcel of the universe that God created.

In God's natural revelation to us, we see that nature is full of competition. Trees stretch to the sky, competing for sunlight; their roots extend deep into the ground, competing for the moisture and nutrients needed to survive. We also observe in God's special revelation that, through his written Word, He and satan are in competition. Athletes need to understand competition is an amoral force. In and of itself it is neither good nor bad. Competition may bring out either the best or the worst in all who compete. However, we cannot blame competition if athletes fail morally, emotionally, or psychologically. It is how athletes choose to react to competition that will determine whether competition is positive or negative.

God's design for competition is to help mold athletes into the men and women He desires them to be. Any attempt to remove competition from our lives will only hamper our spiritual development, not enhance it.

Therefore, competition needs to be redefined. The word *competition* comes from the Latin verb meaning "to seek together." Rainier Martens, in his book *Joy and Sadness in Children's Sport,* has described competition as "activities directed toward attaining a standard or goal in which a person's or group's performance is evaluated relative to select other individuals or groups."[6] Competition assumes cooperation. It demands that "co-competitors" challenge each other to excel. This challenging one another to excel completes the concept of competing "against" someone. When competitors view competition in its proper sense, they will be able to minimize the negatives associated with it and enhance the possibilities of competition being truly a cooperative effort to help develop them into the people they need to become. Therefore, competitors do not compete "against" one another in the classic sense of that word. To help understand this, a closer look at the word *against* is necessary. The word *against* has as its root word *again,* which means "once more," "additionally," or "furthermore." It is from this connotation the following definitions of the word *against* are derived. These definitions are "close beside or in front of," "in anticipation of," or "as contrasted with." Therefore, playing against someone in this sense assumes something is done once more—or again—and in contrast. Competitors contrast their skills "against" other competitors. Thus, competition becomes a gauge or a measuring stick by which competitors judge themselves. One does not compete "against" an enemy, but rather competes "against" a standard that may sometimes be embodied in another individual or team, but may also be embodied by themselves, a clock, or a challenge.

Steroids and Other Performance-Enhancing Procedures

Using this concept of "against" as a foundation, Christian athletes must evaluate their usage of steroids and other performance-enhancing drugs and medical procedures. The sports world is embroiled in a

---

[6]Rainer Martens, *Joy and Sadness in Children's Sports* (Champaign, IL: Human Kinetics Press, 1978).

dilemma caused by athletes who have gone beyond the normal measures of training in their desire to win. Steroid use and blood-doping techniques are being used to increase athletic prowess. These athletes assume their own talents and efforts are not good enough to compete with. They refuse to use only their finely tuned, trained, natural abilities. They fail to understand that by competing with unnatural aids, it is no longer they who compete but rather some human and chemical mutation that competes. In essence, they have changed the whole basis upon which competition is based. No longer do athletes who have been chemically, surgically, or medically altered compete with their own bodies, but they compete as something less than normal. They can no longer evaluate themselves as natural athletes but, rather, they can only evaluate how good a doctor, pharmacist, or surgeon they employ.

Athletes who use performance-enhancing drugs or other medical procedures to give themselves an advantage in their competition have caused sports to be competed at a superhuman level. This is unethical because it forces athletes to use these same superhuman means if they wish to be able to compete at the same level. Any effort to enhance one's performance through illegal or injurious means or to deny legal aids to all participants is unethical. Steroids or other performance-enhancing drugs are not compatible with the ethic based on Christmanship, nor should they be accepted by any understanding of the ethic of Sportsmanship. Only the ethic of Gamesmanship would allow these measures. Even if a few athletes would willingly run the risk of damaging their bodies, while being part of an illegal experience, they must not be allowed to force other competitors to do so also.

Thus, it is imperative for players to always compete at their fullest potential without any artificial aids. Athletes must understand competition is more important than winning and losing. It is a measuring device to gauge one's abilities and progress, and the unnatural enhancement of one's performance is not a true gauge of ability. When athletes use performance-enhancing means that are injurious or illegal, they no longer compete in a cooperative fashion. They have lost the true sense of sport and must be eradicated from any competition so competition may in fact be a true comparison of abilities.

vi. Winning and Losing   Athletes desiring to gain a proper perspective concerning winning, losing, and competition will be aided by answering the following questions:

- Is it fulfilling to win by forfeit?
- Is it fulfilling to win every competition by large margins?
- Is it fulfilling to win a game only by cheating, taking performance-enhancing drugs, or by any other unfair action?
- Is it fulfilling to have my team win a game without my participating?

As evidenced by the answers to these questions, athletes should recognize that winning by forfeit or by having far superior talent is unfulfilling. It is also unfulfilling to achieve victory by cheating, for cheating does not accurately gauge an athlete's abilities, only their morals. Moreover, athletes are rarely totally satisfied if they do not play in a game, even if their team wins. Furthermore, whenever players become so wrapped up in winning and losing, they never truly enjoy the ecstasy and thrill of simply competing. They never find fulfillment in attempting to meet the challenge of competing against a standard. It is sad that so many competitors never experience true exhilaration and excitement in their competition because they are so concerned with winning or worse, their winning was a result of them cheating, not being a superior competitor.

Crowds do not cheer for a forfeit. Adrenaline does not flow in games in which athletes totally outperform and dominate their co-competitors. Records are rarely broken by one team or individual at a time. More often they are exceeded by two or more competitors simultaneously. Winning is important, but only when it is a result of one's dedicated and determined effort. Winning is never as important as competing. Trophies pale beside the memory of the game in which the trophy was won. Only when competitors "remold their minds" can they experience the fulfillment; mere talent is unfulfilling. It is also of simply competing, of simply playing. This understanding of competition then provides the foundation from which to talk about what success is.

vii. Success   Success is not the gift, but rather what a person does with their gift (Matthew 25:14–30). All gifts are of equal value but all uses are not. The gift of music is no more important than the gift of parenting. The gift of drama is no more important than the gift of athletic prowess. All gifts are necessary to human life. All gifts are important. The question becomes "How do athletes utilize their gifts?" Success then becomes not what gift a person has, but rather, what each person does with the gift they are given.

Success is not only being "number one" or being a consistent winner but also includes successfully competing in Christ-like ways and to one's fullest potential—regardless of the score. The professional basketball team the Los Angeles Clippers finished its 1987 season with a record of 12 and 70. Does this losing record make them unsuccessful? The team consisted of a dozen or so of the top 250 basketball players in the world. They were highly successful athletes. Their team may not have been successful as a unit; however, this does not mean they as individuals were not successful. They were not "number one," but they could still be considered successful if they adhered to the true spirit of the word *competition* and thus cooperatively pushed the teams they played to greater heights. One must be careful in establishing criteria for success. Christmanship rejoices with the team or individual that finishes "number one" but never maintains athletes can only be successful by being "number one."

True success is not measured by money, prestige, trophies, or any other earthly treasure. For the Christian success is one thing only: competing in such a way as to maximize one's gifts to the fullest and always competing in the image of Jesus Christ. What makes this so significant is this concept of success actually gives athletics and recreation validity and worth. Christian athletes will feel free to compete only when they understand they can worship Christ in and through their competition, and competition is a force to mold them more into the image of Christ. Competition has worth when athletes seek to worship God through sport. and they conform themselves to Christ while competing. If athletes can be judged by God as being successful by simply using the gifts given to them by God, sport must not be condemned as being of less importance than any other endeavor.

Some may argue sports in and of themselves have no redemptive value, but by using that criteria, what does? The world of finance? Teaching? Medicine? The only endeavor that could possibly claim for itself any eternal significance would be some sort of religious activity. The logical conclusion, therefore, would be for everyone to become full-time religious workers, and that in itself is totally illogical, because the world could not survive without doctors, farmers, teachers, etc. Athletes must realize their efforts are meaningful. They must be set free to utilize their athletic gifts fully and alongside every other gift given. Success is conforming to the image of Christ and worshipping Christ in whatever vocation and avocation He gives a person the ability to do (Philippians 3:7–14).

This view of success will not be easy to accept by a mind-set that believes "winning is everything." Neither should this view of sporting success be used as an excuse for losing consistently. However, for the Christian competitor it will bring fulfillment like nothing else can.

In order for athletes to have their minds remolded, one essential question must be answered. Have you said "yes" to Jesus Christ or asked another way: Do you have a personal relationship with Him? He cannot remold your mind unless you give it to Him. You will not experience an *"overwhelming victory"* unless you decide to compete Christ's way. Are you frustrated by athletic experiences? Has the fun disappeared? Is your life lacking peace and fulfillment? Please consider giving your life—including your sporting life—to Christ. It is as simple as praying: "Dear Jesus, please forgive me for trying to live my life on my own. I want You to come into my life. I want a personal relationship with You. Please give me Your guidance. Amen." That's all there is to it.

If you prayed that prayer, you now have a new "coach." His name is Jesus, and He is overjoyed to be in right relationship to you. Of course your journey toward successful competing isn't over. You'll want to go back over what you've read so far and continue reading on through the specific prescriptions for competing in the Christmanship ethic.

viii. Summary of Christmanship   Christian athletes must emulate Jesus Christ in everything they do, including how they compete. They must step out of the humanistic-based ethic of Sportsmanship and the pragmatic-based ethic of Gamesmanship to follow the principles of Christmanship. The practical aspects of Christmanship are attained by competing in the image of Jesus Christ. These precepts include interacting with teammates, coaches, co-competitors, and officials as Christ would interact. These precepts also demand players not miss the exhilaration of competing by being so caught up in the winning and losing of a game. Athletes must compete with a zeal that is infectious. They must also have a proper view of success and seek to give their ultimate effort utilizing and maximizing their gifts. Christian athletes must compete in the image of Christ and allow their experiences in competition to further mold them into the image of Christ. More specifics will follow in the next chapter.

CHAPTER 7

SPORTS AND LORD'S DAY ISSUES

This chapter provides a thorough investigation of the biblical texts and theological mandates concerning Sabbath and Lord's Day issues as they relate to competition and sport. It establishes general biblical rules and principles and applies them to the realm of sport and athletics. It prescribes specific attitudes, motives, and actions. It is deserving of a separate chapter because it is such a critical component of an overall theology of competition, and yet it is hardly ever considered by any serious Christian athlete or coach.

INTRODUCTION

The 1981 Academy Award for best picture of the year was *Chariots of Fire.* This film depicted the lives of the finest British and American Olympic runners in and around 1924, but its portrayal of Eric Liddell, the Scottish sprinter who later became a missionary to mainland China, is the most deeply moving and unforgettable vignette. The movie depicts each of the athletes' personal struggles, but the most riveting of all is Liddell's dilemma of integrating his faith with his competing. His conviction of "honoring the Lord's Day" collided head-on with the dream of winning Olympic gold. His struggle of whether or not to run in Olympic races held on Sunday exemplifies many issues that should still concern Christian athletes of modern day.

The phrase "should still concern" is chosen because, for most twenty-first-century Christian athletes and coaches, competing on Sunday is no longer an issue. By and large, the Christian community has curiously removed the Sabbath from most discussions about the Ten Commandments, and thus, its relevance has been dismissed from the consciousness of those attempting to follow Christ. This chapter will provide a basis from which sports ministers, Christian athletes, coaches, and athletic directors can make decisions on how they, their athletic endeavors, and their sports programs are to honor the day.

I. INTRODUCTORY CLARIFICATIONS

The terms *Lord's Day* and *Sabbath Day* are often used interchangeably but not so here. For clarity, *Sabbath* will be used in references to the Old Testament, and *Lord's Day* will be used for New Testament and modern-day discussions. Other distinctives will be addressed when appropriate.

The change of the name (from Sabbath to Lord's Day) and the change of the day (from Saturday to Sunday) also need explanation and further clarity. There were three basic reasons why the change from Sabbath to Lord's Day occurred.

A. Theological

Sunday became known as the "Lord's Day" because the Resurrection of Jesus Christ had such a dramatic and significant impact on the early believers. In addition, within a matter of weeks of the Resurrection, a second major event, Pentecost, occurred on a Sunday. Common, everyday conversations describing the day these two events occurred included phrases like: "the day the Lord Jesus was resurrected" or "the day the Holy Spirit fell" and eventually were shortened to "the Lord's Day." The transition from Sabbath to Lord's Day transpired over a period of time but increasingly took on a sacred essence. For early followers of Jesus, Sunday was now a most important day and Lord's Day celebrations evolved, following in the tradition of how other Jewish holy days such as Passover and Hanukah came into existence. Historically a holy day was established to mark a significant occurrence of God's supernatural intervention into human affairs. This held true for the early church as it believed the Lord's Day was a New Testament fulfillment of the Old Testament covenant of Sabbath, much like (a) the Lord's Supper was the fulfillment of the Passover Seder meal and (b) Baptism, the rite symbolizing God's people entering into relationship with Him and His church, was the fulfillment of circumcision. What must not be lost in this discussion was how powerful and significant the Resurrection was and how much it was confirmed through the gift of the Holy Spirit at Pentecost. It was so significant and poignant that a new holy day was acknowledged and continually observed.

B. Pragmatic

Most early Christians still considered themselves Jews, and as Jews, they believed it necessary to partake in Jewish traditions and rituals. They wanted to retain their Jewish heritage and yet also considered themselves followers of the newly resurrected Messiah. This new-found faith inspired them to participate in newly emerging Christian activities celebrating the coming of the Christ, His crucifixion, and His Resurrection. The pragmatic problem this tension created was experienced in two ways:

1. Jewish Christians wanted to participate in both the traditional Jewish rituals and the emerging Christian expressions of faith.

2. Even if the emerging fellowship of Jewish Christians decided to only participate in Christian religious expressions, the buildings needed for such activities (either a home or a synagogue) were occupied on Saturday by Hebraic rituals and services.

Thus, a second day was needed so as to enable participation in the newly developing Christian activities regardless of the theological concerns.

C. Societal

As the new tripartite paradigm of Jews, Jewish Christians, and Gentile Christians evolved, more and more tensions developed between these faith communities. The new community of Christ followers found it necessary to distinguish themselves from the Pharisaical rituals of the Judaizers. The emerging Christ-centered society was a combination of both Jew and Gentile, and they sought new expressions and formats that were more relevant to Gentiles. Many Greeks and Romans, and even many secularized Hebrews, could not appreciate or relate to the Jewish way of worshiping or understanding God. This is all very similar to the reason churches in the late twentieth century began "contemporary worship services" and why Christian rituals changed again in the new millennium.[1] Healthy churches attempt to maintain a relevance to a continually changing society without changing the timeless Christ-centered message. The early church faced a very similar dilemma, and this hastened the move to the Lord's Day becoming the day of worship for the emerging church.

II. INTRODUCTORY ASSUMPTIONS

Though this particular discussion of Sabbath and Lord's Day concepts should be of relevance to any follower of Christ, it is specifically directed to the following groups of people:

- ⚽ Coaches of all levels
- ⚽ Amateur and professional athletes
- ⚽ School administrators, including athletic directors
- ⚽ Tournament and/or league directors
- ⚽ Anyone involved in sports-related ministries, such as FCA, AIA, YMCA

---

[1] By 2010, what was commonly called "contemporary worship" was 40 years old and had become "traditional," while what had been considered "traditional" had faded from any common expression. This is extremely frustrating to churches, which were late adopters of the "contemporary" only to find out it had become passé in the new millennium.

⚽ Anyone who serves as a local church recreator, activities pastor, or sports minister

In addition, this work is written specifically for followers of Christ who wish to honor God in both who they are and in all they do. It is designed to aid Christian athletes, coaches, and anyone involved in sports ministry to live a life consistent with the biblical mandates concerning the Lord's Day by providing practical answers to Lord's Day issues. However, if this work is read by someone who is not currently a follower of Christ, it may be of help as you consider the claims of Christ and what it means to follow Him. This chapter describes God's love for all of humankind as expressed in the Lord's Day offer of rest, peace, and joy to all followers of Jesus Christ. Whether the reader is a follower of Christ or not, my hope is each will be encouraged by understanding that God loved people so much He created a "holiday" once each week for their benefit. This "Lord's Day" is to be celebrated and enjoyed each week. Christ's own words concerning the Sabbath were "The Sabbath was made for man, not man for the Sabbath" (Mark 2:27). When properly understood and lived out, the Lord's Day concept is one of the most significant attractions of the Christian faith. No other religion or worldview offers such a winsome opportunity!

Finally, it is important to read this material in its entirety. The full comprehension for the Lord's Day can only be fully understood by a thorough study of the topic. Only then can one fully appreciate the peace, joy, and strength that results from honoring the Lord's Day. Furthermore, the instructions concerning the day are much more than a list of do's and don'ts. Rather than seeing any of what follows as an unnecessary encumbrance, remember the Lord's Day was designed for the benefit and enjoyment of mankind.

III. HOW THIS STUDY WILL PROCEED

This discussion will follow the traditional Christian procedure for determining ethical behavior.[2] It has three steps:

---

[2]It may be of interest to some to note this is also the origin of the "three-point sermon," which follows the same pattern of (1) Principle Stated—study the scripture; (2) Pattern Observed—declare the doctrine; and (3) Practice Applied—apply the principles.

A. Study the Scripture

This step includes finding scriptures that contain direct commands and rules concerning the Sabbath and Lord's Day as well as any other verses that provide relevant biblical principles concerning the topic. Study of Scripture assumes appropriate use of biblical interpretation (hermeneutics) and includes the application of biblical principles in the twenty-first century of biblical rules established in and for the first century. Even though the first century rule may no longer be relevant for those living in the twenty-first century, its basic principle may well still be applicable.

B. Declare the Doctrine

This step determines what is to be believed as a result of the scriptural study and research. This procedure consists of first establishing any clear-cut specific commands found in the Bible concerning the topic. These will serve as the foundation for all ethical decisions. Added to them will be biblical doctrines based on principles found in other passages, which may not necessarily address the specific topic but are nonetheless relevant for general ethics.

C. Apply the Principles

This final step determines what ethical decisions and subsequent moral actions emerge from the doctrines. It will determine what should or should not be thought, or done, as a result of the first two steps.

The desired result of this study is for readers to find their own way of "honoring the day." To that end, questions rather than statements will often be asked. Rather than mandating a "one size fits all" ethic, readers will be able to determine their own way of observing the day by answering the questions raised throughout the narrative.

It is rare to hear anyone preach or teach about the Lord's Day. Rarer still is the Christian who treats Sunday different from any other day, with the possible exception of attending church! So why be concerned about the Lord's Day? Why read this discussion? Succinctly stated: because the day is important to God! Competitors should be concerned about the Lord's Day because the Lord has communicated a vital concern about it. This importance will be demonstrated by the study that follows.

IV. STUDY THE SCRIPTURE: BIBLICAL BASIS FOR THE LORD'S DAY

The study of the Scriptures concerning the Lord's Day will begin with a study of the Ten Commandments, include other Old Testament references, and then move to the New Testament and study the teachings and observances of Jesus, Paul, and the early church.

A. Significance of the Ten Commandments

The first reference to the Sabbath Day is found in the writings of Moses, beginning with the Creation account and where it is found in both lists of the Ten Commandments. The Ten Commandments are nothing less than God's penultimate for ethics and morality. The following realities concerning the commandments will clearly demonstrate this and will confirm that followers of Christ should also have the same high regard for them.

1. God Gave the Commandments   God gave these commands to Moses to form the basis of the new society. They were to serve as the foundation for the moral, religious, social, and legal structures for the children of Israel when they came into the Promised Land.

2. God Spoke the Commandments   God spoke the commandments with His own voice. Although not the only time in history in which God spoke out in an audible voice, He has only done so a few times and thus the significance is clear. The giving of the Ten Commandments is one time He was determined to clearly alliterate His message and its importance. God spoke audibly so there could be no confusion as to the importance of all of the Ten Commandments, which would include His expectations concerning the Sabbath day (Exodus 19:5, 19:19, 20:1, and Deuteronomy 5:22).

3. God Wrote the Commandments   Not only did God verbally speak the Ten Commandments, but more importantly, He wrote them with His own hand. The significance of the Ten Commandments being the only thing God ever physically wrote cannot be minimized (Deuteronomy 5:22).

4. God Wrote the Commandments a Second Time   Not only did God write the Ten Commandments once, but after Moses shattered the first tablets, God also wrote them a second time. This intensifies the fact God was communicating their importance.

5. God Enforced the Commandments   Not only did God unequivocally write, speak, and thus establish the Ten Commandments, but He also invoked a system of retribution for any who would violate the Commandments (Exodus 31:14f). The penalty for disobedience was death by means of stoning. Stoning (a) was a harsh and brutal means (the violator was so heinously evil as to deserve it); (b) did not defile the executioners (again the violator was so heinously evil to even touch the victim meant defilement to the executioner); and (c) the victim was left under a pile of rocks, and it removed the necessity of burial, which again alleviated the possibility of touching the evil body.

Thus, God clearly demonstrated the significance of the Ten Commandments and expected nothing less than His followers should appropriately honor and obey them. However, some may argue that although this is true in general, a specific command or two may have changed in importance due to a new dispensation of God. To counter such thinking, the following explorations are offered to substantiate the relevance and continuing importance God places on the fourth commandment.

B. Old Testament Significance of the Fourth Commandment

1. It is found in 98 Old Testament passages and mentioned in 22 books of the Bible overall.

2. It is the only one of all Ten Commandments that is listed in all five books of the law—the first five books of the Old Testament, often called the Pentateuch.

3. It was an important part of the establishment of the society of the Promised Land, and a foundational aspect of the reestablishment of the society in Nehemiah and Ezra's day (Nehemiah 8:1–8; 9:38; 10:28–39; 13:15–22).

4. **Its benefits are timeless and would be an aid for every society, even secular societies, by promoting a day for recreation, rest, and relationships.**

The biblical mandate is not just an Old Testament theme, however. It is well supported by the New Testament as well.

C. New Testament Significance of the Fourth Commandment

1. *The Sabbath is referenced in 56 New Testament passages.*
2. *The Sabbath is fulfilled in the teachings of Christ.*

Jesus never taught against the Sabbath, but rather fulfilled it. The Gospels are replete with Jesus's confrontations of the Pharisees and their traditions, which had been superimposed upon the Sabbath, as can be seen in the following examples.

a. Jesus Condemned Pharisees   Jesus condemned the Pharisees for establishing and adhering to human traditions instead of obeying God's commands and purposes for the day (Mark 7:8–9).

b. Jesus Blasted the Pharisees   Jesus also blasted the Pharisee and yet he personally upheld and fulfilled the Law (Matthew 5:17–20).

c. Jesus Modeled for the Pharisees   Jesus modeled the way the day was to be observed when He dined on the Sabbath with a Pharisee. Through this He modeled the day was to be a day of refreshment (Luke 6:1).

d. Jesus Demonstrated Restorative Ministry for All in Need   Jesus demonstrated restoration by the healing He performed at the dinner mentioned in the last point (Luke 6:2–6).

e. Jesus Emphasized the Main Purpose of the Sabbath   Jesus taught and healed on the Sabbath, as seen in the story of His healing a woman while teaching at a Sabbath Day synagogue (Luke 13:10–17).

f. Jesus Again Healed and Empowered on the Sabbath   Jesus also healed the crippled man at the Pool of Bethesda and gave him strength on a special holy Sabbath (John 5:1–9).

g. Summary of Jesus and the Sabbath   Jesus never taught against the Sabbath, only against the onerous, self-inflicted strictures created by the Pharisees. Furthermore, many of the healings Jesus performed took place on the Sabbath, and most of these took place while He was attending Sabbath Day observances in the synagogue. Jesus fulfilled the Sabbath Day law and principles by His actions, His teachings, and His obedience. It is quite clear Jesus:

- Fully adhered to the true meaning and purposes of the Sabbath
- Never dismissed the fact it was to be observed
- Railed against the way in which the Pharisees had corrupted it
- Modeled what He taught about the Sabbath

3. *The Sabbath Is Fulfilled in the Life and Teachings of Paul*   The book of Acts records Paul's model of observing the Sabbath through his regular attendance at the synagogue. His only teaching about the Sabbath centered on two things: (a) He wanted to ensure there would not be a return to the Pharisaical misuse of the day and (b) he wanted to protect Christianity from assimilating any pagan traditions, festivals, or days into the newly forming faith (Romans 14; Colossians 2:16f). Paul's great desire for his Jewish brethren was to combat the Judaizers in an effort to set them free from onerous human tradition. His desire for his Gentile brethren was a complete break from paganism. His overall goal was to encourage all early Christians to fully take part in the New Covenant and relish its joy and freedom.

a. Summary of Paul and the Sabbath   Paul observed both the Sabbath and the Lord's Day. He never taught it shouldn't be observed. He taught followers of Christ they were to live in the New Covenant and not be bound by either the Old Covenant or any pagan entrapments, but he never taught the New Covenant did away with any of the Ten Commandments.

4. *The Sabbath and the Final Rest of the New Testament*   The theme of rest is found throughout the Bible. The final rest is the culmination of the Sabbath Day/Lord's Day theme. The theme of rest is found in the following passages:

⚽ The very first book of the Bible (Genesis) records God resting

⚽ The Pentateuch teaches humankind is to set aside a day for rest

⚽ The prophets and books of history proclaim what happens when the Sabbath rest is obeyed and conversely the problems that follow when it is not obeyed

⚽ Jesus and Paul modeled and taught the principles of rest on the day

⚽ The last book of the Bible states all believers will enjoy an eternal rest

a. Summary of the Final Rest and the Sabbath   This overview helps substantiate the Sabbath Day principle of rest is not just for the Old Testament and not just for a period of time nor for a political/societal reason but rather is one of the foundational theological underpinnings for the Christian church for all time. It finds its ultimate fulfillment in the New Testament through the believer's final rest as found in Paul's letter to the Hebrews and John's Revelation (Hebrews 4:9; Revelation 14:9–13).

5. *The Sabbath Was Also Fulfilled in New Testament Times by the Way in Which the Early Church Observed the Day*   As the church became more and more a Gentile church, the more it moved from observing the Sabbath to observing the Lord's Day. This is evidenced by Paul's teaching to give financially on the Lord's Day and by John being in meditation on the Lord's Day (1 Corinthians 16:2; Revelation 1:10). Nonetheless, the basic theme remained the same. Christians are to observe 1 day a week as unto the Lord.

D. Summary of the Biblical Data

Therefore, the biblical data concerning keeping the Sabbath Day holy can be summarized as follows. It:

⚽ **Was commanded by God**

⚽ **Was emphasized by God as to its importance and continuing relevance**

⚽ **Was to be enforced by capital punishment**

- ✿ **Was supported by Christ and Paul**
- ✿ **Was practiced by the church**
- ✿ **Is to be observed by believers of all generations**
- ✿ **Foreshadows the believer's eternal final rest**

Therefore, the day is firmly rooted in the Scripture, supported by Church traditions, and most importantly is considered extremely important by God and, thus, should be highly esteemed by followers of God!

V. DECLARING THE DOCTRINE: BIBLICAL RULES AND PRINCIPLES FOR OBSERVING THE LORD'S DAY

It is clear the Sabbath and Lord's Day themes are important theological constructs. To be relevant, however, they need to be made more specific. All stated so far can be succinctly summarized and explained by the following three statements: The Sabbath or Lord's Day is created for:

A. A Day Set Aside unto the Lord
- ✿ Set aside for worship
- ✿ Set aside for spiritual renewal
- ✿ Set aside for personal development[3]

B. A Day Set Aside for Rest
- ✿ Set aside for followers of Christ
- ✿ Set aside for others
- ✿ Set aside for the animal world[4]

---

[3] Isaiah 58:13–14 and others call believers to set aside this day for the Lord and not to use the day doing only what pleases them.

[4] The word *Sabbath* is a Hebrew word that means "rest." This concept is based on Exodus 20:8–11 where God commands rest and is founded upon the example of God. If the Creator rested on the seventh day, so must the creation.

C. A Day Set Aside as a Sign of Redemption

⚽ By observing this day, the Christian gives a witness to his belief in God.

⚽ By refraining from working, the Christian has additional time to reach out to those who are not yet believers in Christ.

⚽ By not causing someone else to work, the believer has freed up the nonbeliever to have Sundays free to be able to attend church or other outreach activities.[5]

This quick overview of the biblical data will be used as the scriptural foundation from which to consider the ethical and moral implications and applications.

VI. THE REASON WHY THE FOURTH COMMANDMENT IS DISREGARDED

Before going on, it is necessary to assess why Lord's Day observances have fallen into disregard with the vast majority of the Christian community in spite of church tradition and biblical support for the honoring of the Lord's Day. Insights for how one should honor the day will be gained by understanding why it is disregarded. The cause is threefold:

⚽ There has been *a misappropriation of how Sabbath Day principles* should be applied. This has led to unnecessary and cumbersome burdens being placed upon followers of Christ and thus the day became a dreary duty rather than a freeing holy experience.

⚽ The second cause emerged from *erroneous beliefs* that Christ taught against Sabbath day principles. In fact, He stated the Sabbath was made for man.

⚽ The third cause stems from the *unwillingness of believers* to pay the price for appropriately observing its principles.

Each of these will now be addressed.

---

[5] Deuteronomy 5:15; Ezekiel 20:12, 20; and Matthew 12:1–14 all give biblical mandates for the keeping of the fourth covenant between God and His people.

A. The Misappropriation of Sabbath Day Principles

The Pharisees best exemplify the abuses of Sabbath Day principles in biblical times, while the Puritans are used (often unjustly) as more modern-day examples. However, it must be remembered that although the ill-conceived practices of these and other groups must be reevaluated, their zeal to please Christ by lovingly obeying the law must be emulated. A modern-day example of misplaced zeal occurred in the mid-1980s at an evangelical college. Students at this college were allowed to watch television on Sundays on all but the first floor of their dormitories. The reason stated for this policy was so anyone walking beside the dorms could not see students watching television. Though the administration was honest in admitting its reasoning, this ruling was a rather bizarre way to appease alumni. It attempted to uphold a culturally defined, rather than a biblically based, ethic of obedience to the Sabbath and resulted in students ridiculing rather than appreciating the day. Due to many examples like this, most Christians jettison any attempt to honor the day rather than doing the hard work of making the ancient commands of God relevant to a modern-day application.

B. The Erroneous Beliefs about Christ's Teaching on the Sabbath

The second reason why the Sabbath has been largely disregarded is found in the fact a number of Christians have wrongly interpreted Christ's teachings concerning the Sabbath Day. One such interpretation states Christ did away with all guidelines and mandates concerning Sabbath Day principles. This is an erroneous belief. Although Christ did denounce and correct the ceremonial observances of Sabbath Day adherence, He fully supported the moral aspects of obedience to the Sabbath. Christ explained how to observe the Sabbath in fulfillment to the law, not how to neglect the law. He never taught Christians to evade obeying the fourth commandment. Just as Christ did not do away with the binding nature of the marriage vow just because He outlined a procedure that permitted a few necessary divorces, He also did not teach a disavowal of the entire Sabbath Day principle by correcting the misguided Pharisaic teachings. What Christ taught against was the abuse of the principles that were embodied by Pharisaical and legalistic notions and mandates. Christ taught a fulfillment of the Sabbath Day principles. These fulfillments are found in Matthew 12. The Christian's responsibility to the Sabbath Day mandates concerning work can be summarized by these three phrases:

1. Acts of Necessity

    a. Acts of necessity include duties or responsibilities that ensure and protect the general health, life, and safety of people and the created order. All such duties are exempted from any Lord's Day prohibitions. Those included for exemption would be police or fire patrols and doctors, among others. Even farmers must have their cows milked each day for the health of their herds. These are just a few examples of legitimate acts of necessity (Matthew 12:1–4).

2. Acts of Mercy

    a. Acts of mercy include duties or responsibilities that have to do with aiding someone in need. Visiting shut-ins, helping a stranded motorist fix a flat tire, or any other act that would prove merciful are all exempted from any Lord's Day prohibitions. Milking cows may be considered both an act of necessity and an act of mercy (Matthew 12:9–14)!

3. Acts of Ministry

    a. Christ clearly taught that ministry was to take place on the Lord's Day, and furthermore, this mandate covers two of the three main reasons for the day (worship and ministry). These duties or responsibilities would include anything that would either provide worship, fellowship, Christian teaching, or evangelistic outreach (Matthew 12:5–8).

From these verses and others, it is clear Christ taught the importance of the Sabbath Day; actively lived by them; and moreover, taught His followers how to honor the day.

C. The Unwillingness of Believers — Being Faithful Costs Something

Christians will certainly experience many blessings that come from honoring the day, but they may also be faced with occasional sacrifices and possible ridicule for so honoring it. This, then, is the third reason why many people neglect it. Observation of the Lord's Day may place limits as to the scope and extent of activities or involvements for some and may even include a severe sacrifice as it did for the Scottish Olympian Eric Liddell, who conceivably gave up the opportunity to win three Olympic medals.[6] It is for these reasons some believers seek to find a rationale for Lord's Day involvements that may not adhere to biblical mandates. Though hard to admit, the reality is that many who claim to be followers of Christ simply have nothing more than a faith of convenience. They are willing to follow Christ when it is easy and the cost is not high, but if being a disciple of Christ entails sacrifice, they look to find a way out or ignore clearly marked expectations. It is similar to fasting. Though wonderful, spiritual growth and fulfillment may result from fasting, it is not often partaken of because it means making a sacrifice.

The words of Alastair Begg ring true when he exhorts: "Unless one can recognize the distinction of the day; unless people are absolutely convinced God distinguished the day; unless people are persuaded as to the significance of the day; they will never know its liberation, and its privileges, nor will any of their observances be anything more than empty traditions."[7]

In short, one must come under the influence of the Holy Spirit and have an unshakable conviction to "honor the Sabbath Day (Lord's Day) and keep it holy" in order for any of the following recommendations to make any sense.

---

[6] Liddell won gold in the 400 and bronze in the 200 at the 1924 Paris Olympics. He refused to run in the preliminary heats for the 100; the 4 by 100; and the 4 by 400. It stands to reason Liddell had a strong chance to win a medal in all three of these events as his teammate, Harold Abrams, won the 100 and Eric had beaten him in that race, and the British team had other runners who all did very well in the other races.

[7] These statements are a summary of Begg's comments in his audio series titled "Guidelines to Freedom," which are a series of sermons on the Ten Commandments. "Pathway to Freedom," sound recording. (Cleveland, OH: Truth for Life, 2003). 12 CDs. ID 20501.

Before reading any further, it is imperative the reader of this treatise examine his or her own heart. Are you open to the possibility the Holy Spirit is speaking to you about this issue? Is God drawing you closer to Himself and to the intended purpose of His day for you and your benefit? Is He convicting you of your nonchalant attitude concerning His day? Do you desire to be faithful in these regards? Or do you find yourself already wanting to make excuses or not do the hard work of making proper ethical application in your life? The proper response is a sincere prayer of confession and, where needed, a desire to please God no matter what the cost, followed by a plea for further guidance. Godspeed to you in your endeavors.

VII. MAKING APPLICATION
A. Biblical Ethics Revisited

Now that the Scripture has been studied and its doctrine declared, the attention of this chapter turns toward application. A brief summary of biblical ethics will be helpful in this pursuit. To clearly comprehend proper Christian behavior, one must know the distinction between ethics and morals.

Ethics are defined as the philosophical model for appropriate behavior or action, whereas morals are the actions themselves. Therefore, what Christian ethicists attempt to do is to provide philosophical models (ethics) that serve as foundational ethical guidelines for moral behavior (morals). These models for the Christian must be biblically based and Christ-centered, but must also be relevant with contemporary society and life. They must never be determined in a vacuum without both the theoretical and the practical aspects being taken into consideration. Furthermore, it must be understood there are three basic levels of biblical, ethical teaching.

1. Didactic   The root meaning of this word comes from the Greek language. It denotes the essence of justice and righteous judgment and it also has acquired a usage of teaching righteousness. Sometimes it is referred to as the ontological approach, from a Greek word meaning "truth." Thus, it is specific, mandated teaching about righteousness and truth.[8] Didactic teachings define specific biblical rules.

---

[8] The Ten Commandments are didactic rules and are always applicable. Thus, murder is both defined as being unethical in theory and immoral in action.

2. Casuistic The root meaning of this word has to do with case law. Case law is commonly found in books like Leviticus and enables Christian ethicists to be able to make ethical determinations on any moral dilemma by applying the biblical principles derived from previous relevant cases of a similar nature to the issue in question.[9]

3. General Wisdom General wisdom is generally found in the book of Proverbs and a few other passages. Such wisdom can often be helpful in determining a Godly way to approach the moral dilemma when there is a question.[10]

In addition it must be understood these three levels also form a hierarchy of importance. General wisdom gives way to casuistic law, which in turn acquiesces to the didactic. This does not necessarily imply the three are in conflict with one another—only that a higher weight is placed upon the didactic than the other two, etc.

Didactic teaching is plentiful in Scripture, but it is usually cloaked in an earlier century's culture or is not comprehensive in its mandates and at times is in need of the casuistic or general wisdom for further explanation and clarity. An example of the first dilemma is found in Paul's discourse on eating meat that had been offered to first-century idols. This is a didactic teaching that Christians living in Corinth in the year AD 50 would have had no problem understanding and applying, but of course this teaching is not nearly so clear-cut nor is it nearly so relevant for one living in the twenty-first century. In twenty-first-century America, very little if any meat is offered to idols; however, much of what is called "New Age" music is written for (offered to) false gods (idols) and should be avoided by followers of Christ. This is determined by applying the eternal biblical principle, which emerges out of the first-century biblical rule.

---

[9] Although it is clear that murder is unethical and immoral, the Scripture never addresses the specifics of whether or not abortion is murder. But the case law concerning the injuring or killing of an unborn baby of a pregnant woman gives a precedent for protecting the life of the unborn.

[10] General wisdom passages affirm life and advise caution when in doubt concerning protecting life.

This then outlines the basic formula that will be used in determining the ethics concerning the Lord's Day. An effort will be made to:

⚽ **First**, determine any didactic teachings.

- Is the Lord's Day/Sabbath Day mandated?
- If it is mandated, what are the specific actions required?

⚽ **Second**, establish any guiding principles.

- Such as rest, worship, ministry, etc.

⚽ **Third**, utilize any general wisdom provided by Scripture such as prudence, moderation, etc.

B. Specific Recommendations for Faithful Observance of the Lord's Day

The approach for this section will be to avoid two pitfalls:

⚽ Legalism

⚽ Lawlessness or antinomianism

The first approach will be avoided so as to not create a legalistic do and don't list reminiscent of the Pharisaical legalism that Christ railed against; the second, so as to not communicate observing the day is unimportant. Rather, the hope is to set people free so they can experience the rich renewal and revitalization that come from "setting the day aside unto the Lord." The basic flow will not be to establish a set of prohibitions, but rather it will establish new avenues of involvement that will enhance one's life. Of course, this may necessitate a curtailment or stoppage of some current activity or involvement, but only so a new, more productive and life-enhancing activity can be partaken of. This curtailment is not done out of any attempt to punish or to restrict a person, but more so to set one free and to enable health, happiness, renewal, and joy. There may also be some curtailments or prohibitions recommended for the protection and benefit of other people in society. These prohibitions must be seen as concessions in consideration of others, not as a restriction on personal freedom.

The ensuing recommendations will follow three already established guidelines, which can be summarized as:

- A day set aside unto the Lord (a day with a goal of worship and spiritual development)
- A day set aside for rest (I won't work; I won't cause anyone else to work)
- A day set aside as a sign (a day for witness and good works)

1. A Day Set Aside unto the Lord   For the believer the following question will reveal one's heart.

> *Is it the Lord's Day or just the Lord's hour?*

Most Christians feel they meet their obligation to the Lord's Day by attending a worship service and maybe an additional Christian education hour. These people, while faithfully attending church, have relegated the Lord's Day into the Lord's hour or at most the Lord's morning. They sit in the pew anxiously waiting to get on with "their day."

Using the before-mentioned guidelines of principle and rule, it is important to establish there are no definite biblical commandments or rules that detail specific instructions as to "keeping the day Holy." Therefore, relevant, guiding principles of Scripture must be sought. With this as the basic guideline, the first recommendation is to use the Lord's Day for one of the reasons God set it aside—for spiritual enhancement and improvement.

Many Christians have bemoaned they have so little time for Bible study, Scripture reading, prayer, or fellowship. Multitudes have wanted to read the Christian classics. These same people complain of having so little time for these desired activities. They need only take advantage of the one day each week God has given them for such activities. The issue is not having enough time; it is the utilization of the time one has. It is using the time God requires to be set aside in the best way possible. This is where most Christian athletes and competitors begin to feel the pinch. Coaches believe they have to work on Sunday in order to keep up with other schools, teams, and programs. Players fail to realize that by either competing or training for competition on Sunday, they place great strains on their time and energies, which could be utilized in efforts leading to greater spiritual formation.[11] Although there is certainly no mandate in Scripture that specifically bans any athletic endeavor on Sunday, it is wise for the Christian athlete, coach, and even recreational enthusiast to have a clear understanding and regard for the admonition of the prophet Isaiah, which commands everyone to do what is pleasing to God on the Sabbath, rather than going his own way or doing as she pleases (Isaiah 58:13f). The basic questions that must be answered are: Will this activity lead to honoring the day? and Will this endeavor lead to spiritual renewal and personal growth?

2. A Day Set Aside for Rest   Once again, Scripture is devoid of any detailed commandments that define work and rest. It is, however, full of principles that adequately provide Christian patterns for rest that are pleasing to God. In general, the biblical mandate is for the day to be set aside as a day free from the obligations of normal work. However, as has been previously explained, there are many exceptions that find a biblical mandate in the threefold proposition found in Matthew 12, which includes acts of mercy, acts of necessity, and acts of ministry. How this principle of rest pertains to athletes and athletics follows.

Just as before, one can reveal his or her motives by answering the following questions:

⚽   *What work can be done only on Sunday (or, what must be done on Sunday and not the other 6 days)?*

⚽   *Is one's intent how to circumvent the Sabbath Day principle or is it how to please God?*

The first question is a pragmatic one. Simply put, most of what people do on Sunday can and, therefore, should be done on another day. There is no legitimate reason college or high school games have to be played on Sunday. There is no reason why youth leagues need to be run on Sunday.

---

[11] One issue that cannot be addressed here is the distinctives between professional and amateur competitors. It will be addressed at another place in this discussion.

Any race, marathon, or other event that is held on Sunday could be held on Saturday. It is the author's contention that the only prevailing reason for holding athletic events on Sunday (other than the possibility of professional sports) is the pure and simple preference of the organizers and participants. There is no substantial pragmatic reason other than convenience, preference, and, of course, economic gain.

Therefore, the second question becomes pertinent. If one is combing the Scriptures looking for loopholes that will provide a possible rationale for working or causing someone else to work on Sunday, then the one seeking how to be faithful has already transgressed the Sabbath Day principle. The question should not be what one can get away with, but rather must be what would be most pleasing to God with regard to the Sabbath Day.

Moreover, if one is set to nitpick about the Sabbath Day, he or she should be attempting to intensely protect the day rather than seeking to curtail its observances. In this regard, the Pharisees got it right. They were scrupulous, indeed, overly scrupulous in their attempts to nitpick at what could or could not be done on the Sabbath. In an effort to really honor God and to sincerely love others, Christian athletes and coaches who compete should not be involved in anything that would cause any of the following people to work:

- ⚽ Referees
- ⚽ Score keepers
- ⚽ League directors or officials
- ⚽ Coaches
- ⚽ Custodial and maintenance staffs
- ⚽ Restaurant or food service employees
- ⚽ Gas station attendants
- ⚽ Movie theater workers

Although general recreational activities are certainly profitable Lord's Day endeavors, even these must be evaluated if they cause certain people to work (i.e., lifeguards, park police, camping employees, etc.). The goal for every church involved in sports and recreational ministry; for every Christian sports ministry such as AIA, YMCA, or FCA; and for every Christian college and school should be to distinguish the Lord's Day and to make it holy by not engaging in any activity that would make themselves or others work.

3. A Day Set Aside as a Sign   For the third time, it must be stated that there is no clear-cut commandment mandating specific actions for believers to adhere to as it relates to setting aside the day for a sign. However, once again with a little reflection, some general principles can be established, and as in the first two areas, a clarifying question can reveal motive and can recommend possible direction.

> *What is the goal and/or purpose of the believer's life?*

Or stated another way,

> *Why does God give the believer each day of his or her life?*

Although the writers of the Westminster Confession were wise in assessing the chief aim of mankind is to "glorify God and enjoy Him forever," it must be realized things like prayer (talking with God), praise, and obedience will all be better accomplished in heaven than on earth. The one activity that people can do to glorify God better on earth is to be a "sign" or a witness to the unbeliever. It is imperative for anyone who follows Christ to endeavor to be a positive witness for Christ. It is essential to notice that a joyous and meaningful observance of the Lord's Day can only aid in that witness in the following ways:

- ⚽ *The first witness* comes by personally honoring the Lord's Day, which provides believers and their families with observably better health, happiness, and relationships. Personal observance of the Lord's Day enhances one's life, and such lives are attractive to those seeking this same fulfilled and joyous life.

- ⚽ *The second witness* occurs by demonstrating one's priorities and commitments to church, ministry, and spiritual development. Nonbelievers will be able to observe faith as it is lived out, at least partially, by keeping the Lord's Day holy.

⚽ ***The third witness*** is observed in the acts of mercy rendered by believers on the Lord's Day. Not only will the recipients of the acts notice, but so will others.

⚽ ***The fourth witness*** can be a literal witness of verbal or nonverbal communication of the Gospel message to a nonbeliever through various outreaches performed on the Lord's Day.

VIII. SUMMARY OF APPLICATION

In general Bruce Ray is helpful with his set of four guidelines for observing the Lord's Day. Ray states we are to observe the Lord's Day in four basic ways:

⚽ ***Happily:*** "Shout with joy and worship with gladness"
(Psalms 100).

⚽ ***Holily:*** "Do not forsake the gathering of yourselves together"
(Hebrews 10:19–25).

⚽ ***Honestly:*** "Keep from doing as you please on My Holy Day . . .
call the Sabbath a delight . . . and honor it by not going your own
way . . . then you will find your joy" (Isaiah 58:13f).

⚽ ***Humbly:*** "Not desiring it to end to get back to making money and
doing business"[12] (Amos 8:4–7)

In order to really enjoy and appreciate what God desires for His followers in their observance of His day, it is important to maintain a positive outlook on it and be happy about having one day a week for spiritual formation, rest, and outreach. For unless it is kept *Happily* (with joy), *Holily* (separate and different from the other six), *Honestly* (with integrity not just adhering to outward ritual, but really engaging in its design and purpose), and *Humbly* (with no longing to get it over with), one will never fully experience the blessings, joys, and delights God promises.

For those leading a sports ministry or serving as a coach or athletic administrator, the following questions will help determine

---

[12] Bruce Ray, *Celebrating the Lord's Day: Finding Rest in a Restless World* (Phillipsburg, NJ: P&R Pub., 2000).

appropriate functions that should be entered into on the Lord's Day. Will the activity:

- ⚽ *Refresh the faculty, staff, volunteers, or participants and the participants' families?*
- ⚽ *Occur during the time of the traditional Sunday morning or evening worship services and, even if it doesn't, will it influence those participating to not partake in those services by making the day too busy?*
- ⚽ *Lead to reverence, unity, and worship or will it lead to disharmony and strife?*
- ⚽ *Lead to doing God's thing or the things of people?*

Not only are these good questions for those leading and participating in sports ministries, but they are also excellent questions for any individual or family to ask when contemplating Lord's Day involvements.

IX. SUMMARY OF SPORT AND LORD'S DAY ISSUES

It should be obvious at this point that there is a general biblical rule, or command, for followers of Christ to observe the Lord's Day. It is just as obvious there are no specific delineations of particular actions provided by Scripture concerning sports, recreational, or athletic involvements on the Lord's Day. In spite of this void of specific instruction, the Bible is replete with principles that are extremely helpful in providing believers of the twenty-first century with guidelines that will enable them to honor the Sabbath Day and keep it holy. These guidelines begin with calling believers to a heartfelt desire to keep the day holy. It continues by encouraging believers to use the day for the worship of God and personal spiritual renewal; to use the day for betterment of themselves, others, and society by refraining from work and from causing anyone else to work; and to use the day for spiritual outreach and ministry.

One final question may help to solidify one's stewardship of the day:

Would a casual observer of your life easily recognize the distinctive difference of how you use the day?

If not, then perhaps a change is in order.

X. A PERSONAL TESTIMONY AND CONCLUDING THOUGHTS

"Remembering the Sabbath to keep it holy" and honoring the Lord's Day have been among the most freeing, inspirational, and invigorating aspects of my faith and life.

"Remembering the Sabbath" provides a rootedness and a balance to my life: rooted by being anchored to a repeated rhythmic tension of activity and rest, and balanced by engaging in a healthy mix of work and play. When properly rooted and balanced, I am continually fulfilled, renewed, and refreshed.

"Honoring the Lord's Day" tethers me to the twin principles of personally and corporately worshipping God. I personally practice the presence of Christ in my 6 days of "vocational" endeavors, and I also exalt God each Sunday by engaging in corporate praise, fellowship, and spiritual contemplation centered on the preaching of God's word. Both the personal and the corporate demonstrate a witness of the responsibilities and blessings of being a follower of Christ.

Perhaps Sabbath keeping is best summarized by saying rest (which enables play) is a foreshadowing of the eternal rest Paul writes about in his letter to the Hebrews.[13] I am impressed by the following two quotes: Mark Buchanan writes, "Play hints at a world beyond us" and "when we play we nudge the border of eternity."[14] Abraham Heschel's reflection is indeed profound when he states that remembering the Sabbath "rehearses heaven" and is a "foretaste of heavenly activity."[15]

Perhaps Lord's Day keeping is best summarized by saying worship (which enables spiritual formation) is a foreshadowing of the eternal worship John writes about in the Holy Spirit's Revelation to him.[16] The ancient Celtic saints believed pagan worship of the earth and nature hinted at a heavenly being, who by comparison was far beyond humankind,

---

[13] Hebrews 4.

[14] Mark Buchanan, *The Rest of God: Restoring Your Soul by Restoring Sabbath* (Nashville: Thomas Nelson, 2006), p 141.

[15] Abraham Joshua Heschel, *The Sabbath* (New York: Farrar, Straus & Giroux, 2001), p. 74.

[16] Revelation 4.

and when we praise Him we experience a mere touch of heaven. These Christ-centered Celts believed worship of the "Eternal One" was best experienced in a "thin place" where the veil between heaven and earth is mystically minimized, providing a dim glimpse of glory.

Then again, perhaps **"Remembering the Sabbath"** and *"Honoring the Lord's Day"* are best understood through the two biblical concepts of time: *Chronos* and *Kairos*. *Chronos* monitors time by a clock; *Kairos,* by a calendar. *Chronos* makes a slave of every man by demanding his every moment be filled by frenetic activity. *Kairos* makes time a slave of men by calling men out of the moment-to-moment demands and ushering them into a season of reflection, relationship, and renewal. Play, which happens during *Kairos*, replenishes, renews, and reinvigorates through re-creation. Work, even God-honoring work, which happens during *Chronos*, enables a daily worship of God through vocation but also depletes and deprives through slavish demands of obeisance to a clock. Do not be confused . . . humankind worships God in practicing the presence of God in daily *Chronos*-based vocational activities and by a celebration of *Kairos*-based seasonal experiences. Unfortunately, however, secular culture deems *Kairos* less important, more undervalued, and often preempts it in favor of the "tyranny of the urgent." It promotes a "play is for kids, work is for adults" ethos. I firmly believe when Jesus said we must become like children, He envisioned more than a child-like faith. Certainly, a child-like joy was also hoped for.

Sunsets and sunrises (*Kairos* blessings) radiate intermittently changing hues of colors across luminous clouds. But these celestial displays of a Heavenly Artist's creativity last but a few fleeting minutes each day. Unless intentionally prepared for and contemplatively engaged in, their *Kairos* blessings are only occasionally stumbled upon, and then only by accident.

How many *Kairos* blessings have you missed by being driven by the *Chronos* culture? How many physical, relational, and spiritual blessings have you forfeited by not "Remembering the Sabbath and honoring the Lord's Day"? When will you respond to the joyous offer of Christ to rest, play, and worship? Jesus asks for a change in your commitment, your schedule, and your mind-set, but in exchange He offers renewing rest, joy, and peace, both now and forever. "The Sabbath was made for man . . ."

CHAPTER 8

FREQUENTLY ASKED QUESTIONS CONCERNING SPORT AND FAITH

This chapter answers some of the most frequently asked questions and addresses some perplexing and yet common issues concerning faith and sport integration. It is designed to provide twenty-first-century competitors with answers to sporting dilemmas and to empower the theological and academic world with a rationale for how to answer the criticisms often raised about such issues as violence in sport, church and sport conflicts, and overzealous, out-of-control competitiveness. It will suggest ways for how to truly follow Christ in the world of sport, even if it leads to an athletic loss. It will also present a few "best practices and principles" for break-ing through the occasional negative culture of competition to truly being able to "worship" Christ in and through one's competitive endeavors.

I. INTRODUCTION: ANSWERING DIFFICULT QUESTIONS

Most people believe athletic endeavors are, in general, positive activities, and yet even those who highly value sport sometimes find it difficult to justify such sports as boxing, and possibly football or hockey, among other sports, due to episodic brutality and savagery.[1] Other critics have difficulty justifying the tens of millions of dollars paid to an athlete for hitting, kicking, shooting, or throwing a ball when "millions of people are starving and we can't even pay our teachers a decent wage." Criticisms seem to fall into one of three categories.

A. Three Frequently Voiced Criticisms

Even people who make no claims to faith often voice criticisms about sport. Complaints shared by both secular and spiritually minded people can usually be placed in one of three categories: (a) violence, (b) cheating, or (c) misplaced priorities. The Christian community would add at least three others: (d) sanctity of the human body, (e) idolatry, and (f) Lord's Day/Sabbath Day concerns. This chapter will focus on answering criticisms of, and frequently asked questions concerning, the integration of faith and sport.

Although previous chapters have discussed the basic template for determining the basis for biblically defensible sports in general, and have addressed the actions and attitudes required of competitors in specific terms and situations, there are still many nagging questions frequently raised by Christian competitors. Some stem from questions arising from a few troubling biblical verses, some seek clarification of what was heard in a particular sermon or talk, and others emerge from real-life situations athletes and coaches experience during a competition or game. I'm sure there are a myriad of coaches, athletes, theology students, and sports ministers who are asking one or more of the following questions.

---

[1] Concerns about specific sports and sporting actions and which sports are biblically defensible were addressed in Chapter 4.

II. THREE MEANS OF ANSWERING FREQUENTLY ASKED QUESTIONS

Most ethical dilemmas can be solved through an application of one, or a combination of, the following three means: (a) logic (rational thought), (b) biblical hermeneutics (proper interpretation), and (c) natural revelation (contemplation on truths found in the created order and/or the human experience).

- **Logic** helps in three ways:
  - It clarifies the actual issue in question
  - It accurately defines the issue and all terms used
  - It eliminates fallacious reasoning
- **Biblical Interpretation (hermeneutics)**[2] helps by
  - Establishing an accurate translation of relevant passages
  - Applying hermeneutical structures
  - Applying biblical rules and principles
- **Natural Revelation** helps by
  - Applying God's truths as found in His created order as evaluated through His divine revelation found in His living (Jesus) and written (the Holy Scripture) Word

Each of the answers to the following FAQs will utilize one or more of these.

Question 1: How can I, as a Christian athlete, justify my sporting endeavors when 1 Timothy 4:8 reads "exercise is of little value"?

This is truly a frequently asked question. It is a most important foundational theological query because if Scripture does indeed state "exercise is of little value," then none of the other questions are relevant. The short

---

[2] The official term for biblical interpretation is *hermeneutics*. The discipline of biblical hermeneutics has been developed and utilized by the Christian Church over thousands of years. It is a trustworthy guide to determining Christ-honoring, biblically based ethics.

answer is that the specific version of 1 Timothy quoted here is a very poor English translation of the original Greek, and in addition, it is not congruent with the rest of the biblical teaching (biblical *a priori*) on sport and physical fitness. Furthermore, anyone who interprets this verse in such a way as to condemn physical fitness, and by extension sport and athletics, needs a refresher course on biblical interpretation (hermeneutics). A good and proper hermeneutical study reveals physical exercise has value for anyone, including Christians. It must be noted, however, that a good hermeneutic will also reveal physical exercise is not to extend beyond its God-ordained parameters or exceed its level of importance, including becoming a higher priority than spiritual exercise, which is "profitable for all things."[3]

Question 2: Can God's sanctioning of violence throughout the OT (Jacob wrestling with the Angel; David battling and killing Goliath; the Israelite army killing thousands, etc.) be used to justify more violent sports such as MMA, boxing, and so forth?

Using Old Testament passages that condone, or even mandate, violence to justify violence in sport is a jump too far. This jump can only be made if one makes one of the classic mistakes made by beginning biblical interpreters. Such a jump also necessitates falling for a logical fallacy. The following discussion sheds light on these twin errors and is offered to clear the confusion expressed in this frequently asked question.

Hermeneutics: Biblical Rules and Principles

The error in biblical interpretation is made when a sweeping general application is based upon a very specific and limited command (rule) of God. It is true, God commanded acts of violence in the Old Testament. Yet, these very specific dictates of God were designed for very specific and limited uses of violence. These specific commands of God were issued for His unique purposes. They were not general commands nor were they

---

[3] A review of the longer and much more in-depth answer can be found on pages 46–53 in Chapter 3 of this book.

intended to justify violence for any and every purpose, means, or time. For example, He issued a specific command to institute capital punishment, but that directive is a very specific command, designed to govern one specific aspect of human interaction. God's command to carefully but forcefully incorporate capital punishment is not to be misinterpreted as license to commit violent acts beyond the set of parameters outlined in Scripture. To state that prescriptions of a specific command that rules over a specific aspect of human interaction are principles to be applied to a broader set of ethical dilemmas is a disturbing misuse, and abuse, of the biblical text. Such application can only be expected if and when there is great and widespread corroboration from the rest of Scripture. At best, biblical rules that direct the ethics of specific dilemmas can only suggest general principles for related dilemmas. They may be used as one of many inductive arguments in support of an overall thesis but cannot be considered a definitive, deductive proof for intentional violence in sport.

The general issue concerning violence in sport was, to a large degree, addressed in the "Template for Determining Biblically Defensible Sport" found in Chapter 4. Yet, this specific FAQ needs further attention and explanation. It will now also be considered through the following discussion and viewed through the lens added in this chapter titled "Honor Code for Participating in Biblically Defensible Sport" (see Graph 17 on page I-7). The overarching principles of the Bible affirm Old Testament proscriptions are for very limited and specifically proscribed violence and cannot be used to justify violence in sport.

Logic: Fallacious Arguments

1. Definitions   Violence can be defined as intentionally inflicting harm or death on a person. This would include physical, mental, emotion, relational, and psychological harm. Thus, a sport that (a) mandates intentionally hurting an opponent as its intended goal or (b) harming a co-competitor is required to accomplish its intended goal is by definition a violent activity.

2. Clarifications and Biblical a Prioris   Again, violence can be defined as an act of force committed against a person with the intent to harm, maim, or kill. In contrast, the overwhelming majority of the Christian

Scriptures prohibit such intentional violence. In general, verbal, mental, and physical acts of violence are all condemned.[4] A few biblical mandates, however, do mandate intentional violent acts. God mandates capital punishment in a few specific and limited cases. Similarly, for His own purposes, God occasionally commands His followers to wage war.[5] It must be noted, however, that these biblical mandates are very narrowly proscribed for very specific situations and, thus, cannot be applied to sport nor can they be used to justify intentional violence within sport.

A proper interpretation of the Bible reveals overarching biblical truths that are supported throughout the Bible called *a prioris*. For example, honesty is a biblical *a priori*. However, there are a couple of very specific times in which dishonesty is temporarily allowed. The specific mandate of honesty is not done away with, only superseded by another biblical *a priori* for a specific time and place. For example, Rahab was honored by God for protecting the lives of Joshua and the other spies, even though she had to lie to protect them. This principle of one law temporarily superseding another can best be illustrated by natural revelation.

The natural law of gravity is always in effect. However, for short periods of time it is superseded by the law of aerodynamics. Normally everything is pulled to earth via gravity, but airplanes, via aerodynamics, can temporarily "rise above" the normal law of gravity. Any pilot who enjoys the temporariness of aerodynamics and seeks to make it permanent denies the law of gravity to his own (and to all others on the plane) peril. A good pilot knows how and when to supersede the law of gravity but also knows to keep an eye on the "gas tank."

---

[4] The last six of the Ten Commandments all mandate love toward others and prohibit evil and violence to the person and his/her possessions. The "Sermon on the Mount" is also full of admonitions to love and not hate as are many of the New Testament teachings of Christ, Paul, Peter, and others.

[5] I realize there is some debate about both of these issues. A few Christian theological communities are total pacifists (any act of violence or restraint is condemned). Some decry war only and support capital punishment, while others believe war is biblical but not capital punishment. These intramural debates among Christians have little bearing on the discussion of sport and violence because anyone holding a total or partial pacifistic view will agree with the thesis proposed here because it claims any act of intentional violence within sport is antithetical to biblical theology.

So, a proper clarification of the theological question—can MMA and prizefighting be biblically justified on the basis of God-proscribed military actions and/or capital punishment—becomes clear. The overall biblical *a priori* is to love and not intentionally hurt, maim, wound, or kill any other human being. The specific mandates of war and capital punishment are limited to very proscripted times and purposes. They are not overarching biblical *a prioris* but rather temporary, specifically proscribed mandates designed to rule specific situations and times.

3. A Technical Logical Fallacy The logical fallacy of this inquiry is technically categorized as the overall fallacy of *ambiguity* with a specific subsection of ambiguity termed *division*. The fallacy of division makes a general proposition false by stating the whole is to be considered the same as a part. In this case, it is fallacious logic to state because the Bible condones one specific act of violence it thus condones every act of violence.

Applying the Template for Biblically Defensible Sport

The "Template of Biblically Defensible Sport" (see Graph 16 on page I-7) has been developed as an aid and guide for all athletes and coaches who desire to be biblically based and Christ honoring in all their sporting pursuits. In order for a specific sport to be biblically defensible, it must meet each level of the template.

Most sports that fail to meet the criteria do so at the very first level: *redemptive purpose*. This is true for sports such as prizefighting and MMA. One is hard pressed to claim MMA has a redemptive purpose when the ultimate goal is to physically disable and harm your opponent. At least prizefighting could muster one possible redemptive purpose: earning a living through winning the "prize" money awarded from being victorious in the arena. Even this stretches credulity to the breaking point. Prostitution and drug dealing could also be justified by this same logic. So unless the rules of engagement within prizefighting and MMA can be changed, they do not get past the first step on the biblically based template.

In addition, any sport that has the intentional harming of an opponent as its goal and intended purpose fails to meet standards set in the "Honor Code for Participating in Biblically Based Sport" (see Graph 17 on page I-7). To honor the "Temple of the Holy Spirit" is a key component of this honor code, so obviously, any sport that intentionally harms or maims a human body is problematic and does not meet the honor code criteria.

The key word for this discussion is *intentionality*. Intentional violence is what differentiates prizefighting from rugby, American football, lacrosse, or many other sports. Most sports have the potential for unintentionally harming a human body. This raises the possibility for boxing or MMA to be adapted in ways that could meet the standards of both the "Biblically Defensible Sport Template" and the "Honor Code for Participating in Biblically Defensible Sport Template."[6]

For example, there is a clear difference between Olympic-style boxing and prizefighting. The purpose of Olympic boxing is not to pummel an opponent into unconsciousness but rather to score points by landing certain punches on an opponent's torso. Notice how the Olympic rules of not punching above the neck or below the waist are designed to protect the human body (temple of the Holy Spirit). Thus, Olympic-style boxing could be considered biblically defensible. Could MMA's goals be changed? Could its rules be adapted to come into compliance with the Honor Code? If so, then it too could be considered as legitimately meeting the criteria for biblically based sport.

4. Summary   Ultimate fighting sports have been clearly *defined* as athletic contests that intentionally inflict bodily harm to an opponent. It has also been *clarified* that specifically proscribed violent activities such as capital punishment and war have been mandated, but limited by, God for specific purposes and cannot be used to justify wanton or intentional violence within or outside of sport. Specific mandates are not overarching biblical *a prioris* and thus only apply to the specific time and situations they are referenced to.

In addition, the "Biblically Defensible Sport Template" and "Honor Code for Participating in Biblically Defensible Sport Template" both condemn any sport that has intentionally harming an opponent as its ultimate

---

[6] Graphs 12 and 17 on pages I-5 and I-7 are differentiated by the following: The *Template for Biblically Defensible Sport* is designed to determine which sports are biblically defensible. The *Honor Code for Determining and Participating in Biblically Defensible Sports* is designed to guide sports participants in both determining which sports to participate in and then how to participate within those specific sports. Both have been created to help Christian competitors know if, when, and how to compete in biblical, Christ-honoring ways.

goal and purpose. Such sports must not be conducted or participated in. These two sets of guidelines do, however, suggest ways in which such pursuits could be changed and adapted that would make them biblically defensible and Christ honoring.

Question 3: What should I do when I encounter a sporting situation in which two biblical mandates seemingly conflict? How do I choose which one to operate on?

Key Bible Verse: "whatever does not proceed from faith is sin" (Romans 14:23).

The Dilemma

Almost every moral dilemma in sports occurs when two or more ethical standards collide. This question can be better understood when a real-life scenario is examined. For example, should a pitcher obey his baseball manager when he instructs him to intentionally "bean" an opposing batter with a pitched ball?[7] This dilemma pits one biblical principle (to honor and obey our authorities) against other biblical principles that (a) prohibit violence and (b) mandate the care and protection of the human body.

Determining the Answer

Dilemmas such as this can be addressed by establishing one of, or all of, the following hermeneutical principles:

- Identifying biblical *a prioris*
- Identifying specific biblically based *rules*
- Identifying general biblically based *principles*
- Identifying biblical passages that offer "*general wisdom*" on the issue

---

[7] The word *beaning* is a term used in the sport of baseball to describe the act of a pitcher hitting an opposing batter in the head with a thrown ball. This is especially disturbing because many thrown baseballs reach speeds of 100 miles per hour!

A. Identifying Biblical *a Prioris*

The biblical *a prioris* are summarized in Graphs 16 and 17 on page I-7 and assume the biblical priorities of loving one's co-competitors and honoring one's authorities. Both of these are strong biblical rules based upon the Ten Commandments of the Pentateuch, the Great Commandments given by Jesus, and many other verses. One would be hard-pressed to determine which of these should supersede the other. Thus, a second level or even a third level of biblical interpretation is needed that include specific biblical rules and/or overarching biblical principles.

B. Biblical Rules

There are no biblical rules that specifically address this unique situation. How could there be? Baseball was not created until thousands of years later, and as much as many baseball players would like to have a specific biblical commandment that would tell them whether or not it is biblical and Christ honoring to intentionally hit a batter with a pitched ball, there is no such directive.

C. Biblical Principles

Biblical principles can be derived from biblical commandments that address other specific moral dilemmas. For example, the disciples faced a similar dilemma. They were under the authority of the Sanhedrin (the ruling body of first-century Judaism). The Sanhedrin very clearly demanded the disciples to refrain from doing anything to "preach the Gospel" or spread the message of Jesus (Acts 4:1–22). Rather, they chose to disobey their authority on the basis of the Old Testament principle that relieved a person from obeying an authority who demanded an immoral action. This kind of action was also observed in the New Testament era, when the three Magi refused to honor King Herod's command to report where Jesus was born.

Remember the earlier stated illustration from natural revelation concerning a plane, a pilot, and the law of aerodynamics temporarily superseding the law of gravity? That illustration can be applied here to help clarify what a baseball pitcher should do. He should recognize the biblical principle that to honor and obey earthly authority is to be temporarily disregarded whenever those in leadership demand unbiblical actions or endeavors. Pitchers should follow the biblical principles as summarized in Graphs 16 and 17 on page I-7. Specifically this means to honor one's co-competitor, honor "the temple of the Holy Spirit," and be governed by the "Biblically Based Rules" that prohibit the intentional "beaning" of an opposing player.

Question 4: Can my sporting activity really be considered worship?

Key Bible Verse: "by the mercies of God . . . present your bodies as a living sacrifice, holy and acceptable to God, which is your spiritual worship" (Romans 12:2).

The story of Cain and Abel (the first two sons of Adam and Eve) provides some insights. Cain was "a worker of the ground." Abel was "a keeper of sheep." Both "brought to the Lord an offering." "And the Lord had regard for Abel and his offering, but for Cain and his offering He had no regard" (Genesis 4:1–5).

Some interpret these verses in such a way as to communicate God only accepts a certain kind of offering: a blood sacrifice, but this cannot be verified by other verses. Many times the Scriptures direct the Israelites to offer grain offerings, sheaf offerings, and wine offerings (Leviticus 23:9–22). Certainly the burnt offerings of animals are a most acceptable offering, perhaps even a preferred offering, but it cannot be concluded God rejected Cain on the basis of what he brought as an offering. Rather God's acceptance of Abel had to do with his faith as is verified in Hebrews (Hebrews 11:4). Other passages indicate Cain's deeds were evil even before he killed his brother (1 John 3:12; Jude 11). Therefore, it becomes obvious Abel's offering was accepted because of his faith, not because of what he sacrificed. Moreover, Cain's offering was rejected on the basis of Cain's heart, not on what he brought to worship God.

These two men offered God their "produce" (what they "produced"). They were working men, not priests. They brought what they had—the fruit of their labors—and offered it up to God as a sacrifice. God accepted one and rejected the other. This suggests each person is to bring to God a sacrificial offering that represents their unique skills and labors, but . . . always with a pure heart in faith.

The lesson for athletes has to do with presenting their unique gifts, skills, and sporting opportunities as offerings to God. The key is whether or not they offer their athletic endeavors and results to God out of a pure heart of faith. If their heart is hard toward God, their athletic offerings will be rejected as was Cain's. If their goal is to seek self-glorification and honor, their offerings are not done in faith with a pure heart. Moreover, a pure heart of faith is more than what is being offered. For the pure heart of faith, the action of making an offering to God is sacramental! A sacrament is an outward sign of an inward reality; in this case it represents love and honor for God. Any athlete who "goes through the motions" of attending a pre-game "chapel," saying a pre-race prayer, or making the sign of the cross prior to swinging a bat or bowling a ball will have these religious actions rejected by God. A true sacrament is a visual expression of heartfelt worship, which will be received by God.

Paul explains this in more detail in the letter he wrote for God to the Romans of the first century. "I appeal to you brothers, by the mercies of God, to present your bodies as a living sacrifice, holy and acceptable to God, which is your reasonable worship" (Romans 12:1).

The word which is translated *worship* in this verse comes from the Greek word from which the English word *liturgy* is derived. Liturgy really means worship and, thus, Paul is encouraging the Romans (and by extension: us) to worship God through their bodies as living sacrifices. This is a true fulfillment of the Old Testament's admonishment to make sacrifices to God. Furthermore, humankind cannot worship God except through their bodies! Singing, praises, the lifting up of hands, dancing in the spirit, etc., are all bodily expressions of praise. Once again, it is impossible to worship God without one's body. Athletes may understand this as well as, or better, than anyone. Worship is a bodily experience.

Music—A Helpful Comparison

I find it amazing that musicians are never subjected to questions about whether or not they can worship God through various musical expressions. Musical pursuits such as singing, playing an instrument, conducting an orchestra, arranging musical scores, and other musical endeavors are accepted as appropriate ways to worship God, and so should they be! Yet why are gifts of music accepted and athletic gifts are not? Is musical giftedness more blessed by God than athletic giftedness (a blood sacrifice over a grain offering)? Certainly not! Cannot actors and playwrights worship God through the dramatic arts? Cannot scientists worship God through research that leads to curing catastrophic diseases? Cannot doctors worship God through healing; teachers through educating; and lawyers and judges through ensuring justice? Are all of these vocations; are all of these gifts and abilities not honorable? Surely these vocations are all ordained by God and these gifts and abilities are honorable. Likewise, athletic giftedness is equally honorable.

Summary of Sport and Worship

So yes, athletes can indeed worship God through athletic activities as long as (a) their hearts are pure; (b) their motives are to honor and worship the Lord of the universe, not the lord of sport; and (c) they compete in ways and times proscribed within the Christmanship ethic. Not to do so would be to "hold God in contempt"!

Question 5: Would Jesus intentionally commit a personal foul in the game of basketball?

Key Bible Verse: "whatever you do, do all for the honor and glory of the Lord" (1 Corinthians 10:31; compare with: Colossians 3:17, 23).

The answer to this frequently asked question is aided by consulting: (a) the "Template for Determining Biblically Defensible Sport" (items B, C, D, and E) and (b) the "Honor Code for Determining Biblically Defensible Sport" (Item 3)—Graphs 16 and 17 on page I-7. It also introduces one aspect of competition that has not yet been addressed: strategy.

Strategy and the Bible

Nowhere does Scripture condemn strategy or strategic plans and actions. Therefore, an intentional foul that strategically enhances a player's performance and/or a team's chances for success cannot be condemned simply because it is strategic. More importantly, many Scriptures indicate appropriate strategy is to be praised.

Adherence to the Honor Code of Biblically Defensible Athletic Actions

There is a marked difference between an intentional foul that minimizes a co-competitors advantage and a violent act that masquerades as a strategic game plan. What would make an intentional foul problematic for a Christian would be either a wrongful motivation or action that does not adhere to specific aspects of either of the two templates mentioned earlier. For example, the intentional foul must be condemned if in committing an intentional foul a player had to cheat, maim, or intimidate a co-competitor. Cheating (breaking the rules) violates letter "B" of the "Template for Determining Biblically Defensible Sport" governing rules (Graph 12 on page I-5). Maiming violates letter "B" of the "Template for Determining Biblically Defensible Sport" and also runs contrary to the third item of the "Honor Code for Determining Biblically Based Sport" as both seek to honor the "temple of the Holy Spirit" (Graph 17 on page I-7). And finally, intimidating violates letter "E" of the "Template for Determining Biblically Defensible Sport" because it does not treat co-competitors in Christ-like ways (Graph 12 on page I-5).

Summary

So, the answer to the question of Jesus intentionally fouling another player is both yes and no. Yes, if the foul would strategically aid Christ's own performance or increase His team's chances for success; no, if the intentional foul would not (a) honor the redemptive goals of the game; (b) adhere to the rules of the game; or (c) causes intentional physical, psychological, or emotional harm to another player.

Clarifying questions that a Christian athlete or coach should ask are "Would this action honor Christ?" and "Would I commit this foul on Christ?" If the answer to either question is no, then it should be clear any such action would not be within the Christmanship ethic.

Question 6: Since I committed to being a faithful member of my team, should I participate in a team game, practice, activity, or meeting if it conflicts with a spiritual commitment such as personal devotions, a church service, or Bible study?

Key Bible Verse: "For where your treasure is, there your heart will be also" (Matthew 6:21; compare with: Luke 12:34).

This FAQ is really a question of determining where the heart of the questioner is. Is the inquiring player or coach looking for an "excuse" to avoid attending a worship service or Bible study, or are they sincerely seeking God's direction and blessing? Has the inquiring competitor already determined sport to be his or her priority, or are they sincerely open to God's setting their priorities?

The vital importance of this question cannot be overstated. This is the most important question ever asked by athletes, because how one answers this will greatly determine the vitality and future of the questioner's faith. Simply put, those desiring a rationalization for opting out of spiritual disciplines and endeavors so they can participate in sporting activity are well on the way to the eventual *accommodation* or even *capitulation* of their faith (see Chapter 5). The answer to this question is a clear indication of a sporting person's priorities and commitments. It communicates whether or not Jesus Christ is the Lord of the athletic person's life.

I don't want to be misunderstood. I fully believe in being committed to one's team, and this entire book is an attempt to provide athletes with a strong apologetic for sport and faith integration. I hope what I've written will not only encourage Christians to participate in sport but also provide them with insights to ensure truly Christ-honoring sporting activity. So, what follows should not be perceived at any level to be a discouragement for Christian involvement in sport. Rather, it is provided to encourage and empower biblically based and Christ-honoring sporting endeavors. To that end, each Christian athlete and coach must answer one foundational question: Is Christ the Lord of you and your sport, or is sport the lord of your life? Your answer has eternal significance for you and all whom you might influence. First, however, a few thoughts about influence and impact will help clarify the issue.

God Determines Our Impact and Influence

The prevailing wisdom among most sports ministries in the early twenty-first century has been to encourage Christian athletes to strive for the highest level of sporting success possible because the higher the level of athletic success an athlete attains, the higher and wider his "platform" will be. An enhanced platform enables a wider influence and a deeper impact for the gospel. This kind of counsel from well-meaning sport ministry advisors, at times, even goes so far as to recommend athletes sacrifice participation in spiritual activities (church and Bible study attendance, etc.) if it would enable a "higher sports-related platform for the gospel." My response is simply this: "Only God can truly determine our impact and influence. Our role is simply to be faithful!"

For example, Eric Liddell has not competed in a sanctioned athletic competition since 1925 and yet his gospel influence and impact continue to grow and expand! It may seem to be counterintuitive, but his "gospel platform" is stronger than ever because he chose not to run—not to seek a higher platform. Instead, during the 1924 Paris Olympics, Liddell chose to be faithful to honor the Lord's Day, including being willing to sacrifice the opportunity to be a five-time medalist! His faithfulness included attending a Lord's Day church service while one of the heats he qualified for was run.[8] He did what is unthinkable in today's sports ministry world. He willingly chose the spiritual over the athletic and in so doing trusted God rather than human wisdom to determine what his platform would be.

Sadly, it seems athletes of other faith traditions have been more willing to take stands for their faith than Christians. Jewish athletes such as Sandy Koufax and Mormons such as Eli Herring made national headlines when they choose to follow their religious convictions over their sport. Koufax refused to pitch on Jewish holy days, and Herring refused the

---

[8] At the 1924 Paris Olympics, Liddell won a gold medal in the 400 and a bronze in the 200 but relinquished the opportunity to win medals in the 100, 4 by 100, and 4 by 400 because the finals and/or heats all fell on the Lord's Day. The reality of winning three additional medals and the importance of his presence to the British track team was seen at a meet held a week after the Paris Olympics, when the four-man British relay teams beat the Americans (winners at Paris) with Liddell anchoring.

offer to sign a contract worth millions of dollars because the NFL plays its games on "the Sabbath."[9]

I also recognize there are many Christians who, because they don't have a national profile, will never be known to the general public, but have had an incredible impact on their local school and community. One such champion was a female high school basketball player who took the courageous stand to not play in a championship game because it was scheduled on a Sunday. Her decision to honor Christ over her sport provided her a brief national platform, but more importantly, she had a significant impact on her high school coach and local community. She sought faithfulness and left her platform up to God. Again I repeat: The Christian athlete or coach cannot determine their influence or impact, only their faithfulness. So the question remains for all Christian sports people: Is Christ the Lord of you and your sport, or is sport the lord of your life?

Dangerous Waters

Beyond platform and impact issues, a major consideration is the detrimental impact a long-term absence from attending church will have on the spiritual health of athletes. The command to "forsake our gathering together" (Hebrews 10:25) is not just to boost church attendance but, more importantly, is for the benefit of the individual church member. A core cause for the faltering faith of elite athletes is the lack of regular and consistent church fellowship. Failure to stay connected to corporate and personal Christ-honoring worship, Bible study, Christian fellowship, and accountability inevitably leads to spiritual anemia.

The journey away from faith usually starts innocently enough. Sporting priorities are intended to be short term in endurance but soon overshadow and preclude spiritual commitments. Missing one Bible study or worship service won't, in and of itself, cause a falling away from faith,

---

[9] My intent in placing Mormons outside the Christian faith is not meant to be offensive to Mormon beliefs and traditions. In fact, I fully support and appreciate many Mormon tenets, especially their strong convictions about the Sabbath. I also have enjoyed a deep, multi-decade friendship with a person who was a sincere Mormon (who subsequently came to faith in Jesus and converted to Christianity), but Mormon and Christian theologies are quite different and, thus, I reference them as people of a different faith tradition here.

but extended periods of neglecting one's spiritual disciplines has consequences. At best, athletes enter into a period of spiritual stagnancy. At
worst, they experience a complete *capitulation* of one's faith. Once more,
I ask the question: Is Christ the Lord of you and your sport, or is sport
the lord of your life? No one would knowingly swim in shark-infested
waters, yet many Christians choose to enter into very dangerous spiritual
waters when they "forsake gathering together" with the Christian family.

The Bottom Line

Christian athletes would be wise to seriously count the cost before making any commitments to a team or athletic endeavor. To pursue athletic
excellence is a high, Godly calling: one that can be honoring and pleasing
to God; one that can be utilized to enhance and expand the kingdom of
God. However, even a high, Godly calling can become a "false idol" and
lead to spiritual death.

Participation on sports teams that consistently and regularly conflict with church participation is almost never in the best interest of
anyone. Any athletic endeavor that prevents and precludes personal
spiritual disciplines such as personal worship, Bible study, prayer, and
contemplative Christ-centered meditation is a recipe for spiritual disas-
ter. Athletes and coaches facing these choices should evaluate them in
light of Matthew 16:6:

> "For what will it profit a man if he gains the whole world and for-
> feits his own soul? Or what shall a man give in return for his soul?"

What is your priority? What is your God? What is your soul worth: a college
scholarship? a pro career? Another biblical passage is worth considering:

> "Do not be deceived; God is not mocked, for whatever one sows,
> that will he also reap. For the one who sows to his own flesh will
> reap from the flesh corruption, but the one who sows to the
> Spirit will from the Spirit reap eternal life." (Galatians 6:7, 8)

So, the bottom line is although a Christian athlete will earn and maintain the respect of her non-Christian teammates when she chooses to

miss an occasional personal spiritual activity, such as individual or group Bible study, to maintain a commitment to one's team, her faith will be completely compromised and dismissed as irrelevant if she consistently and regularly skips spiritual pursuits in favor of sports. In addition, it is almost never acceptable to miss a corporate church service or misuse the Lord's Day.[10]

Afterthought 1

Perhaps the most ironic part of this discussion has to do with the unintended consequences of seeking a higher sports platform. Not only do most athletes who make sport their priority run the risk of failing in their personal walk with Christ, but more profound is that the very act they hope will provide them with opportunities to share their faith actually renders their words null and void. Their actions communicate the exact opposite of what they verbally espouse. Choosing to play in a game or participate in athletic training rather than attend a church service communicates church participation is a lower priority than sport! What we say doesn't really matter if our lives don't verify and affirm our words. And so the very reason we want to achieve athletic success—to establish and enhance a platform to speak about Christ—is nullified. By compromising our faith pursuits we will lose credibility with our non-Christian teammates, and our words are drowned out by our actions.

So, Christian athletes and coaches should consistently, regularly, and with great exuberance choose spiritual commitments over sporting commitments; choose church attendance over sporting activity. Then and only then will they have anything to say.

Afterthought 2

Most of the frequently asked questions emanate from interactions with other athletes and coaches. For the most part, the answers to these questions emerge from the latter part of the Ten Commandments

---

[10] Chapter 7 outlines the biblical perspective on the Lord's Day and its relevance for sports people. It is must reading for all athletes and coaches who are serious about competing in Christ-honoring ways.

(Commandments 5–10). FAQ 7: "Can I participate in sporting activities when they conflict with spiritual activities" is addressed by the commandments addressing humankind's interactions with God (Commandments 1–4). The essence of the first four commandments addresses the sin of idolatry. Idolatry is condemned because it honors something other than, and above, God. The connection is obvious. Is God or sport the Lord of your life?

ATHLETICS IN THE FIRST CENTURY

The New Testament is replete with athletic words, analogies, concepts, and descriptions. Under the guidance of the Holy Spirit, some of the New Testament writers even used technical athletic terms, which when understood in the athletic context provide additional spiritual enlightenment and truth. It is for these special enlightenments and insights into the biblical texts this is written. It is believed when one knows the social, chronological, historical, and cultural backgrounds of first-century athletics, one will be better able to accurately interpret the biblical passages of the first century that are athletic in nature. In addition, it is hoped this review of first-century athletics and Christianity will pique the interest of those currently interested in sports (but not necessarily in Christ) and eventually lead them into a personal relationship with Him. Thus, what follows is a brief look into the history of ancient athletics and the sporting context in which the New Testament was written. A particular emphasis will be placed on Paul and his interactions with the sports world of his day.

I. HISTORY OF ATHLETICS LEADING UP TO THE FIRST CENTURY AD

A. Greece

Although it is true that Egypt and other societies had some forays into athletics, play, and games, Greece is unsurpassed in historic athletics. Greek athletic culture continues to shape modern-day sport, including many specific traditions or concepts that include the following:

- Sports academies
- Trainers and coaches
- Sports facilities that are still built upon the same principles and shapes as in ancient Greece
- The Olympic Games themselves

Greek games and competitions began mainly as military endeavors, but eventually evolved into an overall training for Greek citizens. The exercises and practices were called "gymnastics," while the competitions that developed were termed "athletics." The gymnastics became part of a comprehensive educational system that included mental, physical, and spiritual training. The Greeks believed the most virtuous man was one who was well rounded and complete in every way. Their term *kalokagathia* described the highest ideal of "the beauty of goodness and the goodness of beauty." The goal of the ancient academies was to produce men of virtue, strength, and character.

Athletic training began as early as age 7 and lasted for most boys until at least 14 years of age. For many the training would continue until age 18, and some underwent special, extended training as part of the group called the *epheboi*. These additional two years of strenuous training was often in preparation for the military. For most men, the training of the academy did not end with school, however. They often continued to exercise well into middle age and even later. Aristotle even records an insightful interlude of his mentor Plato, wrestling with one of Plato's students.[1] The athletes trained to music. The music was to prevent them

---

[1] H. A. Harris, *Greek Athletes of the Ancient World* (London: Oxford University Press, 1930), p. 117.

from becoming too brutal, and the athletics kept the young men from becoming too effeminate.

The Greeks were extremely competitive, infatuated with the human body, and committed to overall excellence and virtue of the human soul. This part of their culture as much as anything was what clashed with the Roman and Jewish cultures that they encountered.

B. Rome

E. N. Gardiner succinctly states "the Romans of the Republic despised athletics."[2] Though they may have despised athletics, they still thoroughly enjoyed strenuous exercise, including pursuits such as hunting, riding, and swimming. This disdain of Greek athletics originated from at least six causal factors.

1. The typical Roman predilection toward practicality and pragmatism drove them away from what they considered to be frivolous enterprises such as athletics. The Romans had developed a rather grisly and grim view of life, which grew out of their experiences of war. Exercise could be a means to better health or strength, but it was certainly not to be an end in itself. To spend all of one's effort training to be an athlete was deemed a waste of time.

2. A second reason Romans could not entirely value exercise and athletics was because it would be unthinkable to a high-born Roman to submit to the demands of a trainer, who often was a man of no important family or position.

3. As if the pragmatic passions of the Romans would not have been enough to preclude any leanings toward full-time athletics, the third fact that made Greek athletics unpalatable to the Roman was the Greeks performed their exercises sans clothes. To be publicly naked was to ensure the complete disdain of the Roman world. To appear naked in public was probably the most revolting aspect of Greek athletics to any sensible Roman.

4. In addition to these issues, the fourth causal factor had to do with the fact that Rome had no political rivals and thus had no one to compete with. Each Greek city was a rival of all the other Greek cities,

---

[2] E. N. Gardiner, *Athletics of the Ancient World* (London: Oxford University Press, 1930), p. 117.

and athletic competitions played a vital role in the balance of power. Conversely, Rome simply crushed its victims by brute, military force and thus had no need of any other way of competing. This may also have led to the fifth reason why Rome never fully appreciated Greek athletics.

5. Rome had been so brutalized by the ravages of war that its sensitivities had been dulled, and thus it was much more intrigued by the gore of gladiatorial battles than the finesse of athletics. They had a certain blood-thirst, which the seemingly tame Grecian games could not satisfy. They wanted entertainment, not athleticism.

6. Moreover, the last reason the pragmatic Romans held Grecian athletics in contempt was because for all of the attention the Greeks gave to athletics, none of it had helped Greece to withstand the power of Rome. As Gardiner points out, even the Roman word *ludi* represented their view that the games were nothing more than entertainment.[3]

C. Jerusalem and the Hebrew Culture

It has been postulated that Jews of the first century did not participate in the athletics of the day, and there are some very worthy arguments favoring this perspective. Before anything so conclusive can be decided upon, a quick overview of Jewish community in the first century is needed.

First-century Jews were split into two major groups of people: those of the *diaspora* and those living in or near Jerusalem. The most obvious difference would be those living throughout the Roman Empire were much more likely to be influenced by the Roman and Hellenistic cultures. Some specifics of this become increasingly clear throughout this discussion, but in general, the Jew of the dispersion was more likely to have participated in the Greek and Roman athletic activities than would have the Jews of Judea. At the very least the *diaspora* Jew would have had much more exposure to Greco-Roman sports culture and thus would have more likely succumbed to its influences.

Generally speaking the Jewish culture held a very dim view of the sports world based on four major reasons. The first was based on a religious and theological foundation that argued Greek

---

[3] Ibid., p. 119.

athletics were in violation of many of the Jewish tenets of faith, which included:

- Athletic festivals being dedicated to pagan gods
- Athletes making sacrifices, taking vows, giving offerings, and praying to pagan gods
- Statues honoring victorious athletes (which violated their beliefs concerning idolatry)
- Promotion of self-glorification of the athlete rather than seeking to glorify God
- Deification of athletes and emperors
- Proliferation of unashamed nakedness
- Pagan festivals, rituals, and parades included as an integral part of the games

In addition, to these theological concerns was added the basic pragmatic issue of simple survival. For most Jews just eking out an existence was a constant struggle; therefore, few if any had opportunity to take part in anything so "frivolous" as athletics. One cannot make too much of the survival issue, however, because although it was a deterrent to many Jews of the first century, even the more wealthy Jews would still not have taken part in athletics on the basis of their relative unimportance. Thus, the third area in which the Jews collided with the Greek philosophy was their view toward things eternal, rather than temporal, and in addition, they wished to pursue issues of weightier consequence.

An even greater survival issue—particularly for those Christian Hebrews of the first century—was their forced participation as the victims in the usually fatal activities of the Coliseum and other gladiatorial-based spectacles.

It is because of these four major issues, among others, that many historians and theologians have reasoned it all but impossible for first-century Jews to be involved in athletics. Though the significance of these objections cannot be totally dismissed and must have certainly curtailed Jewish involvements in sports, there are a few equally significant factors of another perspective that demand evaluation before a definitive decision can be made.

1. Evidence Indicating Some Jewish Involvement in Sport There is much to suggest there were Jews who were involved in athletics and even participated as athletes. Four of these reasons include the following:

a. H. A. Harris cites historical and archaeological data that demonstrate Jewish association with athletics. Two of these include athletic pictures in the Jewish catacombs at Rome and a letter from the emperor Claudius to Alexandrian Jews concerning their participation in athletics.[4] These historical evidences, along with other references, would suggest Jewish involvement in athletics—at least by those living in a Hellenized setting.

b. Second, it is naive to believe Jews who lived a great distance from Jerusalem would not have been tremendously affected by a long-term exposure to Hellenic culture.

c. Third, any enlightened mind would be able to see through the obvious theological shortcomings of condemning sports and athletics as a whole. There is nothing intrinsically evil with athletics any more than there is anything intrinsically evil with sex, automobiles, or alcohol. Each of these is without morality in and of themselves and is described as amoral. Therefore, any wise Jew could make a case for participation in athletics as at the worst amoral. Moreover, it was likely many would have observed the many positives stemming from the high ideals of Greek athletics and consequently been involved in them.

d. Of deeper saliency, however, are the life and writings of Paul himself. It is apparent even to the casual reader of the Pauline Corpus that Paul was well acquainted with the athletics of his day. His insightful perspectives; his coherent and profound usages of technical athletic terms, coupled with his ingenious ability to use these sporting motifs to communicate deep spiritual truths, all give credence to acknowledge it is all but certain Paul personally participated in, and/or was an observer of, the athletics of his day. Paul did not just know about athletics. He exhibits an intimate, firsthand knowledge. I am in full agreement with H. A. Harris

---

[4] H. A. Harris, *Greek Athletes and Athletics* (Indiana: Indiana University Press, 1967), p. 133.

when he observes that "St. Paul knew his athletics, while Epictetus did not."[5] One cannot read the words of Paul without recognizing his insightful comprehensions, which could only come from a firsthand experience. The significance of this is fully realized upon the recognition there was none more dedicated to Judaism than Paul as is recorded in the Acts of the Apostles.

II. DESCRIPTION OF FIRST-CENTURY ATHLETICS
A. General Trends

One of the best pictures of the athletic festivals of the first century AD comes from Dio Chrysostom when he writes his description of the activities that surrounded the Isthmian Games:

> Then round the temple of Poseidon you could see and hear the accursed sophists shouting and abusing one another, and their so-called pupils fighting with each other, many authors giving readings of their works, which no one listens to, many poets reciting their poems and others expressing approval of them, many conjurors performing their tricks, and many fortune-tellers interpreting omens, thousands of lawyers arguing cases, a host of cheap-jacks selling everything under the sun.[6]

This description accurately details why Paul would have taken Timothy to the Isthmian Games during the years they were involved in ministry at nearby Corinth. He recognized the opportunity to interact with people from all over the world who either attended or participated in the Isthmian Games. Athletes, the wealthy, and even emperors often attended. It is intriguing to entertain the possibility that Paul may even have witnessed his future tormentor when he watched Nero's pathetic attempt at being a victorious athlete the year Nero made a mockery of the Isthmian Games. At the very least Dio Chrysostom provides a wonderful insight into an athletic realm during the days of the Apostles.

---

[5] Ibid., p. 131.
[6] Ibid., p. 139.

What Paul, Timothy, and possibly even Peter, among other first-century Christians, observed at the Isthmian Games was only a remnant of the former glory of Greek athletics. For most sports historians, the golden age took place in ancient Greece from approximately the eighth through the third century BC. This time was marked by its commitment to the development of the entire person of the amateur athlete. The desire was to produce well-rounded individuals full of virtue. Gradually this ideal fell into disfavor, however, and athletic training was eventually removed from the academy setting and into a separate sports-only setting. As the athletic aspects of the training became the sole focus, the overall integrity of the athletic world was greatly damaged and eventually was fraught with a pervasive corruption and decadence.

This movement away from the Classical Greek ideals began in the second century BC and was best symbolized by the destruction of Corinth in 146 BC. When Corinth ceased to exist, the Isthmian Games were all but destroyed. This blow, to one of the four most prestigious athletic festivals, was representative of what was occurring generally to the ancient ideals of Grecian life and sport. It was followed by the unthinkable as even the famed Olympic Games were moved to Rome for one Olympiad in 80 BC. In addition, the international significance of the crown games was lost, as evidenced by the list of Olympic winners during this time, which bore only the names of local athletes. The reduction of the prominence and importance of Greek athletics lasted for at least 100 years, and the previous greatness was not again approached until much later in the first century AD.

Although there was much degradation from the ideals of the Ancient Greeks in the everyday life of the gymnasiums, there remained an underlying desire and appreciation for the old ways. An especially insightful account by Lucian (AD 125–180) indeed demonstrates how Greeks of the later Roman Empire still held on to the ideals of former centuries. In his delightful dialogue between Solon and Anacharsis, Lucian champions all of the best of the early Greek athletes, academies, and festivals, but even though many were desirous of the past, this time continued to be one in which corruption increased and amateurism decreased as professionalism became the norm. Professional athletics in itself removed the higher ideals of cooperative competition and replaced them with the one ideal of being victorious. Only by winning could athletes ensure their professional status and thus their livelihood. Athletes were well cared for by both the grants bestowed upon them by their home cities (which could include lifelong stipends and freedom from any civic taxes or liabilities) and by the gifts awarded to them at the festival in which they were victorious. By most accounts the moral underpinnings of athletics had reached an all-time low. Into this setting Imperial Rome emerged as a catalyst toward a revival of sorts for a floundering institution.

B. Roman Influences

The Caesars took a significant interest in Grecian-styled games. The Romans realized the political significance the athletic realm could have in stabilizing a conquered province. In addition, by providing entertainment and involvement for local citizens, athletics helped to maintain peace as well as garner support for a foreign ruler. Roman support for Greek athletics began with Julius Caesar, expanded under Augustus, and possibly reached its zenith under Trajan and Hadrian.

Augustus established the Augustan games in AD 2 at Naples and in addition the Actian Games held at Actium every 4 years. In the summary of his lifetime achievements, Augustus included the fact he provided three athletic festivals—two in his own name and a third in the name of his grandson. These games were titled "the Italica–Romaia–Sebasta–Isolympia Games."[7] The term *Isolympia* originally defined youth participation in the Greek festivals, but under the Romans took on a new distinction of any festival so deemed to be under the same rules and way of management as the Olympic festival. In essence they became a rival to the Olympics and other Olympic-styled festivals. These Isolympic festivals were to be found throughout the Empire in cities such as Athens, Ephesus, and even Rome. At first the right to bestow such status and prestige upon a festival was exclusively left up to the officials of the Olympic and Delphic games, but later this authority was usurped by the Emperors.

---

[7] Rachel Sargent Robinson, *Sources for the History of Greek Athletics* (Cincinnati: Published by the author, 1955), p. 162.

Another festival initiated during this time period (AD 44) would be of interest to New Testament historians and theologians because it was founded by Antiochus Epiphanes at the city of Antioch. It was this festival and its games that were often referred to by St. Chrysostom.[8]

Another significant influence the Romans brought to Greek athletics was their ability to build new, larger, and better athletic facilities. Most of the major improvements occurred in the second century AD, and many were completed under the Emperor Hadrian, including such things as the gymnasium and library at Athens and the baths in Corinth.[9] Hadrian also instituted a winter festival at Nemea and founded quinquennial festivals in honor of his beloved Antinous at Mantinea and Argos.[10] Other significant buildings of the second century AD came from the munificence of a wealthy Athenian, Herodes Atticus. His contributions included a rebuilt stadia at Delphi and Athens (the latter in marble from Pentelicus); a Roman theater (odeum) in Athens on the south slope of the Acropolis; another odeum in Corinth; a new aqueduct to provide fresh water to Olympia; and a semicircular exedra at Olympia dedicated to Zeus in the name of his wife Regilla, who was a priestess of Demeter. Statues of Herodes, his wife, Hadrian, Antoninus, and others of the imperial family were erected in the exedra as to be a reminder they would be forever spectators of the Olympic Games.[11]

Although these improvements were not accomplished in the first century AD, they are significant from the perspective they would not have been built unless there was a resurgence in athletics. Though at first the Romans may have caused a decline in athletics, under the Empire they were somewhat helpful in reinstating their prominence. With the added interest of the Empire and its Caesars, the Greek festivals not only

---

[8] E. N. Gardiner, *Greek Athletic Sports and Festivals* (London: Macmillan and Company, 1910), p. 170.

[9] Ibid., p. 176.

[10] Ibid., p. 176.

[11] The information concerning Herodes comes from two sources. The first is from the previously cited E. N. Gardiner's *Greek Athletic Sports and Festivals*, p. 178. The second is John McCray, *Archaeology and the New Testament* (Grand Rapids, MI: Baker Book House Company, 1991), pp. 57, 58.

grew in popularity but also in their number. However, all this imperial involvement was certainly a mixed blessing. Though it brought new money, prestige, festivals, and buildings, it also brought a Roman decadence that forever polluted the high Greek ideals and literally robbed Greece of many of its precious treasures as can be acknowledged by the following few examples.

The emperor Caligula (who ruled AD 37–41), wished to remove the 40-foot statue of Zeus to Rome and was only prevented from doing so by the fact that the sheer size and weight of Phidias's magnificent work made it humanly impossible. Nero, however, successfully removed a plethora of smaller statues and other works of athletic art.

Another mark of Roman influence was the athletic guild that spread throughout the Hellenized world, and wherever these associations of athletes went, the mark of professionalism went with them. These guilds were called *Xystoi,* which received their name from the covered colonnades of the gymnasiums called *Xystos.*

Though there were many atrocities that could be leveled at Rome, one of the most despicable was the mockery the Emperor Nero (AD 54–68) made of the games. He went to Greece and personally entered many of the contests and though bested repeatedly by far superior athletes, he was always crowned the winner. Not only did he participate in the athletic contests, but also the contests for musicians and heralds. He desired to win the herald contest to fulfill his own ego needs to be the one to proclaim his own name as winner in the other contests.

One of the events in which he did not participate was the wrestling match. Although he did not wrestle, he was still involved as a wrestling official (*brabeutes*), occasionally pulling back wayward contestants. Nero rewarded each of the controllers of the games (*hellanodicae*) with such things as Roman citizenship and large amounts of money for their forced acquiescence in crowning him victorious.

Nero's arrogance went far beyond his mockery of the games. It included even his unabashed immodesty when he proclaimed at the Isthmian Games that he was the restorer of liberty to Greece. This was a most malicious attempt to reenact the historical event of 196 BC, when Flamininus actually did announce at the Isthmian Games the restoration of Greece's liberty.[12] It continued with his conceited self-aggrandized triumphal return to Rome. At Naples he and his 1,808 crowns were supposedly welcomed back in an unprecedented style (which was repeated at the cities of Antium and Albanum). New, special entrances were created in the cities' walls for the arrival of this "victorious" athlete, who was ushered in on a chariot pulled by white horses. At Rome his vanity swelled even more as was evidenced by his entering on the very chariot in which Augustus had triumphed years earlier. Nero was clothed in purple, wore an Olympic crown, held in his hand a Pythian crown, and was preceded by a procession of courtiers—each who carried a crown Nero had supposedly won. The whole proceeding was a farce of enormous magnitude and symbolized the worst of the Roman involvement in Greek athletics.

C. Grassroots Influences

The many negative influences Roman and professional involvements foisted upon first-century athletics must be kept in balance with the grassroots athletic communities and their involvements. These undertakings of local and amateur athletes must not be completely overshadowed by higher profile festivals and persons. The constant media reports on the latest fiasco seemingly dominate the modern sports world, but they simply do not begin to definitively describe the athletic world of the contemporary person. This is verified by the countless millions of amateur athletes who compete and train each day throughout the world. Though these amateurs may have a passing or even insatiable interest in professional sports, and while the entire world pauses every fourth year to witness new athletic feats in the modern rendition of the Olympic festival, the world of the professional or world-class athlete is but a fraction of the overall athletic endeavors known today. It was the same for the person in the first century. While headlines were dominated by the exploits of the professional athlete, the local gymnasium was filled with young boys and occasionally young girls who all received training and coaching toward an athletic goal.

---

[12] Gardiner, p. 218.

Galen (born in Pergamum in AD 130) illustrates some of this in his instructions written in the second century. He states the health benefits associated with ball-playing. For the following reasons, he recommends ball-playing for the common person:

- It is cheap.
- It is not time consuming like hunting (perhaps like golf).
- It can be played at varying levels of intensity to fit the needs of various individuals.
- It exercises every part of the body.
- It gives pleasure to the mind and strength to the body.
- It is safer than wrestling.
- It teaches many lessons for life.[13]

Rachel Robinson also verifies this by pointing out there were far too few professional athletes to utilize the many gymnasiums and far too many local festivals for the few professional athletes to attend. Thus, the first century was a mix of the high-profile festival and athletes with the grassroots involvements of local athletes and their endeavors.

One further insight into this era is needed and is related to the pervasiveness of athletics into the life of the common person. To illustrate this, another perusal of modern life is helpful. For years, in America, schools have required students to take part in physical education classes. In addition, countless millions more are enrolled in extracurricular activities both at their school and also at various other organizations such as the YMCA. First-century children were no different; in fact, there may have even been a higher degree of emphasis placed upon this training for youth—at least for boys. It is thus all but certain the Apostle Paul and other first-century Christians received this training. As Harris states, Paul "may have owed something to boyhood memories of happy days spent in running and wrestling with young pagans in the sunny sports grounds of Tarsus."[14] It is a well-documented fact that athletics were

---

[13] Gardiner, p. 186f.
[14] Harris, p. 135.

pervasive throughout the lives of first-century people just as they are today, and therefore, these involvements could well have become part and parcel of the lives of the people who made up the early church.

D. Athletic Facilities of the First Century

Though there were sports facilities in most if not all of the cities visited by Paul, only two will be highlighted so as to provide a representative overview of first-century athletic buildings. These two cities occupied the most prestigious events and buildings of any of the cities visited by Paul.

1. Ephesus Ephesus was frequently mentioned in writings and inscriptions of antiquity in association with athletics. One Marcus Aurelius Asclepiades (also called Hermodorus), in recounting his exploits (in approximately AD 180), includes the city of Ephesus and its festival in a list that includes the more prestigious Crown Games.[15] John McRay describes three different gymnasiums built in Ephesus during the first two centuries AD,[16] and the elaborate terraced stadium at Ephesus was reconstructed during the reign of Nero. A first-century inscription adds there was a gladiatorial show in this stadium.[17] This would lend support to the possibility that Paul's statement about facing wild beasts in Ephesus could have been accurate. The stadium was certainly built with a rounded end designed just for such events. The stadium was outfitted not only with the typical seating upon an accompanying bank overlooking the site of competition, but it was also equipped with the innovation of seating upon the vaulted wall that arched over the athletes' dressing rooms. This vaulted seating was built along the north side of the stadium. With these just being a few of the myriad of references to the Ephesian athletic community, there can be little doubt Ephesus had a well-established athletic community with a long and famous history.

2. Corinth The second city to be reviewed must be Corinth, with its world-renowned Isthmian Games. These games were one of the four Crown Festivals, which also included the Pythian Games at Delphi, the Nemean Games that during the time of Paul were held at Argos, and the

---

[15] Ibid. pp. 127, 128.
[16] McRay, p. 260.
[17] Harris, p. 142.

premier games of Olympia. While standing behind the Olympic and Pythian Games in terms of athletic prestige, the Isthmian festival was by far the best attended of any athletic festival, and because of its being held every 2 years (unlike the 4-year intervals at Olympia and Delphi), it became the most important of all the festivals with regard to its popularity and its influencing the current athletic trends.

Although Corinth itself also had athletic accommodations, the facilities for the festival lay a few miles outside of the city at Isthmia. It was here the temple of Poseidon stood upon a small acropolis, which was surrounded by a wall. The 650-foot stadium was constructed with seats of marble and lay in a ravine that had been formed by a stream. Corinth and Isthmia were connected by a road known as the "sacred way."[18] This passageway was bordered on the one side by statues of victorious Isthmian athletes, and by the lush greenery of pine trees on the other. One can easily imagine Paul and Timothy walking down this road on their way back to Corinth, discussing the athletes and events of the day. It was these very experiences shared by the two evangelists Paul alluded to in his last words to Timothy about his finishing the race, fighting the good fight, and being crowned by the judge.[19] It is easy to believe this master teacher used the hike back as a time to communicate to his protégé eternal truths derived from their observations at Isthmia.

Another item describing the athletic facilities has to do with an old stoa being secured by Publius Licinius Priscus in the second century AD and then remodeling it into living quarters for athletes at Isthmia.[20] This would demonstrate the Isthmian Games were proving profitable by this time and thus provides another indication the event Paul and others would have attended was in fact a significant affair of some magnitude.

E. Athletes of the First Century

1. Appollophanes   Though it would be quite interesting to discuss all of the known athletes of the first century, only two will be cited in an effort to again be representative rather than exhaustive. The two chosen would have had some relevance and possible significance to Paul. The first was

---

[18] Gardiner, p. 219.

[19] 2 Timothy 4:6–8.

[20] Harris, p. 158; Gardiner, p. 219.

the only Olympic champion known to have been from Tarsus. His name was Appollophanes, and he was crowned the victor of the stade (the shortest foot race and most prestigious of all the foot races—approximately 200 yards in length) in AD 85. It is obvious Appollophanes was an athlete of some reputation and more than likely competed in many of the games of that era. This means he may have competed at Isthmia, Ephesus, or some other city in which Paul might have been living. At the very least it is possible Paul would have known of him and would have been interested in the exploits of a fellow "homeboy" from Tarsus.

2. The Children of Hermesianax   The second athlete that may have been known by Paul would more accurately be described as a family of athletes. What makes the members of this family of particular interest is:

(a) They competed in the middle of the first century AD,

(b) They were citizens of Corinth, and

(c) Even more intriguingly, they were all female athletes.

They are known by the inscription written on a base that at one time supported all three of their statues. This inscription was found in Delphi, written by the father of the three girls, and was dedicated to the Pythian god Apollo.[21] Again, it can easily be speculated that Paul would have at least been acquainted with their names and accomplishments, if he had not personally met them.

III. BIBLICAL CONNECTIONS WITH FIRST-CENTURY ATHLETICS
A. The Church at Ephesus and Paul's Epistle to It

Once more in an effort to be representative rather than exhaustive, only three connections between sport and first-century Christianity will be explored. The first relates to how Christianity intersected with the sports world at Ephesus. So as not to be redundant, the aforementioned connections with Ephesus will not be revisited, but only built upon, particularly as it relates to the letter to the Ephesians.

---

[21] Harris, p. 180f.

Ephesus had a well-established athletic community and in particular was well known for its athletes' prominence in what was known as the heavy athletics. These consisted of boxing, wrestling, and a particularly rough sport called the *Pankration,* which combined the elements of both boxing and wrestling and in addition allowed any other bodily contact except the gouging out of the eyes or the grasping of the sex organs of an opponent. From this background it is easy to understand why Paul was inspired by the Holy Spirit to use the analogy he did in the sixth chapter of his epistle to the Ephesians.

When read by the Ephesians, this illustration would immediately invoke the seriousness of the battle with the powers of darkness. Another passage concerning Ephesus is found in 1 Corinthians 15:32, where Paul makes a statement about fighting with beasts at Ephesus. It is not within the scope of this treatise to comment definitively about whether or not Paul actually battled wild beasts in the Ephesian stadium and yet at the very least it must be agreed Paul's statements would prove Ephesus was known to have had this type of spectacle. This statement indicates Paul was certainly aware of such activities, and his comments bear out the archaeological findings concerning the stadium at Ephesus.

B. The Church at Corinth and Paul's Epistle to It

The second intersection has similar bearings and is found in 1 Corinthians 9:24–26. There is little doubt as to the relevance such a passage would have had to those who lived in the city that orchestrated one of the three most significant athletic festivals of the day. The spiritual truths that were communicated by and from the athletic realm would have held a deeper significance for those who lived every day in a city that had a prevalent athletic culture.

Another modern-day example will aid in clarifying and explaining this. Canton, Ohio, is the home of the Professional Football Hall of Fame. Once each year it becomes the focus of all those who love and follow football. Though it is true the city is deluged by tourists and football enthusiasts only one week each year, the Hall of Fame nonetheless has an influence on the city of Canton that is felt every week of the year. This is manifested by the ongoing industry needed to support the yearly festival and its Hall, as well as by the constant stream of people stopping by on the way to somewhere else. This is why I must take issue with McRay's analysis when he states Paul did not choose Corinth because of its sports venues. McRay's view demonstrates an ignorance of how the sports-related industries have a constant impact on their host cities. It is obvious from his writings that Paul understood the relevance of athletics, and though it cannot be conclusively proved Paul established long-term ministry sites at cities such as Corinth and Ephesus solely on the basis of their athletic credibility, certainly this knowledge impacted his reasoning for using these two cities as major bases for operation.

C. The Apostle Paul

The final connection between Christianity and the sports world of the first century is the Apostle Paul himself. From all of the information available, it is clear Paul was first exposed to Greek athletics as a young boy in his home city of Tarsus and even took part in the athletic training that occurred in the gymnasium situated on the banks of the Cydnus river. Harris declares there were at least four important athletic festivals that were regularly held during imperial times and these would help to verify a prominence of athletics in Tarsus.[22]

This involvement of Paul's probably did not enjoy a long life, however, as he went to study in Jerusalem under Gamaliel while still a young man. In addition from every account, it is apparent Paul became inflamed with his religious activities and would have had precious little time or energy left for anything else. Even if Paul would have desired to continue his gymnastics, he would have been hard pressed to find any suitable facility near Jerusalem. Yet as was mentioned earlier, he carried on a lifetime appreciation of the sports world, which becomes clear in not only his writings, but also in the choices of cities in which he visited. Moreover, this is made evident by his physical and mental strength and endurance. There is little doubt he had been conditioned both physically and mentally to compete and strive. H. A. Harris, after quoting the Corinthian passage where Paul lists his physical accomplishments that included beatings, stonings, shipwrecks, robberies, and his sufferings from cold, starvation, and thirst (this passage itself resembles

---

[22] Ibid., p. 133.

inscriptions found concerning the accomplishments of athletes), states: "The man who could write that was tough by any standards."[23] There is little doubt Paul was greatly influenced by the athletics of his day, but there is one additional possibility that is intriguing, and it has to do with Paul's thorn in the flesh.

A long-standing tradition has been that Paul's "thorn in the flesh" had to do with poor eyesight or another related problem with his eyes. This topic is in need of a much more thorough investigation of the arguments given in favor of Paul's eyes being his thorn in the flesh, but poor eyesight has been one of the leading explanations for Paul's thorn in the flesh. And, when this proposed scenario is coupled with the possibility of Paul being an athlete, interesting speculations occur. For instance, history records Paul was not a physically large man; rather, he was comparably smaller to others he associated with. This then would preclude him from being successful in most of the athletic events of his day. Long legs aided the speed of runners, and long arms favored the boxer by providing a longer reach. A larger man was also typically stronger, and thus, Paul would have been at a disadvantage in events needing brute strength, such as wrestling and throwing the javelin or discus. One event left to a smaller man may have been the aforementioned *Pankration*. Although strength was necessary, in this event quickness was just as important. Not only did this event better suit Paul's physical strengths of quickness and stamina, but it also would fit with his psychological strengths of being a fierce competitor and master strategist. If this scenario can be established, it is just possible it was during a contest in the *Pankration* as a youth that one of Paul's eyes was gouged by another lad from Tarsus. Of course, this would have been illegal, but there were referees in those days for a reason, and furthermore, anyone associated with athletics knows athletes will regularly attempt to stretch or even break the rules in order to gain success. Now of course all of this is obviously speculation, and yet it is speculation within a reasonable possibility. Even if Paul did not receive his physical malady as an athlete, it is still clear he had a long, biding interest in athletics and brought those interests and insights into his teachings and activities.

---

[23] Ibid., p. 133f.

IV. SUMMARY

Much more research and thinking need to be done in considering what is known about the athletics of the first century and how this information can aid in unpacking the Holy Scriptures. For instance, one of the great New Testament mysteries is whom the Holy Spirit inspired to write Hebrews. If only the athletic passages of Hebrews were to be considered, it would lend great weight to Paul being the human part of the authorship equation. The similarities of not only the words used in the letter to the Hebrews but also the insightful use of the analogies are strongly Pauline. It is this example and many others that should inspire wider and deeper scholarship and investigation of first-century athletes and athletics. Hopefully this research and inquiry will provide a more enlightened and, therefore, more relevant message of Christ and His redeeming love to those who compete in the late twenty-first century.

APPENDIX B

LORD'S DAY ISSUES AND THE NFL

This appendix provides a few brief thoughts on Professional Sport (in specific, the National Football League) in light of the theological foundations outlined in Chapter 7 of this book.

CONSIDERATIONS OF PROFESSIONAL SPORTS AND THE LORD'S DAY

It has been clearly delineated that any organized athletic activity that prohibits (or curtails) one's involvement in using the Lord's Day as a day for spiritual development (including preventing one from attending church) or that makes someone work unnecessarily must not be organized or participated in. This would include all recreational, amateur, scholastic, and collegiate endeavors. This is called for so as to give the day a distinctive difference that will promote physical, psychological, relational, and spiritual health and in addition allow for worship, ministry, and outreach to occur. The benefits to individuals, families, and society at large are obvious and significant. This, however, must not be construed as to deny all activity on the Lord's Day. Family softball or volleyball games at the park or croquet matches in the backyard along with barbeques and parties can all be great ways to not only *re-create*, but also be renewed and even be a loving witness to those still contemplating a relationship with Christ. Once again caution must be used so as to not unduly cause someone to work, but because Sunday is designed to benefit people ("the Sabbath is for man and not man for the Sabbath"), recreation that needs a few park rangers, lifeguards, etc., is well within the intended purposes of the day. Such work is a legitimate example of an act of necessity. A similar case then needs to be discussed regarding professional sports.

WHAT CAN BE DONE ONLY ON THE LORD'S DAY

As previously discussed, one of the guiding principles for determining a proper honoring of the day is to discern what has to be done on the Lord's Day. It must be determined which activities cannot be done on any day other than the Lord's Day. In today's secular society, it is unquestionably assumed all professional, along with many collegiate, scholastic, and amateur athletic events, will take place on Sunday. But is this assumption valid? Although it can be understood how those who do not follow Christ would engage in activity that leads to not honoring the day, it is mystifying as to how those who do follow Christ could so profane the day. This basic concept has already been addressed, but a further explanation of why a secular society sponsors athletic events will aid in both understanding how and why these practices began and also will lead to a better concept of the day.

The most fundamental reason sports events began to be held on Sundays has always been money. In an earlier American era in which there were more religious observances such as Lord's Day work prohibitions, professional sports maximized the opportunity to attract large numbers of people who did not work on Sundays. Professional sports moguls realized that millions of people had more time on Sundays to attend a ball game than on any other day of the week and sought to take full advantage of this. Initially the owners did not interfere with organized religion. That is, contests were not scheduled on Sunday mornings or evenings, but this was only so as to not lose potential revenues on ticket sales to fans who would not come to a game due to their devotion to church. However, this has continued to change as athletic promoters have realized fewer and fewer people attend church. At first some contests were held on Sunday evenings and then the NFL began to inch its way into Sunday mornings: first, by starting games at 1:00 AM; then at 12:30 PM; and at times even earlier. The NFL is increasingly more intrusive with its pre-game analysis, which now often begins in the late morning.

It should be obvious at this point the major reason for professional sports being held on Sundays is an economic one. Although making money is a worthy endeavor, it must be balanced and given direction by other biblical ethics, in this case by Lord's Day directives. To make money, sports leagues naturally select a time frame where there was no competition for fans and their dollars. This means not encroaching upon the time-honored Friday or Saturday domains of amateur football. This points out that a day for professional football other than Friday or Saturday was necessary for its survival. Sunday became that day.

This explanation does not in itself justify the use of Sunday as the chosen day for professional football. The day could be Thursday or Monday (and for one game each week, it is), and yet for the aforementioned economic reasons, Sunday was chosen and has proved wildly successful.[1]

---

[1] Although the current Monday Night Football has been successful, it is doubtful each franchise could survive a complete schedule of Monday night games. It is successful now due in part to its infrequency and, thus, novelty. It is more likely to move high school and college games to weeknights. Sadly, the opposite is occurring with great rapidity: Colleges, high schools, and even youth leagues are increasingly being played on the Lord's Day.

Moreover, it must be understood professional football could not maintain its current financial status without being played on Sunday. Whereas baseball, hockey, basketball, and other sports can have multiple games each week and, therefore, be financially profitable, it is unlikely professional football could survive on the smaller crowds that it would attract if limited to competing on weekday nights. Thus, if football is moved to a weekday occurrence and subsequently loses much of its financial benefits, the result will be the loss of revenue for not only the owner, but also for the players and everyone else who makes a living working in football. Beyond all else, Sunday afternoons in the fall and early winter have become synonymous with football for most Americans. It has almost become a secularized version of a holy (separate) day. In fact the Super Bowl comes as close to a true secular holiday as can be found in the American culture.

It is, therefore, the author's contention that professional football is the only exception that can even be postulated as fulfilling the Lord's Day/ Sabbath Day mandates.[2] Yet even this is a huge stretch. Even if relegated to afternoons, and even if it can be said to provide a few hours of diversion and recreation, and even if it does not interfere with worship, spiritual development, and acts of ministry or mercy, it is still not deemed wise. As the Scripture says, it may be "permissible" but still not "profitable" for followers of Christ to partake of.

Further cautionary statements are in order. The major danger in allowing one sporting endeavor to encroach upon the Lord's Day is the natural progression that may ensue. For if one exception is made, then there will be another and another and soon no distinction of the day is left; thus, the whole of the matter will become self-defeating. Although this tension is fraught with difficulty, it must be held to or else the end result will indeed be a day without distinction. A day with only professional football will certainly make the day distinctively different. When any and every other sport is allowed, there will no longer be any distinction.

It is my opinion our society in general and all individuals would be better served by not having professional football played on Sunday. It certainly would be the preferred choice for honoring the Lord's Day.

---

[2] Of course, this is a very "Americanized" context. Each culture must wrestle with its own situation and decide what would be God honoring. I cannot be so arrogant as to make any definitive statement about other cultures.

BIBLIOGRAPHY

Akabusi, Kriss, and Stuart Weir. *Wisdom for the Race of Life*. Oxford: Bible Reading Fellowship, 1999.

Aldrich, Joseph C. *Life-Style Evangelism: Learning to Open Your Life to Those Around You*. Portland, OR: Multnomah Press, 1993.

Anderson, J. Kerby. *Christian Ethics in Plain Language*. Nashville, TN: Thomas Nelson, 2005.

Atcheson, Wayne. *Impact for Christ: How FCA Has Influenced the Sports World*. Grand Island, NE: Cross Training Publ., 1994. About the Fellowship of Christian Athletes.

Baker, William J. *Playing with God: Religion and Modern Sport*. Cambridge, MA: Harvard University Press, 2007.

Barton, Bruce. *The Man Nobody Knows*. New York: Collier Books, 1987, c1925.

Bateman, Charles T. *The Life of General Booth*. New York: Association Press, 1912.

Begg, Alastair. *Pathway to Freedom*. Sound recording (12 CDs). Cleveland, OH: Truth for Life, 2003. ID 20501. Series of sermons on Exodus 20, the Ten Commandments.

Beisser, Arnold R. *Madness in Sports*. New York: Appleton-Century Crofts, 1977. Quoted in *The Plain Dealer*, section G, January 18, 1987, p. 3.

Belcher, Richard, and Richard P. Belcher, Jr. *A Layman's Guide to the Sabbath Question.* Southbridge, MA: Crowne Publications, 1991.

Benge, Janet, and Geoff Benge. *Eric Liddell: Something Greater Than Gold.* Seattle, WA: YWAM Publishers, 1998.

Braisted, Ruth Evelyn Wilder. *In This Generation: The Story of Robert P. Wilder.* New York: Published for the Student Volunteer Movement by Friendship Press, 1941.

Broneer, Oscar. *The Odeum.* Cambridge, MA: Published for the American School of Classical Studies at Athens by Harvard University Press, 1932. (American School of Classical Studies at Athens. Corinth; v. 10)

————. *The South Stoa and Its Roman Successors.* Princeton, NJ: American School of Classical Studies at Athens, 1954. (Corinth; v. 1, pt. 4)

————. *Temple of Poseidon.* Princeton, NJ: American School of Classical Studies at Athens, 1971. (Isthmia; v. 1)

Browne, Leonard. *Sport and Recreation, and Evangelism in the Local Church.* Bramcote, Nottingham, England: Grove Books, 1991.

Buchanan, Mark. *The Rest of God: Restoring Your Soul by Restoring the Sabbath.* Nashville, TN: Thomas Nelson, 2006.

Byl, John. *Intramural Recreation: A Step-by-Step Guide to Creating an Effective Program.* Champaign, IL: Human Kinetics, 2002.

————. *Organizing Successful Tournaments.* Champaign, IL: Human Kinetics, 1999.

Byl, John, and Tom Visker. *Physical Education, Sports and Wellness: Looking to God As We Look at Ourselves.* Sioux City, IA: Dordt Press, 1999.

Chariots of Fire (video recording)/Warner Bros. Pictures; a Warner Bros. and Ladd Company release; presented by Allied Stars; an Enigma production; original screenplay by Colin Welland; produced by David Puttnam; directed by Hugh Hudson. Burbank, CA: Warner Home Video, 2003. DVD. Originally produced as a British motion picture in 1981.

Church Sports International (website): www.csi.org.

Coakley, Jay J. *Sports in Society: Issues and Controversies.* 9th ed. Boston: McGraw Hill Higher Education, 2007.

Conner, Ray. *The Ministry of Recreation.* Nashville, TN: Convention Press, 1992.

Connor, Steve. *A Sporting Guide to Eternity: A Devotional for Competitive People.* Fearn, England: Christian Focus, 2002.

_____. *Sports Outreach: Principles + Practice for Successful Sports Ministry.* Ross-shire, Scotland: Christian Focus Publications, 2003.

Conrad, Tim. *Game Plan.* Florissant, CO: Thistle Productions, 2009 (Sapphire Lake series).

_____. *Go the Distance.* Florissant, CO: Thistle Productions, 2010 (Sapphire Lake series).

Couey, Richard B. *Building God's Temple.* Minneapolis: Burgess Pub. Co., 1982.

CSRM: *The Association of Church Sports and Ministers* (website): www.csrm.org.

Dahl, Gordon. *Work, Play and Worship: In a Leisure-Oriented Society.* Minneapolis: Augsburg Pub. House, 1972.

Daniels, Graham, and Stuart Weir. *Born to Play!* Bicester, England: Frampton House, 2004.

_____. *The Sports Stadium: How to Share Your Faith in the World of Sport.* Bicester, England: Frampton House Publications, 2005.

Darden, Robert. *Into the End Zone.* Nashville, TN: Thomas Nelson, 1989.

Davis, John Jefferson. *Evangelical Ethics: Issues Facing the Church Today.* 3rd ed., rev. and expanded. Phillipsburg, NJ: P&R Pub., 2004.

Dickson, John. *The Best Kept Secret of Christian Mission: Promoting the Gospel with More Than Our Lips.* Grand Rapids, MI: Zondervan, 2010.

Digby, Andrew Wingfield, and Stuart Weir. *Winning Is Not Enough: Sports Stars Who Are Going for Gold and for God.* London: Marshall Pickering, 1991.

Doggett, Lawrence Locke. *The Life of Robert R. McBurney.* Cleveland, OH: F.M. Barton, 1902.

Dorsett, Lyle W. *A Passion for Souls: The Life of D.L. Moody.* Chicago: Moody Press, 1997.

Driscoll, Mark. *The Radical Reformission: Reaching Out without Selling Out.* Grand Rapids, MI: Zondervan, 2004.

Ehrmann, Joe. *Inside Out Coaching: How Sports Can Transform Lives.* New York: Simon & Schuster, 2011.

Eisenman, Tom. *Every Day Evangelism: Making the Most of Life's Common Moments.* Downers Grove, IL: InterVarsity Press, 1987.

The English Standard Version Bible: Containing the Old and New Testaments with Apocrypha. New York: Oxford University Press, 2009.

Evans, Tony, Jonathan Evans, and Dillon Burroughs. *Get in the Game.* Chicago: Moody Publishers, 2006.

Finney, Charles G. *How to Promote a Revival.* Antrim, Ireland: Revival Pub. Co., 1948.

Gardiner, E. Norman. *Athletics of the Ancient World.* Oxford, England: Clarendon Press, 1930.

Garner, John, ed. *Recreation and Sports Ministry: Impacting Postmodern Culture.* Nashville, TN: Broadman & Holman, 2003.

Gough, Russell Wayne. *Character Is Everything: Promoting Ethical Excellence in Sport.* Fort Worth, TX: Harcourt Brace College Publishers, 1997.

Green, Michael. *Evangelism Through the Local Church.* Nashville, TN: Oliver-Nelson, 1992.

Grubb, Norman P. *C. T. Studd, Athlete and Pioneer.* Atlantic City, NJ: World-Wide Revival Prayer Movement, 1947.

Guttman, Allen. *Sport Spectators.* New York: Columbia University Press, 1986.

Harris, Harold Arthur. *Greek Athletes and Athletics.* Bloomington: Indiana University Press, 1966, c1964.

_____. *Sport in Greece and Rome.* Ithaca, NY: Cornell University Press, 1989. Originally published 1972.

Heschel, Abraham Joshua. *The Sabbath: Its Meaning for Modern Man.* New York: Farrar, Straus & Giroux, 2005, c1951.

Higgs, Robert. *God in the Stadium: Sports and Religion in America.* Lexington: University Press of Kentucky, 1995.

Hodder-Williams, J. E. *The Life of Sir George Williams: Founder of the Young Men's Christian Association.* New York: A.C. Armstrong, 1906.

Hoffman, Shirl James. *Good Game: Christianity and the Culture of Sports.* Waco, TX: Baylor University Press, 2010.

Hoffman, Shirl James, ed. *Sport and Religion.* Champaign, IL: Human Kinetics Books, 1992.

Holy Bible, Containing the Old and New Testaments: Authorized King James Version, With a New System of Connected References. New York: Oxford

University Press, 1945. Originally published 1611, the most published English Bible, available in countless editions.

The Holy Bible: New Century Version, Containing the Old and New Testaments. Dallas, TX: Word Bibles, c1991.

The Holy Bible: New International Version, Containing the Old Testament and the New Testament. Grand Rapids, MI: Zondervan Bible Publishers, c1978.

Hopkins, Charles Howard. *History of the Y.M.C.A. in North America.* New York: Association Press, 1951.

Hughes, Thomas, 1822–1896. *The Manliness of Christ.* Philadelphia: H. Altemus, 1896.

_____. *Tom Brown at Oxford.* First published: Cambridge, England: Macmillan, 1861. Many modern editions are available.

_____. *Tom Brown's School Days.* First published: Cambridge, England: Macmillan, 1857. Many modern editions are available.

Hunter, George G. *How to Reach Secular People.* Nashville, TN: Abingdon Press, 1992.

Johnson, Elliot. *Focus on the Finish Line: Hurdles Female Athletes Face in the Race of Life.* Grand Island, NE: Cross Training Pub., 1997.

_____. *Heroes of the Faith: Advice from God's Athletes.* Grand Island, NE: Cross Training Pub., 1995.

_____. *The Point After: Advice from God's Athletes.* Grand Rapids, MI: Zondervan, 1987.

_____. *Strong to the Finish.* Grand Island, NE: Cross Training Pub., 1998.

Johnson, Elliot, and Al Schierbaum. *Up Close with The Savior.* Grand Island, NE: Cross Training Pub., 1994.

Kaltsas, Nikolaos. *Olympia.* 2nd ed. Athens: Ministry of Culture, Archaeological Receipts Fund, 2000.

Keddie, John W., and Sebastian Coe. *Running the Race: Eric Liddell, Olympic Champion.* New York: Evangelical Press, 2007.

Kluck, Ted. *The Reason for Sport: A Christian Fanifesto.* Chicago: Moody Press, 2009.

Kohn, Alfie. *No Contest: The Case Against Competition.* Boston: Houghton Mifflin, 1986.

Krattenmaker, Tom. *Onward Christian Athletes: Turning Ballparks into Pulpits and Players into Preachers.* Lanham, MD: Rowman & Littlefield, 2010.

Ladd, Tony, and James A. Mattheson. *Muscular Christianity: Evangelical Protestants and the Development of American Sport.* Grand Rapids, MI: Baker Books, 1999.

Larson, Knute. *The Great Human Race: How to Endure in the Marathon of Life.* Akron, OH: The Chapel Press, 2002.

Linville, Greg. *A Contemporary Christian Ethic of Competition.* Canton, OH: First Friends Church, 1990.

_____. *Does Sport Ministry Aid Local Church Evangelism?* Ashland, OH: Ashland Theological Seminary, 2007. Thesis (D. Min.)—Ashland Theological Seminary.

_____. *Executive Director's Blog.* www.csrm.org/blog.html (accessed April 8, 2013). This blog contains many of Greg Linville's writings.

_____. *Overwhelming Victory: A Coaching Manual.* Ashland, OH: Ashland Theological Seminary, 1987. Project (M.A.)—Ashland Theological Seminary.

_____. *Surrounded by Witnesses.* Canton, OH: Association Press, 2005.

_____. *Theology of Competition.* Canton, OH: Overwhelming Victory Ministries, 1990.

Locke, Tates, and Bob Ibach. *Caught in the Net.* West Point, NY: Leisure Press, 1982.

Long, Jimmy. *Generating Hope: A Strategy for Reaching the Postmodern Generation.* Downers Grove, IL: InterVarsity Press, 1997.

Magnusson, Sally. *The Flying Scotsman.* New York: Quartet Books, 1981. Biography of Eric Liddell.

Martens, Rainier. *Joy and Sadness in Children's Sports.* Champaign, IL: Human Kinetics Press, 1978.

Mason, Bryan. *Beyond the Gold: What Every Church Needs to Know About Sports Ministry.* Milton Keynes, England: Authentic Media Ltd., 2011.

_____. *Into the Stadium: An Active Guide to Sport and Recreation Ministry in the Local Church.* Milton Keynes, England: Authentic Media Ltd., 2003.

Mattingly, Don. *Recreation for Youth.* Nashville, TN: Convention Press, 1986.

McCasland, David. *Eric Liddell: Pure Gold: A New Biography of the Olympic Champion Who Inspired Chariots of Fire.* Grand Rapids, MI: Discovery House, 2001.

McCown, Lowrie, and Valerie J. Gin. *Focus on Sport in Ministry.* Marietta, GA: 360° Sports, 2003.

McLemore, Clinton W. *Street Smart Ethics: Succeeding in Business Without Selling Your Soul.* Louisville, KY: Westminster John Know Press, 2003.

Michener, James A. *Sports in America.* New York: Random House, 1976.

Moore, R. Laurence (Robert Laurence). *Touchdown Jesus: The Mixing of Sacred and Secular in American History.* Louisville, KY: Westminster John Knox Press, 2003.

Morrow, Greg, and Steve Morrow. *Recreation: Reaching Out, Reaching In, Reaching Up.* Nashville, TN: Convention Press, 1986.

Morse, Richard Cary, 1841–1926. *History of the North American Young Men's Christian Associations.* New York: Association Press, 1913.

_____. *My Life with Young Men: Fifty Years in the Young Men's Christian Association.* New York: Association Press, 1918.

Neal, Wes. *The Handbook on Athletic Perfection.* 3rd ed. Grand Island, NE: Cross Training Publishing, 1981.

Neal, Wes. *The Handbook on Coaching Perfection.* 2nd ed. Milford, MI: Mott Media, 1981.

New Testament in Modern English. Translated by J. B. Phillips. New York: Macmillan, 1958.

Newman, Louis E. *An Introduction to Jewish Ethics.* Upper Saddle River, NJ: Pearson Prentice Hall, 2005.

Newman, Wendell T. *Organizing for Recreation Ministry.* Nashville, TN: Convention Press, 1990.

Nix, Stan. *Sports Stories and the Bible.* Carlsbad, CA: Magnus Press, 2003.

Olivova, Vera. *Sport and Games in the Ancient World.* New York: St. Martin's Press, 1985.

Oswald, Rodger. *Sports Ministry and the Church: A Philosophy of Ministry.* Campbell, CA: Church Sports International, 1990s.

_____. *A Theology of Sports Ministry.* Campbell, CA: Church Sports International, 1993.

Parrott, Mike. *Team Huddles: Sports Devotionals*. Grand Island, NE: Cross Training Pub., 2000.

Peterson, Eugene H. *The Message: The Bible in Contemporary Language*. Colorado Springs: NavPress, c2002.

Piggin, Stuart, and John Roxborough. *The St. Andrew Seven: The Finest Flowering of Missionary Zeal in Scottish History*. Edinburgh; Carlisle, PA: Banner of Truth Trust, 1985.

Pollock, John Charles. *The Cambridge Seven: A Call to Christian Service*. London: Inter-Varsity Press, 1969, c1955.

Prebish, Charles S. *Religion and Sport: The Meeting of Sacred and Profane*. Westport, CN: Greenwood Press, 1993.

Prime, Derek. *Active Evangelism: Putting the Evangelism of Acts into Practice*. Ross-shire, Scotland: Christian Focus, 2003.

Putney, Clifford. *Muscular Christianity, Manhood and Sports in Protestant America, 1880–1920*. Cambridge, MA: Harvard University Press, 2001.

Rader, Benjamin G. *American Sports: From the Age of Folk Games to the Age of Televised Sports*. Englewood Cliffs, NJ: Prentice Hall, 1990.

Rainer, Thom S., and Lewis A. Drummond, eds. *Evangelism in the Twenty-First Century: The Critical Issues*. Wheaton, IL: Harold Shaw Pub., 1989.

The Random House College Dictionary. rev. ed. Edited by Jess Stein. New York: Random House, 1975.

Ray, Bruce A. *Celebrating the Sabbath: Finding Rest in a Restless World*. Phillipsburg, NJ: P&R Pub., 2000.

Reich, Frank. "Competition and Creation." *IIIM Magazine Online*, 4, no. 6 (February 11–17, 2002), 1–9. http://thirdmill.org/magazine/issues.asp/volume/4/number/6 (accessed April 8, 2013).

Roques, Mark, and Jim Ticknor. *Fields of God: Football and the Kingdom of God*. Carlisle, PA: Authentic Lifestyles, 2003.

Sauer, Erich. *In the Arena of Faith: A Call to a Consecrated Life*. Grand Rapids, MI: Eerdmans, 1955.

Sjogren, Steven, Dave Ping, and Doug Pollock. *Irresistible Evangelism*. Loveland, CO: Group, 2004.

Spalding, Greg. *Run the Greatest Race: Be a Disciple Who Makes a Difference*. Pittsburgh, PA: City of Champions Pub. Co., 1996.

Sport: An Educational and Pastoral Challenge: Seminar of Study on the Theme of Sport Chaplains, Vatican, September 7–8, 2007/Catholic Church. Pontificium Consilium pro Laicis. Citta del Vaticano: Libreria Editrice Vaticana, 2008.

Stanley, Andy. *Louder than Words.* Sisters, OR: Multnomah Press, 2004.

Stoll, Sharon Kay, and Jennifer M. Beller. *Who Says This Is Cheating? Anybody's Sports Ethics Book.* Dubuque, IA: Kendall Hunt Publishing, 1993.

Strobel, Lee. *Inside the Mind of Unchurched Harry and Mary: How to Reach Friends and Family Who Avoid God and the Church.* Grand Rapids, MI: Zondervan, 1993.

Thiessen, Gordon. *Cross Training Manual: Playbook for Christian Athletes.* Grand Island, NE: Cross Training Pub., 1991.

Tinley, Josh. *Kneeling in the End Zone: Spiritual Lessons from the World of Sports.* Cleveland, OH: Pilgrim Press, 2009.

Verhey, Allen. *The Great Reversal: Ethics and the New Testament.* Grand Rapids, MI: Eerdmans, 1984.

Walker, Dan. *Sport and Sundays: Christian TV Presenter Dan Walker Tells His Story.* Rev. and updated ed. Leominster, England: Day One Publications, 2010, c2009.

Warner, Gary. *Competition.* Elgin, IL: David Cook, 1979.

Webb, Bernice Larson. *The Basketball Man: James Naismith.* Lawrence: University Press of Kansas, 1973.

Wier, Stuart. *Kriss.* London: Marshall Pickering, 1996.

_____. *More Than Champions: A Sport Stars' Secrets of Success.* London: Harper Collins, 1993.

_____. *The Ultimate Prize: Great Christian Olympians.* London: Hodder Christian, 2004.

_____. *What the Book Says About Sport.* Oxford, England: Bible Reading Fellowship, 2000.

Young, David C. *A Brief History of the Olympic Games.* Malden, MA: Blackwell Pub., 2004.

Patrons Page

First Friends Church—Offering a comprehensive Sports Outreach for all ages. Contact Information: 5455 Market Ave., Canton, OH 44714, www.firstfriends.org.

Children of Promise Inc. exists to benefit the youth of our nation as they grow in wisdom, in stature, in spirit, and in favor with their fellow man. Contact information: 330-323-2012.

Eastview Christian Church Sports Outreach. A local church using sport as a platform for outreach to the local community. Contact information: 1500 N. Airport Rd, Normal, IL 61761, 309-451-5000, www.eastviewchurch.net.

Uncharted Waters—Reaching Kids for Christ Through Church Sports Camps. Contact Information: uwsportsministry.org.

Regis Judy Family

Steven Stocker Family

Subject Index

Note: Page numbers with n indicates footnotes.

Index of Bible Books